Drug, Set, and Setting

Drug, Set, and Setting

The Basis for Controlled Intoxicant Use

NORMAN E. ZINBERG, M.D.

Yale University Press
New Haven and London

Designed by James J. Johnson
and set in Caledonia Roman type by The Composing Room of
Michigan, Inc.
Printed in the United States of America by
Vail-Ballou Press, Binghamton, New York.

Library of Congress Cataloging in Publication Data

Zinberg, Norman Earl, 1921–
   Drug, set, and setting.

   Bibliography: p.
   Includes index.
   1. Drug abuse—Social aspects.   2. Drug abuse—
Prevention.   3. Drug abuse—Research—United States.
I. Title.   II. Title: Controlled intoxicant use.
[DNLM: 1. Substance abuse.   2. Research design.
3. Research—Standards.   4. Social environment. WM 270
Z77db]
HV5801.Z56   1984   306'.1   83-16803
ISBN 0–300–03110–6

10   9   8   7   6   5   4   3   2   1

Contents

Preface

The viewpoint toward the use of illicit drugs expressed in this book has developed gradually during more than twenty years of clinical experience with drug users. Initially I was concerned, like most other people, with drug abuse, that is, with the users' loss of control over the drug or drugs they were using. Only after a long period of clinical investigation, historical study, and cogitation did I realize that in order to understand how and why certain users had lost control I would have to tackle the all-important question of how and why many others had managed to achieve control and maintain it.

The train of thought that has resulted in the writing of this book was set in motion in 1962. At that time, after a decade of teaching medical psychology to nonpsychiatric physicians at the Beth Israel Hospital in Boston by making rounds with them each week to see both ward and private patients, I began to puzzle over the extreme reluctance these sensible physicians felt about prescribing doses of opiates to relieve pain. Their hesitation, based on a fear of addicting patients, was surprisingly consistent, even where terminal patients were concerned. So, in conjunction with Dr. David C. Lewis, then Chief Resident in Medicine at Beth Israel, I began to make a study of this phenomenon. As we surveyed clinical data and then looked into the history of drug use, a picture emerged that scarcely resembled the one we had received in medical school.

Finding little clinical evidence to support our doctors' extreme concern about iatrogenic addiction, except in the case of one obviously demanding group of patients, we turned to the history of drug use for an explanation. There we found ample reason for the medical apprehension about opiates. A whole set of traditional cultural and social attitudes toward opiate use had apparently been internalized by our physicians and was governing their thoughts and actions, engendering fears that were undermining their capacity to relieve suffering. In addition, the doctors' attitudes were not only determining their willingness or unwillingness to prescribe opiates but were also influencing the effect these drugs had on their patients. This was my first exposure to the power of what in this book is called the "social setting" to modify behavior and dictate responses in drug users.

I had no plans to continue investigating drugs after our Beth Israel study was finished, but two papers on our work (Zinberg & Lewis 1964; Lewis & Zinberg 1964) happened to be published just as interest in drug use was reaching fever pitch. Many physicians, confused about the new habits of "tripping" or "turning on" reported to them by patients (or by patients' parents), were looking for a psychiatrist who was knowledgeable about drugs. Some of them began referring such patients to me, even when the drug was marihuana or a psychedelic rather than an opiate.

As my clinical experience with drug users grew, I became aware that the traditional views about marihuana and the psychedelics were even more inaccurate than those about opiates. In the case of marihuana use I found repeatedly that the drug's reputation for destroying normal personality functioning and for harming a variety of bodily processes was based on misunderstanding and misconception. It is rather ironic now, when approximately fifty-seven million Americans have tried marihuana (Miller & Associates 1983), to recall that less than two decades ago most informed citizens believed that any use of marihuana would turn the brain to jelly.

Some of my public pronouncements in this area were made in collaboration with a valued colleague and friend, Dr. Andrew T. Weil. In the fall of 1967, during his fourth year of medical study at Harvard, he decided that if our statements were to be regarded as credible, we had to have experimental data. He proposed that we do an experiment with marihuana that rigorously followed scientific methodology, one in which neither researchers nor subjects would know whether the substance used was active or only a placebo. First, we had to find out whether marihuana had been standardized pharmacologically and whether legal obstacles could be overcome so that it could be used experimentally with human beings.

These two aims so occupied our thought that the question of how users developed control over their drug use seemed light-years away. At the time, the notion of giving marihuana to human beings and in particular to naive subjects seemed very daring, and our fear that such an experiment would be considered presumptuous proved to be well founded. Getting permission from the Bureau of Narcotics and Dangerous Drugs (BNDD), the Food and Drug Administration (FDA), and the National Institute of Mental Health (NIMH), all of which claimed jurisdiction over this area, was a labor of Hercules. Weil, who made the experiment his senior project, had more time than I had to write scores of letters answering the minute inquiries of these agencies and also to take several trips to Washington, but we both made innumerable phone calls to unravel the "Catch-22" relationships of primacy among the agencies until, at last, permission came through.

The authorities stipulated that our subjects must be driven to and from the experiments; that they must promise not to touch any machinery, electrical or otherwise, for twenty-four hours after using marihuana; and that they must sign an elaborate informed-consent form including lifetime guarantees that they would not sue if they became addicted.

But even these stringent requirements did not satisfy Harvard University. The Executive Committee of the Medical School refused permission for the experiment on advice of counsel, who said to me on the telephone: "I have checked into this proposal carefully and find nothing specifically illegal. However, I have also checked my conscience and have decided that I must recommend that Harvard not countenance your giving this dangerous drug to human beings."

Dr. Robert Ebert, then Dean of Harvard Medical School, was uneasy about this decision. So, when Dr. Peter Knapp, Director of Psychiatric Research at Boston University Medical School, generously and courageously arranged to have us do the work under his roof, Dr. Ebert procured legal counsel for us at Harvard's expense to deal with any problems that might arise in satisfying the requirements of the governmental agencies and in obtaining proper informed consent.

The experiments, which took place the following year (1968), went smoothly and uneventfully, largely because of Dr. Knapp's thoughtful advice and the help of his talented laboratory assistant, Judith Nelsen. Not one of our subjects, whether experienced or naive, was at all disturbed by the experiments, and we learned something about the effect of acute marihuana intoxication on various physiological and psychological functions. I felt then and still feel, however, that the main achievement of these first controlled experiments in giving a widely condemned illicit drug to human beings was to show that such experiments could be conducted safely (Weil, Zinberg & Nelsen 1968).

The next year (1968–69) I was invited to lecture in social psychology at the London School of Economics, and at the same time I received a Guggenheim award to study the British system of heroin maintenance (Zinberg & Robertson 1972). I was fortunate enough to arrive in England in July 1968, just as the British were beginning to send heroin addicts to designated clinics instead of permitting private physicians to prescribe heroin for them, a change that greatly facilitated my study. I found that in Britain there were two types of addicts, both of which differed from American addicts: the first functioned adequately, even successfully, while the second was even more debilitated than the American junkie. But although the second type of junkie behaved in an uncontrolled way and did great harm to himself, he, like the American alcoholic, was not a cause of social unrest, crime, or public hysteria.

Gradually I came to understand that the differences between British and American addicts were attributable to their different social settings—that is, to the differing social and legal attitudes toward heroin in the two countries. In England, where heroin use was not illicit and addicts' needs could be legally supplied, they were free from legal restraints and were not necessarily considered deviants. British addicts had a free choice: either they could accept drug use as a facet of life and carry on their usual activities, or they could view themselves as defective and adopt a destructive junkie life-style. Thus my year in England revealed the same phenomenon I had observed at the Beth Israel Hospital several years earlier: the power of the social setting, of cultural and social attitudes, to influence drug use and its effects. It was becoming obvious that in order to understand the drug experience, I would have to take into account not just the pharmacology of the drug and the personality of the user (the set) but also the physical and social setting in which use occurred.

On my return to the United States in 1969, I was aware that a change had occurred in the social setting surrounding the use of the psychedelics and particularly of LSD, for public reaction to the "drug revolution" had shifted from hysteria about psychedelics to terror of a "heroin epidemic" (Zinberg & Robertson 1972). In 1971, after these feelings had been further fueled by reports of overwhelmingly heavy heroin use by the troops in Vietnam, The Ford Foundation and the Department of Defense arranged for me to go to Vietnam to study that situation as a consultant. Vietnam was a strange and frightening place for American enlisted men (EMs). Hated by the Vietnamese and hating them, the American troops were easily attracted to any activity, including drug use, that blotted out the outside world (Zinberg 1972).

As it became clearer to me that the social setting (the EMs' Vietnam) was the factor leading either to preoccupation with the use of drugs or to feverish absorption in some other distracting activity, I decided to advise the Army to take drug users out of their existing social setting, out of Vietnam. This advice was rejected. General Frederick Weygand said that if the EMs knew that heroin use would get them out of Vietnam, there would be no nonusers and therefore no Army. He did not realize that heroin was so easy to get in Vietnam that anybody who wanted to use it was already doing so. Nor did he share my sense that the troops' interest in heroin was attributable to the bad social setting—the destructiveness of the war environment and even of the rehabilitation centers—in which controlling social sanctions and rituals had no chance to develop. At that time, my theory of the way in which groups evolve viable social controls to aid controlled use was not well enough formulated to be convincing. Hence the Army paid little attention to what hindsight indicates was basically good advice.

Of course, the using EMs were eventually sent home, and as my small follow-up study and Lee N. Robins' large and comprehensive studies showed (Robins 1973, 1974; Robins, Davis & Goodwin 1974; Robins, Helzer & Davis, 1975; Robins et al. 1979), once the users were taken out of the noxious atmosphere (the bad social setting), the infection (heroin use) virtually ceased. About 88% of the men addicted in Vietnam did not become readdicted after their return to the United States.

In 1972, back in America, I began to think more coherently about drug use. I had known for many years that there were old-time "weekend warriors" (those who used heroin on occasional weekends), and my study with Lewis in 1962 had confirmed the existence of numerous patterns of heroin use. The vast social experiment with psychedelics in the 1960s and the later drug scene in Vietnam had highlighted the power of the social setting and made me wonder whether that power could be applied in a beneficial way to the control of intoxicants, including heroin. My reading on alcohol use showed that the history of alcohol, like that of the opiates, was exceedingly complex and gave me some ideas concerning the further study of drugs. At the same time I had the opportunity to encourage new research on the use of opiates. As consultant to the newly formed Drug Abuse Council (DAC), I approved a small grant to Douglas H. Powell, who wanted to locate long-term heroin "chippers" (occasional users). By putting advertisements in counterculture newspapers, he turned up a group that was small but sizable enough to demonstrate his thesis that controlled users existed and thus that factors other than the power of the drug and the user's personality were at work (Powell 1973).

During this same period, Richard C. Jacobson (with whom I had worked earlier on a drug education project) and I were planning a study of the way in which "social controls," as we called them, operated. The ideas we had then seem confused and rudimentary now, but only scattered clinical data were available to work from, and very few of them had been collected systematically. We planned to make a comparative study of the controlled use of three illicit drugs with different powers and different degrees of social unacceptability: marihuana, the psychedelics, and the opiates (particularly heroin).

Because of what now seems a paucity of knowledge about the specifics of heroin use (not just occasional but also heavy use) (Zinberg et al. 1978), I was unprepared for the complex moral and philosophical problems this research raised. Of course, I was well aware of the difficulty of maintaining an objective stance in the field of drug research. Here the investigator is seen as either for or against drug use. On every panel, radio show, and TV show, and even at professional meetings, where one would expect objectivity, the program must be "balanced." A speaker who is seen as pro-drug is "balanced" by someone who is considered anti-drug. Since the "anti's" take the position that prohibition and abstinence are essential, any opposing view is perceived as pro-drug.

As a result of my earlier work on marihuana, which showed it to be a relatively mild though not harmless intoxicant, I have often been classified with the "pro's." This has caused me little anxiety because I have been firmly committed, in private and in print, to principles of moderation and to a concern about such things as driving when intoxicated, age of the user, and dissemination of the drug. Undoubtedly, too, my conviction that marihuana was not a terribly destructive drug made it easier to shrug off the charge of being pro-drug. It seemed more important to make known the facts about marihuana than to cooperate in promulgating misconceptions, putting people in jail for simple possession, and creating an unnecessary climate of fear. Thus I naturally opposed the unreasonable punishment of anyone who did not agree that the Emperor's raiment was the finest ever seen—that is, that marihuana was a deadly intoxicant.

After my research on social control and illicit drug use had been funded by the DAC in 1973, the question of placing limits on my inquiry became far more pressing. What would be the result of reporting that some people were able to control their heroin use? Might this statement lead certain individuals to try heroin who would not otherwise have done so and who might not be able to handle it?

By 1974 Jacobson had returned to graduate school, and Wayne M. Harding had become my associate in this enterprise. We pondered these painful questions earnestly. Neither of us could accept at face value the time-honored maxim, "The truth will set you free." Both of us remembered the LSD explosion of the mid-1960s, caused partly by the publicity given by professionals and the media to the use of LSD. At first, when we had difficulty in locating people who used heroin occasionally, we felt little concern because it looked as though such use might be insignificant. But when it became clear that there were many such users, we realized that this finding had to come to public attention. Indeed, during the course of our work, other investigators, notably Leon G. Hunt (Hunt & Chambers 1976) and Peter G. Bourne (Bourne, Hunt & Vogt 1975), began to refer to the occasional use of heroin as a stable pattern of use.

At this point the frequency with which I was asked if I was "for" unrestricted heroin use began to bother me. The question not only revealed a misunderstanding of my position on drugs but also showed that it would be an uphill struggle to present effectively any way of dealing with heroin use that did not demand total abstinence. It is my firm conviction, however, that our findings must be reported and explained and that the possibilities they reveal for controlling drug use should be put forward as a scientifically practical way of preventing drug abuse.

It was not an easy task to choose material from so many years' work that would do justice to the project and at the same time preserve readability. For example, it seemed felicitous to place in an appendix the review of the previous literature which demonstrates that many other workers had been aware of the kinds of people I studied but had not found a conceptual framework in which to put their findings. The literature review contains valuable and convincing material as to the historical existence of controlled users, but including it in the body of the book seemed to interfere with the flow of the presentation of the project.

As the book stands now, this personal account of how the project developed is followed by a review of the background from which the conceptual framework of the project was derived (chapter 1).

Chapter 2 attacks the ambiguous terminology responsible for much of the confusion surrounding discussions of intoxicant use. Then the methodology of the research and the data it produced are presented from an objective and quantitative point of view. The next two chapters (4 and 5) translate those hard figures into the subjective data by quoting extensively from the interviews. These two chapters describe qualitatively how the subjects managed to live with and maintain their controlled use of intoxicants. The subjects' own voices emerge to answer questions about use in purely human terms and at the same time indicate how such subjective research data could be translated into numbers.

One factor that has hampered the appreciation and understanding of the interaction between the individual's personality and his or her larger and more circumscribed milieu—that is, the physical and social setting in which the use takes place—has been the ambiguity in psychoanalytic theory. Chapter 6 addresses that problem and shows how a psychodynamic personality theory can encompass both set and setting variables. The problem of developing social policies which can distinguish use from misuse and develop effective formal social controls to interact with the informal control mechanisms discovered by this research, as well as recommendations for treatment and further research, make up the last chapter.

Acknowledgments

The work on which this book is based has been funded by three organizations. The Drug Abuse Council, Inc. (DAC) supported a pilot project, in operation from 1 July 1973 to 30 June 1976, that determined the feasibility of the main study. The National Institute on Drug Abuse (NIDA) funded the research from 1 July 1976 to 30 June 1979, and extended its grant from 1 July 1979 to 30 June 1981 (#Ro1-DA-01360-01). Standard Fittings Company generously provided funds to help with the final drafting of the manuscript of this book. I owe a huge debt of gratitude to each of these organizations.

From 1 July 1974, Wayne M. Harding was indispensable to the inception and continuation of each step of the work. In particular, credit is due him for the methodology and development of the quantification presented in chapter 3 and appendix C. The one other person who was with the project from its beginning and whose intelligence and devotion saw this manuscript through to completion is Miriam Winkeller. To both of them I want to express my thanks and deep indebtedness.

I want to express my appreciation to a number of other people for their help in getting this project under way and working on it once it was in progress: Thomas E. Bryant, M.D., J.D., James V. DeLong, J.D., and Peter Goldberg of The Drug Abuse Council, Inc.; Dan J. Lettieri, Ph.D., of the National Institute on Drug Abuse; Irwin H. Davlin, president of Standard Fittings Company; Andrew T. Weil, M.D.; Robert Apsler, Ph.D., Jack Barrett, Michael Barry, Ellen Dubach, Richard C. Jacobson, Robert A. Marblestone, Deborah Patt, Thomas H. Seay, and Shirley A. Stelmack for their research assistance; and finally, Dorothy W. and Leonard C. Whitney for their editorial assistance.

1

Historical Perspectives on Controlled Drug Use

CARL IS AN OCCASIONAL HEROIN USER. HE IS A SINGLE, WHITE MALE, TWENTY-six years old, a graduate student who emigrated to the United States from South Africa when he was eighteen. His father died when he was two years old, and his mother remarried eighteen months later. His stepfather, a physician, already had a son and daughter, and there were two sons from the new marriage. Carl regards them all as his own family. No one in the family evidences alcoholism or heavy involvement with drugs, including prescription drugs.

Carl's parents are both moderate social drinkers, as he is. They serve beer or wine at almost every evening meal, and Carl was permitted an occasional sip from about age ten or eleven. When he was twelve he tried tobacco and by nineteen had become the one-pack-a-day smoker he still is. At sixteen he tried marihuana and used it on weekends until he was eighteen. Now he uses marihuana up to three times a week but only in the late evening after completing his work or studies or on social occasions.

Amphetamines were popular with one group of Carl's friends, and between the ages of sixteen and eighteen, when he left South Africa, he used these drugs with them on social occasions about once every two weeks. He has used amphetamines only two or three times since then.

At seventeen, when Carl and his closest friend, whose father was also a physician, were experimenting with drugs, they took a bottle of morphine sulfate from the friend's father's office. They also took disposable syringes and injected each other intramuscularly. Both found the experience extremely pleasurable, and from then on they injected each other on weekends until the bottle was exhausted.

At eighteen, after moving to the United States, Carl entered a college in San Francisco, where he became friendly with a psychedelic-using group. His

1

initial psychedelic experience was very pleasant, and for the next year he tripped about two or three times a month. Then his interest in that sort of drug experience waned. Now he uses psychedelics very occasionally—no more than twice a year.

At twenty, when Carl was teaching in southern California, he ran into a group of "hippies" with whom he snorted heroin. Upon returning to San Francisco he began to ask questions about opiate use. Within a short time his discreet inquiries turned up a group of occasional heroin users that included a close friend who had not told Carl about his use. Carl began using with this group once a month on average, but not on a regular basis.

The irregularity of Carl's heroin use was due entirely to his social life. If he was otherwise engaged and did not see his heroin-using friends, he would use less frequently; if he saw them more often, he tended to use more frequently. This pattern has continued except for two periods of two weeks each when Carl was visiting Amsterdam during a European trip. In that wide-open city he used virtually every day, but this had no effect on his using pattern when he returned to the United States.

After moving to Boston and entering graduate school, Carl, then twenty-two, met a new using group to whom he was introduced by friends from California. He likes two or three of them very much but sees them only occasionally. Neither his "best" friend, a fellow graduate student, nor his apartment mate, a thirty-one-year-old engineer who is not a particularly close friend, knows of his heroin use. "I don't want to be deceptive," Carl says, "but some people have an exaggerated fear of heroin and make a big fuss about it. I don't like to have to explain myself. I just like to get high that way once in a while. It's nobody's business what I like, and I don't want to be judged for it."

His use takes place only in a group, and he either "snorts" or injects intramuscularly. "The trick," he says, "is to get high with the least amount possible. If I take too much, I get nauseated, constipated, and have trouble urinating." As a member of a doctor's family, he is fully aware of the possibility of infection, is meticulous about sterilizing his needles, and never lends them to anyone. At his current level of use the high price of heroin is no hardship. One of his friends with "good connections" procures the drug, and when a good buy is made, Carl purchases a little extra to keep for another occasion. He is not sure what he would do if his friend moved away. He hopes to be able to continue use at his current level, which he has maintained for six years.

Carl has a very active social life in which heroin and marihuana play only a small part. His parents are on excellent terms with him and have visited him recently in this country. When he first arrived in the United States, he thought he might have a problem with women because he was not aggressive; but he formed a long-term, satisfying relationship with a woman before he left California. Since moving to Boston he has dated a lot, including seeing one friend quite consistently for more than a year. When that relationship broke up, he was at loose ends for a while; but for the past three months he has been going with someone he thinks may be the most important person in his life.

Carl liked his college in America more than his secondary school in South Africa, which he did not enjoy either socially or intellectually. He likes graduate school even more. He has a tentative job offer in the Boston area that depends on his finishing his thesis before September, and he is working very hard toward that goal.

Until quite recently it was not recognized that Carl and others like him could use illicit drugs in a controlled manner. But the studies that underlie this book on the controlled (moderate, occasional) use of marihuana, psychedelics, and opiates bear witness to the new interest in people like Carl that began to appear during the 1970s.[1] Before then it had been assumed that because of their pharmacological properties, the psychedelics, heroin, and, to a lesser extent, marihuana could not be taken on a long-term, regular basis without causing serious problems. The unfortunate condition of heroin addicts and other compulsive users was invoked as "proof" of this "pharmacomythology" (Szasz 1975). It was also widely held that these "dangerous" substances were almost always sought out by people with profound personality disorders. Most drug research was strongly influenced by the moralistic view that all illicit drug use was therefore "bad," inevitably harmful, or psychologically or physiologically "addictive," and that abstention was the only alternative (Zinberg & Harding 1982).

Not surprisingly, studies of drug consumption, which burgeoned during the 1960s, tended to equate use (any type of use) with abuse and seldom took occasional or moderate use into account as a viable pattern (Heller 1972). To the limited extent that the possibility of nonabusive use was acknowledged, it was treated as a very brief transitional stage leading either to abstinence or (more likely) to compulsive use. Researchers sought first to determine the potentially harmful effects of illicit drugs and then to study the personality disorders resulting from use of these substances—disorders which, ironically, were considered responsible for the drug use in the first place.

Even before the 1960s, however, it had been known that in order to understand how control of a substance taken into the body could be developed, maintained, or lost, different patterns of consumption had to be compared. This principle had long been applied to the comparative study of patterns of alcohol

1. For a survey of previous research on drug addiction, abuse, and controlled use, see appendix C.

use: alcoholism as opposed to social or moderate drinking. Not until after 1970 was the same research strategy rigorously applied to the study of illicit drug use, and only since the mid-1970s have the existence and importance of a still wider range of using patterns been recognized by the scientific community.

The New Perspective on Control

The new interest in the comparative study of patterns of drug use and abuse is attributable to at least two factors. The first is that in spite of the enormous growth of marihuana consumption, most of the old concerns about health hazards have proved to be unfounded. Also, most marihuana use has been found to be occasional and moderate rather than intensive and chronic (Josephson 1974; National Institute on Drug Abuse 1977; *Marijuana and Health* 1982). It has been estimated, for example, that 63% of all Americans using marihuana in 1981 were only occasional users (Miller & Associates 1983). These developments have spurred public and professional recognition of the possibility that illicit substances can be used in moderation and that the question of how control operates at various levels of consumption deserves much more research. A second factor responsible for the new research perspective is the pioneering work of a few scientists who have been more impressed by the logic of their own results than by the mainstream view of illicit drug use. The most influential work has been that of Lee N. Robins, whose research on drug use among Vietnam veterans (discussed in appendix C) indicates that consumption of heroin (the "most dangerous" illicit drug) did not always lead to addiction or dysfunctional use, and that even when addiction occurred it was far more reversible than had been believed (Robins 1973, 1974; Robins et al. 1979).

As the belief lessened that illicit drugs were in a class by themselves, they began to be compared with licit drugs and other substances. At the same time an inverse shift in attitude was taking place toward licit substances. Research indicated that a wide assortment of these substances—tobacco, caffeine, sugar, and various food additives—were potentially hazardous to health (Pekkanen & Falco 1975; Marcovitz 1969). Other research demonstrated that prescribed drugs, if not used in the way the physician intended, could also be hazardous and might constitute a major public health problem. Thus the public became increasingly aware that even with the advice of a physician, "good" drugs used for "good" reasons could be difficult to control. It seemed that just as the mythology that illicit drugs were altogether harmful was losing ground, so too was the mythology that most licit substances were altogether benign. The result has been a new interest in discovering ways of controlling the use of a wide variety of substances, both licit and illicit.

I came to appreciate these changes in perspective largely through my own research. In 1973, when The Drug Abuse Council gave its support to my study of controlled drug users, the conventional attitude of research agencies was that ways should be sought to prevent drug abuse, which at that time meant preventing all drug use (Zinberg, Harding & Apsler 1978). Since in 1973 marihuana, psychedelics, and opiates were causing the greatest concern, these were the drugs I chose to study. The year 1973 was crucial for several reasons. It just preceded the marked rise of cocaine use, as well as the enormous publicity given to PCP, although the use of PCP (under the pseudonyms of angel dust and THC) had long been fairly widespread. It just followed the year in which the National Organization for the Reform of Marihuana Laws (NORML) began formal efforts to decriminalize the private use of marihuana. It was also the last year in which psychedelic drug use increased at a great rate (131%, according to the National Commission on Marihuana and Drug Abuse, 1973). And finally, it marked the decline of overwhelming concern about a heroin "epidemic."

The two related hypotheses underlying this project were far more controversial in 1973 than they would be today, although they are still not generally accepted. I contended, first, that in order to understand what impels someone to use an illicit drug and how that drug affects the user, three determinants must be considered: drug (the pharmacologic action of the substance itself), set (the attitude of the person at the time of use, including his personality structure), and setting (the influence of the physical and social setting within which the use occurs) (Weil 1972; Zinberg & Robertson 1972; Zinberg, Harding & Winkeller 1981). Of these three determinants, setting had received the least attention and recognition; therefore, it was made the focus of the investigation (Zinberg & DeLong 1974; Zinberg & Jacobson 1975). Thus the second hypothesis, a derivative of the first, was that it is the social setting, through the development of sanctions and rituals, that brings the use of illicit drugs under control.

The use of any drug involves both values and rules of conduct (which I have called social sanctions) and patterns of behavior (which I have called social rituals); these two together are known as informal social controls. Social sanctions define whether and how a particular drug should be used. They may be informal and shared by a group, as in the common maxims associated with alcohol use, "Know your limit" and "Don't drive when you're drunk"; or they may be formal, as in the various laws and policies aimed at regulating drug use (Zinberg, Harding & Winkeller, 1981; Maloff et al. 1982). Social rituals are the stylized, prescribed behavior patterns surrounding the use of a drug. They have to do with the methods of procuring and administering the drug, the selection of the physical and social setting for use, the activities undertaken after the drug has been administered, and the ways of preventing untoward drug effects. Rituals thus serve to buttress, reinforce, and symbolize the sanctions. In the case of alcohol, for example, the common invitation "Let's have a drink" automatically exerts some degree of control by using the singular term "a drink." By contrast "Let's get drunk" implies that all restraints will be abandoned.

Social controls (rituals and sanctions together) apply to the use of all drugs, not just alcohol, and operate in a variety of social settings, ranging all the way from very large social groups, representative of the culture as a whole, down to small, discrete groups (Harding & Zinberg 1977). Certain types of special-occasion use involving large groups of people—beer at ball games, marihuana at rock concerts, wine with meals, cocktails at six—despite their cultural diversity, have become so generally accepted that few if any legal strictures are applied even if such uses technically break the law. For example, a policeman may tell young people drinking beer at an open-air concert to "knock it off," but he will rarely arrest them; and in many states the police reaction would be similar even if the drug were marihuana (Newmeyer & Johnson 1982). If the culture as a whole fully adopts a widespread social ritual, it may eventually be written into law, just as the socially developed mechanism of the morning coffee break has been legally incorporated into union contracts. The T.G.I.F. (Thank God It's Friday) drink may not be far from acquiring a similar status. But small-group sanctions and rituals tend to be more diverse and more closely related to circumstances. Nonetheless, some caveats may be just as firmly upheld: "Never smoke marihuana until after the children are asleep," "Only drink on weekends," "Don't shoot up until the last person has arrived and the doors are locked."

The existence of social sanctions and rituals does not necessarily mean that they will be effective, nor does it mean that all sanctions or rituals were devised as mechanisms to aid control. "Booting" (the drawing of blood into and out of a syringe) by heroin addicts seemingly lends enchantment to the use of the needle and therefore opposes control. But it may once have served as a control mechanism that gradually became perverted or debased. Some old-time users, at least, have claimed that booting originated in the (erroneous) belief that by drawing blood in and out of the syringe, the user could gauge the strength of the drug that was being injected.

More important than the question of whether the sanction or ritual was originally intended as a control mechanism is the way in which the user handles conflicts between sanctions. With illicit drugs the most obvious conflict is between formal and informal social controls—that is, between the law against use and the social group's approval of use. The teenager attending a rock concert is often pressured into trying marihuana by his peers, who may insist that smoking is acceptable at that particular time and place and will enhance his musical enjoyment. The push to use may also include a control device, such as "since Joey won't smoke because he has a cold, he can drive," thereby honoring the "don't drive after smoking" sanction. Nevertheless, the decision to use, so rationally presented, conflicts with the law and so may cause the user anxiety. Such anxiety interferes with control. In order to deal with the conflict the user may display more bravado, exhibitionism, paranoia, or antisocial feeling than would have been the case if he or she had patronized one of the little bars near the concert hall. It is this kind of personal and social conflict that makes controlled use of illicit drugs more complex and more difficult to achieve than the controlled use of licit drugs.

Of course, the application of social controls, particularly in the case of illicit drugs, does not always lead to moderate use. And yet it is the reigning cultural belief that drug use should always be moderate and that behavior should always be socially acceptable. Such an expectation, which does not take into account variations in use or the experimentation that is inevitable in learning about control, is the chief reason that the power of the social setting to regulate intoxicant use has not been more fully recognized and exploited. This cultural expectation of decorum stems from the moralistic attitudes that pervade our culture and are almost as marked in the case of licit as in that of illicit drugs. Only on special occasions, such as a wedding celebration or an adolescent's first experiment with drunkenness, is less decorous behavior culturally acceptable. Although such incidents do not necessarily signify a breakdown of overall control, they have led the abstinence-minded to believe that when it comes to drug use, there are only two alternatives—total abstinence or unchecked excess leading to addiction. Despite massive evidence to the contrary, many people remain unshaken in this conviction.

This stolid attitude inhibits the development of a rational understanding of controlled use and ignores the fact that even the most severely affected alcoholics and addicts, who may be grouped at one end of the spectrum of drug use, exhibit some control in that they actually use less of the intoxicating substance than they could. Moreover, as our interviews with ordinary citizens have shown, the highly controlled users and even the abstainers at the other end of the spectrum express much more interest in the use of intoxicants than is generally acknowledged. Whether to use, when, with whom, how much, how to explain why one does not use—these concerns occupy an important place in the emotional life of almost every citizen. Yet, hidden in the American culture lies a deep-seated aversion to acknowledging this preoccupation. As a result, our culture plays down the importance of the many social mores—sanctions and rituals—that enhance our capacity to control use. Both the existence of a modicum of control on the part of the most compulsive users and the general preoccupation with drug use on the part of the most controlled users are ignored. Hence our society is left longing for that utopia in which no one would ever want drugs either for their pleasant or their unpleasant effects, for relaxation and good fellowship, or for escape and oblivion.

The cultural insistence on extreme decorum overemphasizes the determinants of drug and set by implying that social standards are broken because of the power of the drug or some personality disorder of the user. This way of thinking, which ignores the social setting, requires considerable psychological legerdemain, for few users of intoxicants can consistently maintain such self-discipline. Intoxicant use tends to vary with one's time of life, status, and even geographical location. Many who have made heavy use of intoxicants as adolescents slow down as they reach adulthood and change their social setting (their friends and circumstances), while some adults, as they become more successful, may increase their use. For instance, a man born and bred in a dry part of Kansas may change his habits significantly after moving to New York City. The effects of such variations in social circumstances are readily perceived, but they have not been incorporated into a public understanding of how the social setting influences the use and control of intoxicants.

Enormous variations from one historical epoch to another can also be found in the social use of intoxicants, especially alcohol, in various countries. From the perspective of alcohol use, American history can be divided into three major epochs, differing in the power of the mores to moderate the use of alcohol. In considering these epochs it is useful to bear in mind the following social prescriptions for control, summarized from cross-cultural studies of alcohol use (Lolli et al. 1958; Chafetz & Demone 1962; Lolli 1970; Wilkinson 1973; Zinberg & Fraser 1979).

1. Group drinking is clearly differentiated from drunkenness and is associated with ritualistic or religious celebrations.
2. Drinking is associated with eating or ritualistic feasting.
3. Both sexes and all generations are included in the drinking situation, whether they drink or not.
4. Drinking is divorced from the individual effort to escape personal anxiety or difficult (even intolerable) social situations. Moreover, alcohol is not considered medicinally valuable.
5. Inappropriate behavior when drinking (violence, aggression, overt sexuality) is absolutely disapproved, and protection against such behavior is exercised by the sober or the less intoxicated. This general acceptance of a concept of restraint usually indicates that drinking is only one of many activities and thus carries a low level of emotionalism.

During the first period of American history, from the 1600s to the 1770s, the colonies, though veritably steeped in alcohol, strongly and effectively prohibited drunkenness. Families ate and drank together in taverns, and drinking was associated with celebrations and rituals. Tavern-keepers had social status; preserving the peace and preventing excesses stemming from drunkenness were grave duties. Manliness and strength were not measured by the extent of consumption or by violent acts resulting from it. This pre-Revolutionary society did not, however, abide by all the prescriptions for control: "groaning beer," for example, was regarded as medicine and consumed in large quantities by pregnant and lactating women.

The second period, from the 1770s to about 1890, which included the Revolutionary War, the Industrial Revolution, and the expansion of the frontier, was marked by alcoholic excess. Men were separated from their families and in consequence began to drink together and with prostitutes. Alcohol was served without food, its consumption was not limited to special occasions, and violence resulting from drunkenness became much more common. In the face of increasing drunkenness and alcoholism, people began to believe (as is the case with regard to some illicit drugs today) that the powerful, harmful pharmaceutical properties of the intoxicant itself made controlled use remote or impossible.

Although by the beginning of the third period, which extended from 1890 to the present time, moderation in the use of alcohol had begun to increase, this trend was suddenly interrupted in the early 1900s by the Volstead Act, which ushered in another era of excess. American society has not yet fully recovered from the speakeasy ambience of Prohibition in which men again drank together and with prostitutes, food was replaced by alcohol, and the drinking experience was colored by illicitness and potential violence. Although the repeal of the prohibition act provided relief from excessive and unpopular legal control, it left society without an inherited set of clear social sanctions and rituals to control use.

Social Sanctions Internalized

Today this vacuum is gradually being filled. In most sectors of our society informal alcohol education is readily available. Few children grow up without an awareness of the wide range of behaviors associated with alcohol use, learned from that most pervasive of all the media, television. They see cocktail parties, wine at meals, beer at ball games, homes broken by drink, drunks whose lives are wrecked, along with all the advertisements that present alcohol as lending glamor to every occasion.

Buttressed by movies, the print media, observation of families and family friends, and often by a sip or watered-down taste of the grown-ups' potion, young people gain an early familiarity with alcohol. When, in a peer group, they begin to drink and even, as a rite of passage, to overdo it, they know what the relevant sanctions are. The process of finding a limit is a direct expression of "know your limit." Once that sanction has been internalized—and our culture provides mores of greater latitude for adolescents than for adults—youngsters can move on to such sanctions as "it is unseemly to be drunk" and "it's OK to have a drink at the end of the day or a few beers on the way home from work or in front of TV, but don't drink on the job" (Zinberg, Harding & Winkeller 1981).

This general description of the learning or internalization of social sanctions has not taken into account the variations from individual to individual that result from differences in personality, cultural background, and group affinity. Specific sanctions and rituals are developed and integrated in varying degrees by different groups (Edwards 1974). Some ethnic groups, such as the Irish, lack strong sanctions against drunkenness and have a correspondingly higher rate of alcoholism. In any ethnic group, alcohol socialization within the family may break down as a result of divorce, death, or some other disruptive event. Certainly a New York child from a rich, sophisticated home, accustomed to having Saturday lunch with a divorced parent at The 21 Club, will have a different attitude toward drinking from that of the small-town child who vividly remembers accompanying a parent to a sporting event where alcohol intake acted as fuel for the excitement of unambivalent partisanship. Yet one common denominator shared by young people from these very different backgrounds is the sense that alcohol is used at special events and in special places.

This kind of education about drug use is social learning, absorbed inchoately and unconsciously in daily life (Zinberg 1974). The learning process is impelled by an unstated and often unconscious recognition by young people that drug use is an area of emotional importance in American society and that knowledge about it may be quite important to their personal and social development. Attempts made in the late 1960s and early 1970s to translate this informal process into formal drug education courses, chiefly intended to discourage use, have failed (Boris, Zinberg & Boris 1978). Such formal drug education, paradoxically, by focusing on drug use has stimulated such use on the part of many young people who were previously uncommitted, and while acting to confirm the fears of many who were already excessively concerned. Is it possible for formal education to codify social sanctions and rituals in a reasonable way for those who have been bypassed by the informal process, or does the reigning cultural moralism preclude the possibility of discussing reasonable informal social controls that may condone use? This question will remain unanswered until our culture has accepted the use not only of alcohol but of other intoxicants so that teachers will be able to explain how these drugs can be used safely and well. Teaching safe use is not intended to encourage use. Its main purpose is the prevention of abuse, just as the primary purpose of the few good sex education courses in existence today is to teach the avoidance of unwanted pregnancy and venereal disease rather than the desirability of having or avoiding sexual activity.

Whatever may happen to formal education in these areas, the natural process of social learning will inevitably go on for better or for worse. The power of this process is illustrated by two recent and extremely important social events: the use of psychedelics in the United States in the 1960s and the use of heroin during the Vietnam War.

Shortly after Timothy Leary's advice to "tune in, turn on, and drop out" was adopted as a counterculture slogan in 1963, the use of psychedelics became a subject of national hysteria. The "drug revolution" was seen as a major threat to the dominant cultural values of hard work, family, and loyalty to country. Drugs, known then as psychotomimetics (imitators of psychosis), were widely believed to lead to psychosis, suicide, or even murder (Mogar & Savage 1954; Robbins, Frosch & Stern 1967). Equally well publicized was the contention that they could bring about spiritual rebirth and mystical oneness with the universe (Huxley 1954; Weil 1972). Certainly there were numerous cases of not merely transient but prolonged psychoses following the use of psychedelics. In the mid-1960s psychiatric hospitals like the Massachusetts Mental Health Center and New York City's Bellevue Hospital reported that as many as one-third of their admissions resulted from the ingestion of these drugs (Robbins, Frosch & Stern 1967). By the late 1960s, however, the rate of such admissions had dropped dramatically. At first, many observers concluded that psychedelic use had declined in response to the use of "fear tactics"—the dire warnings about the various health hazards, the chromosome breaks and birth defects, that were reported in the newspapers. This explanation proved false, for although the dysfunctional sequelae had radically declined, psychedelic use continued until 1973 to be the fastest growing drug use in America (National Commission on Marihuana and Drug Abuse 1973). What then had changed?

It has been found that neither the drugs themselves nor the personalities of the users were the most prominent factors in those painful cases of the 1960s. Although responses to the drugs varied widely, before the early 1960s, they included none of the horrible, highly publicized consequences of the mid-1960s (McGlothlin & Arnold 1971). Another book, entitled *LSD: Personality and Experience* (Barr et al. 1972), describes a study made before the drug revolution of the influence of personality on psychedelic drug experience. It found typologies of response to the drugs but did not discover a one-to-one relationship between untoward reaction and emotional disturbance. In 1967 sociologist Howard S. Becker, in a prophetic article, compared the current anxiety about psychedelics to anxiety about marihuana in the late 1920s, when several psychoses had been reported. Becker hypothesized that the psychoses came not from the drug reactions themselves but from the secondary anxiety generated by unfamiliarity with the drug's effects and ballooned by media publicity. He suggested that the unpleasant reactions had ceased to appear after the true effects of marihuana had become more widely known, and he correctly predicted that the same thing would happen in the case of the psychedelics.

The power of social learning also brought about a change in the reactions of those who expected to gain insight and enlightenment from the use of psychedelics. Interviews (ours and others') have shown that the user of the early 1960s, with his great hopes of heaven or fears of hell and his lack of any sense of what to expect, had a far more extreme experience than the user of the 1970s, who had been exposed to a decade of interest in psychedelic colors, music, and sensations. The later user, who might remark, "Oh, so that is what a psychedelic color looks like," had been thoroughly prepared, albeit unconsciously, for the experience and thus could respond in a more restrained way.

The second example of the enormous influence of the social setting and of social learning on drug use comes from Vietnam. Current estimates indicate that at least 35% of enlisted men (EMs) tried heroin while in Vietnam and that 54% of these became addicted to it (Robins et al. 1979). Although the success of the major treatment modalities available when these veterans became addicted (therapeutic communities and civil commitment programs) cannot be precisely determined, evaluations showed that relapse to addiction within a year was a more common outcome than abstinence, and recidivism rates as high as 90% were reported (DeLong 1972). Once the extent of the use of heroin in Vietnam became apparent, the great fear of Army and government officials was that the maxim, "Once an addict, always an addict," would operate; and most of the experts agreed that this fear was entirely justified. Treatment and rehabilitation centers were set up in Vietnam, and the Army's slogan that heroin addiction stopped "at the shore of the South China Sea" was heard everywhere. As virtually all observers agree, however, those programs were total failures. Often servicemen used more heroin in the rehabilitation programs than when on active duty (Zinberg 1972).

Nevertheless, as Lee N. Robins and her colleagues have shown (1979), most addiction did indeed stop at the South China Sea. For addicts who left Vietnam, recidivism to addiction three years after they got back to the United States was approximately 12%—virtually the reverse of previous reports (DeLong 1972). Apparently it was the abhorrent social setting of Vietnam that led men who ordinarily would not have considered using heroin to use it and often to become addicted to it. Still, they evidently associated its use with Vietnam, much as certain hospital patients who are receiving large amounts of opiates for a painful medical condition associate the drug with the condition. The returnees were very much like those patients, who usually do not crave the drug after the condition has been alleviated and they have left the hospital.

For some individuals dependence on almost any available intoxicating substance is likely. But even the most generous estimate of the number of such individuals is not large enough to explain the extraordinarily high rate of heroin use in Vietnam. The number of addiction-prone personalities might even have been lower than that in a normal population because the military had screened out the worst psychological problems at enlistment. Robins found that heroin use in Vietnam correlated well with a youthful liability scale. This scale included some items that are related to set—that is, to emotional difficulties (truancy, dropout or expulsion from school, fighting, arrests). But it also included many items related to the social setting, such as race or living in the inner city, and even then it accounted for only a portion of the variance in youthful heroin use.

A better explanation for the high rate of heroin use and addiction in Vietnam than the determinant of set or personality might be the drug and its extraordinary availability. Robins noted that 85% of veterans had been offered heroin in Vietnam, and that it was remarkably inexpensive (Robins et al. 1979). Another drug variable, the method of administration, must also have contributed to widespread use in Vietnam. Heroin was so potent and inexpensive that smoking was an effective and economical method to use, and this no doubt made it more attractive than if injection had been the primary mode of administration. These two drug variables also help to explain the decrease in heroin use and addiction among veterans following their return to the United States. The decreased availability of heroin in the United States (reflected in its high price) and its decreased potency (which made smoking wholly impractical) made it difficult for the returning veterans to continue use.

Although the drug variable may carry more explanatory power in the case of Vietnam than the various set variables, it also has limits. Ready availability of heroin seems to account for the high prevalence of use, but it alone does not explain why some individuals became addicted and others did not, any more than the availability of alcohol is sufficient to explain the difference between the alcoholic and the social drinker. Availability is always intertwined with the social and psychological factors that create demand for an intoxicant. Once a reasonably large number of users decide that a substance is attractive and desirable, it is surprising how quickly that substance becomes plentiful. For instance, when the morale of U.S. troops in Germany declined in 1972, large quantities of various drugs, including heroin, became readily available, even though Germany is far from opium-growing areas. In the early 1980s cocaine is the best example of drug availability.

In the case of both heroin use in Vietnam and psychedelic use in the 1960s, the setting determinant, including social sanctions and rituals, is needed for a full explanation of the appearance, magnitude, and eventual waning of drug use.

Control over the use of psychedelics was not established until the counter-culture developed social sanctions and rituals like those surrounding alcohol use in the society at large. The sanction "The first time use only with a guru" told neophytes to try the drug with an experienced user who could reduce their secondary anxiety about what was happening by interpreting it as a drug effect. "Use only at a good time, in a good place, with good people" gave sound advice to those taking the kind of drug that would make them highly sensitive to their inner and outer surroundings. In addition, it conveyed the message that the drug experience could be a pleasant consciousness change instead of either heaven or hell. The specific rituals that developed to express these sanctions— just when it was best to take the drug, how it should be used, with whom, what was the best way to come down, and so on—varied from group to group, though some rituals spread between groups.

It is harder to document the development of social sanctions and rituals in Vietnam. Most of the early evidence indicated that the drug was used heavily in order to obscure the actualities of the war, with little thought of control. Yet later studies showed that many EMs used heroin in Vietnam without becoming addicted (Robins, Davis & Goodwin 1974; Robins, Helzer & Davis 1975). Although about half of the men who had been addicted in Vietnam used heroin after their return to the United States, only 12% became readdicted to it (Robins et al 1979).

Some rudimentary rituals do seem to have been followed by the men who used heroin in Vietnam. The act of gently rolling the tobacco out of an ordinary cigarette, tamping the fine white powder into the opening, and then replacing a little tobacco to hold the powder in before lighting up the OJ (opium joint) seemed to be followed all over the country even though units in the North and the Highlands had no direct contact with those in the Delta (Zinberg 1972). To what extent this ritual aided control is impossible to determine, but having observed it many times, I know that it was almost always done in a group and that it formed part of the social experience of heroin use. While one person was performing the ritual, the others sat quietly and watched in anticipation. Thus the degree of socialization achieved through this ritual could have had impor-tant implications for control.

My continuing study of various patterns of heroin use, including con-trolled use, in the United States confirmed the lessons taught by the history of alcohol use in America, the use of psychedelics in the 1960s, and the use of heroin during the Vietnam War. The social setting, with its formal and informal controls, its capacity to develop new informal social sanctions and rituals, and its transmission of information in numerous informal ways, is a crucial factor in the controlled use of any intoxicant. This does not mean that the pharmaceutical properties of the drug or the attitudes and personality of the user count for little or nothing. All three variables—drug, set, and setting—must be included in any valid theory of drug use. It is necessary to understand in every case how the specific characteristics of the drug and the personality of the user interact and are modified by the social setting and its controls.

Illicit Drugs and Social Learning

Our culture does not yet fully recognize, much less support, controlled use of most illicit drugs. Users are declared "deviant" and a threat to society, or "sick" and in need of help, or "criminal" and deserving of punishment. Family-centered socialization for use is not available. Parents, even if they are willing to help, are unable to provide guidance either by example (as with alcohol) or in a factual, nonmoralistic manner.

If parents tell their sons or daughters not to use drugs because they are harmful, the youngsters disregard that advice because their own experiences have told them otherwise. Their using group and the drug culture reinforce their own discovery that drug use in and of itself is not bad or evil and that the warnings coming from the adult world are unrealistic. If parents try a different tack and tell young people that some drugs are all right but others have a high risk component and should be avoided, their position again is vulnerable. "They were wrong about marihuana; why should I believe what they say about cocaine?" think the youngsters (Kaplan 1970). Moreover, by counseling their children that some illicit drugs are "more all right" than others, parents are placed in the position of having to approve an illegal activity. Thus their role as conveyors of the public morality becomes glaringly inconsistent.

The interviews conducted by my research team have indicated that if parents try to obtain first-hand knowledge of the drug experience by smoking marihuana, taking a psychedelic, or shooting heroin, similar difficulties occur. At the very least, they not only are condoning but are themselves engaging in a deviant act. This problem pales, however, before those that arise when the parents try to find out where to get the drug and then how to interpret the high. If they ask their children to get the drug for them or to be with them while they are experiencing the high, the traditional roles of instructor and pupil are reversed. While the youngsters may enjoy this novel authority, it places them in an extremely difficult caretaking role. Above all, such a situation creates enormous anxiety for the parents. Many parents interviewed by my team had never achieved a high because of the dynamics of the social situation, and others had experienced a major panic reaction that convinced them the drug was bad and their children were indeed on the road to destruction (Jacobson & Zinberg 1975). Parents could avoid this pitfall by obtaining the drug in question from their own peers, but even then they would be placed in the position of participating in an illegal activity. In short, illicit drug use is a no-win situation for everyone, even for those trying to plan and teach useful drug education courses.

In the case of the mass media, most of the information provided is dramatically opposed to drug use and to the possibility of controlled use. Heroin consumption is viewed as a plague, a social disease. Stories about bad psychedelic trips resulting in psychosis or suicide have served for years as media staples, and more recently there has been a new spate of marihuana horror programs. In the early 1980s, when extreme care is being taken not to offend any ethnic group, it seems that drug users and peddlers, along with hopeless psychotics, are the only villains left to be featured in the innumerable "cops and robbers" serials and movies shown on television.

When parents, schools, and the media are all unable to inform neophytes about the controlled use of illicit drugs, that task falls squarely on the new user's peer group—an inadequate substitute for cross-generation, long-term socialization. Since illicit drug use is a covert activity, newcomers are not presented with an array of using groups from which to choose, and association with controlled users is largely a matter of chance. Early in their using careers, many of our research subjects became involved either with groups whose members were not well schooled in controlled use or with groups in which compulsive use and risk-taking were the rules. Such subjects went through periods when drug use interfered with their ability to function, and they frequently experienced untoward drug effects. Eventually these subjects became controlled users, but only after they had realigned themselves with new companions—a difficult and uncertain process. Unfortunately, many adolescent users never make this transition.

Cultural opposition complicates the development of controlled use in still another way: by inadvertently creating a black market in which the drugs being sold are of uncertain quality. With marihuana, variations in the content do not present a significant problem because dosage can be titrated and harmful adulterants are extremely rare; the most common negative effect of the black-market economy is that the neophyte marihuana user pays more than he should for a poor product. For the other drugs there are wide variations in strength and purity that make the task of controlling dosage and effect more difficult. Psychedelics are sometimes misrepresented: LSD, PCP, or the amphetamines may be sold as mescaline. With heroin, the potency of a buy is unknown and the risk of an overdose is thus increased. If adulterants are present, the risk of infection may be heightened when the drug is injected.

The present policy of prohibition of drug use by legal means would be justifiable if it persuaded some people never to use drugs and led others to abandon them. Undoubtedly prohibition discourages excessive use, a goal with which I sympathize. But no one knows whether the number of users would be increased if prohibition were to be suspended. Would many people who had not tried illicit drugs choose to use them? Would many who had tried them go on to become compulsive users?

Aside from its questionable effect on the number of drug users, the prohibition policy actively contributes to the prevailing dichotomy between abstinence and compulsive use. It makes it extremely difficult for anyone who wishes to use drugs to select a moderate using pattern. This outcome may have been acceptable before the 1960s, when there were few potential drug experimenters, but it could prove catastrophic in the 1980s when adolescent experimentation approaches statistically normal behavior. Since 1976 more than 50% of high-school seniors report having tried marihuana or hashish at some time in the past, and over 44% have tried within the past two years (Johnston, Bachman & O'Malley 1982).

Although the opportunities for learning how to control illicit drug consumption are extremely limited, rituals and social sanctions that promote control do exist within subcultures of drug users. Our interviews have shown that these controlling rituals and sanctions function in four basic and overlapping ways.

First, sanctions define moderate use and condemn compulsive use. Controlled opiate users, for example, have sanctions limiting frequency of use to levels far below that required for addiction. Many have special sanctions, such as "don't use every day." One ritual complementing that sanction restricts the use of an opiate to weekends.

Second, sanctions limit use to physical and social settings that are conducive to a positive or "safe" drug experience. The maxim for psychedelics is, "Use in a good place at a good time with good people." Two rituals consonant with such sanctions are the selection of a pleasant rural setting for psychedelic use and the timing of use to avoid driving while "tripping."

Third, sanctions identify potentially untoward drug effects. Rituals embody the precautions to be taken before and during use. Opiate users may minimize the risk of overdose by using only a portion of the drug and waiting to gauge its effect before using more. Marihuana users similarly titrate their dosage to avoid becoming too high (dysphoric).

Fourth, sanctions and rituals operate to compartmentalize drug use and support the users' non-drug-related obligations and relationships. For exampel, users may budget the amount of money they spend on drugs, as they do for entertainment; or they may use drugs only in the evenings and on weekends to avoid interfering with work performance.

The process by which controlling rituals and sanctions are acquired varies from subject to subject. Most individuals come by them gradually during the course of their drug-using careers. Without doubt the most important source of precepts and practices for control is the peer using group. Virtually all of our subjects had been assisted by other noncompulsive users in constructing appropriate rituals and sanctions out of the folklore and practices circulating in their drug-using subculture. The peer group provided instruction in and reinforced proper use; and despite the popular image of peer pressure as a corrupting force pushing weak individuals toward drug misuse, our interviews showed that many segments of the drug subculture have taken a firm stand against drug abuse.

2

Addiction, Abuse, and Controlled Drug Use: Some Definitions

THE USE OF ILLICIT DRUGS HAS BEEN A TOPIC OF ENDLESS DISCUSSION IN both professional and lay circles. Most discussions have centered on specific aspects of "drug abuse," such as damage to the user's health and his consequent inability to function effectively. While such effects are undoubtedly felt by some users, it is equally true that many others are able to use drugs moderately rather than destructively. Yet the term "drug abuse" continues to be applied to all styles of drug use, and little or no effort has been made to distinguish abuse from use. In addition, scientific writers as well as the mass media use the term "drug abuse" without defining it explicitly, and even when concerned and informed professionals attempt to formulate precise definitions, their attempts reflect the prevailing cultural values and do not clearly differentiate use from abuse. Many people use "drug abuse" rather than "addiction" because drug abuse is a loose term meant to convey whatever the person using the term thinks is bad. Addiction is a more specific term used to define physiological dependence and, although sometimes used loosely, has a strictly defined meaning.

Users or Abusers? Three Cases

Not surprisingly, the greatest problem I faced in studying controlled users of illicit drugs was that of differentiating between drug use and drug abuse. This difference was fairly evident at the extremes of behavior, but it was by no means so obvious in the gray area where the majority of cases in my study fell. At one extreme were those who used no drugs except marihuana and used that only once a week, along with those who used psychedelics only three or four times a year. All these subjects were so clearly responsible in their drug use that it would not have been rational to define them as drug abusers. At the other extreme were several compulsive users who were included in the research only because my staff and I failed to screen them out during the initial telephone contact. These obvious drug abusers proved useful in helping us to understand how wide the range of using patterns was. Finally, many of our subjects fell into the gray area of more or less controlled use. The case histories of three such subjects—Michael, Jim and Dawn—illustrate that some individuals can keep their drug use under control, avoiding the excessive use and destructive effects that characterize the drug abuser. Michael and Jim's cases have been condensed. Dawn's story is told more fully because it shows the value of approaching the use-abuse problem longitudinally (over time) rather than only cross-sectionally (at a particular point in time).

Michael is a thirty-one-year-old, single, white male social worker, the third of nine children born to a strict, lower-middle-class Catholic family. He has always done well in school (A.B. in Philosophy and M.A. in Social Work) and has a regular and exemplary work history. The members of his immediate family have no history of alcoholism or other serious involvement with drugs, including prescription drugs, but his father uses tobacco heavily. Both of his parents are light drinkers, and from the age of nine or ten Michael was allowed to taste wine on such formal occasions as weddings, baptisms, and birthdays. He began to drink occasionally with his friends at age fourteen or fifteen and after getting sick two or three times reverted to an occasional drink about twice a week and occasional wine or beer with certain meals: "Much less often than my friends." This pattern has continued to the present time. He smoked surreptitiously until age sixteen, when his parents grudgingly gave him permission to continue openly, and he now averages one pack a day. He did not use marihuana until age twenty-seven when, after two or three unsatisfactory experiences, he began to find it pleasurable. Now he uses the drug socially once or twice every other week.

Michael enjoys his job and also takes pleasure in woodworking and handicrafts, and he is renovating his apartment. He has two separate groups of friends, one from work and the other whom he met through tennis, skiing, and craft work. He has had two moderately serious relationships with women, each lasting about a year, as well as several short-term affairs. He has been sexually active in all his adult relationships, including the one with his current girlfriend, whom he has known for three months. He finds that marihuana use "makes sex more pleasurable, more spontaneous, but not easier." After acknowledging his marihuana use in the course of family discussions, Michael was persuaded by two of his brothers, a sister, and a sister-in-law to "turn them on" also.

With characteristic conservatism Michael says of marihuana and alcohol,

"In the use of both I have a take-it-or-leave-it attitude although I like what I do." He regards the dangers of drug use as greatly exaggerated and the drug laws as archaic and unworkable. His friends experiment with psychedelics and this has intrigued him, but Michael does not plan to use other drugs: "I'm afraid of physical or psychological damage, and I don't want to risk it." He does plan to continue his current pattern of marihuana use, however.

Jim, a twenty-four-year-old black male, has always lived with some member of his family. His father, who was a habitual alcoholic until twelve years ago, spent little time at home. His mother worked in the evenings as a maid. Jim and his two brothers were left unsupervised and "went to the streets" in early adolescence.

Jim was first arrested at age eleven for purse-snatching. Each year further arrests followed, for armed robbery, attempted murder, possession of heroin with intent to distribute, and assault and battery on a police officer. During his school years, his criminal activities took precedence over studies and he quit in the tenth grade, although he felt he was capable of doing well academically. At age eighteen he was incarcerated for nine months on a drug charge.

By age thirteen Jim was a daily tobacco user; on weekends, at dances, and on other special occasions he was drinking to get drunk; and he was also using amphetamines five or six times on weekends. By age sixteen he was using marihuana several times a day and had tried heroin. He began by snorting but in a few months was injecting and within nine months had experienced the first of his five "habits" (periods of physiological addiction). His longest heroin habit coincided with participation in a methadone maintenance program at about age nineteen, and it lasted almost two years. His last habit started some six months later and lasted three or four months. At the time he was pimping, and his earnings enabled him to use at least $100 worth of heroin a day. Then he decided to quit using because of the size of his habit and the increasing risk; as he said, "I felt myself going to jail." After withdrawing without anyone's help— an unpleasant but less dramatic experience, he reported, than is often portrayed on television—he started "chipping." He began use at the rate of three times a week, but more than two years ago he cut down to his present level of "twice a week, and sometimes only once a week."

Jim is especially particular about keeping his "works" clean and will not share them with friends. Hence he prefers to use alone, often at his brother's apartment, and then go out and meet friends. The day after using he invariably exercises because he believes this activity helps cleanse his system of heroin. Jim's use of other drugs has also fallen off. He uses beer and wine occasionally ("Me and alcohol don't get along"), marihuana twice a day or less, cocaine once or twice a week, and Valium and Quaaludes erratically.

Jim has had many "temporary jobs here and there" but is ordinarily unem-

ployed. His chief activities and means of support are dealing heroin and hustling of various sorts—usually breaking and entering. He lives either with a
brother or with a girlfriend whom he has known for five years. His drug use is
important to him but less important than the criminal activity he takes pride in:
"I put my business first before I use a drug, and there's got to be extra money to
buy some stuff with."

Jim has indicated some interest in obtaining a high school equivalency
degree and eventually attending college and becoming a physical education
instructor. He plans to continue heroin use, but would like to reduce it to once
or twice a month.

Dawn is a twenty-seven-year-old, single, white female employed by the
court to work with juveniles to avoid criminal sentencing if possible. She was
brought up in New York City, the only child of middle-class, achievement-
oriented parents. She has always been on much better terms with her father
than with her mother. Her parents are moderate social drinkers. There is no
history of alcoholism or of the heavy use of other drugs, illicit or prescribed, in
her immediate family.

Dawn was exposed to marihuana when she went out with a young man who
was a regular user, but she did not begin to use it herself until she had stopped
seeing him. She tried it first at age sixteen with her friend Susan, and the two
girls then began to smoke in school and on the school bus, apparently quite
provocatively. This came to the attention of their parents and the school administrators, who regarded Dawn and Susan as a pair of "rebellious kids." About
five months after she had begun smoking marihuana Dawn started experimenting with psychedelics, which she liked. She continued to use both drugs—
psychedelics only occasionally—throughout her school and college years.

Dawn went through the only period of regular drinking in her life during
the summer of her eighteenth year, consuming about two six-packs of beer a
week. She and her parents were much at odds that summer and have never
been close since; but they had little objection to her alcohol use. If anything,
they expressed surprise when she later gave it up.

She first used heroin at age eighteen, shortly after arriving at a college in
Boston. She and a friend, Lois, were exploring what was then Boston's "hippie"
section, looking for "downs" (Seconal). They were unable to make any drug
connections except with a young man who offered them "junk." They declined
and went back to the dorm. Then, as Dawn put it, "I felt depressed and lonely
and none of my roommates were home. And I wanted to get high, and so I said
to myself, 'Well, the hell with this. I'll go back there and I'll ask him one more
time and I'll just buy something to get high on and I don't care what it is.'" She
went back alone. The dealer sold her a bag of heroin at a very low price but

warned her not to "ever get into it" or come back again. She immediately went into a bathroom in her dorm and snorted some of it. "I felt great, I was high, and I felt really good." Later she went to the room of "some sophisticated girls" who had previously intimidated her, felt quite comfortable, and snorted the rest with them. When she told Lois what had happened after they parted, Lois became very upset and begged her not to do it again. Because this made her feel that "somebody really cared," Dawn stayed away from heroin use for the next two years.

During those two years she spent the summers in a communal living situation with her boyfriend, Paul, and a large group of other people. Paul and the others were using heroin regularly: "People were constantly coming over and getting off that year and the next year, and I just never tried it. I was repulsed by the whole thing and I wouldn't do it." She did try methadone in this house, however, two years after her first heroin use. She recognized and enjoyed the opiate high and felt safe in drinking rather than shooting it.

A year later, at age twenty-one, Dawn again tried heroin when Susan, her old school friend, came to visit and told Dawn she had been shooting heroin once a week. "I was like in a really depressed, really angry, really rebellious sort of mood . . . so when Susan said, 'Oh, let's get some,' I said, 'Great.'" This was the first time Dawn had injected a drug. She next used heroin a month later, after dropping out of college and moving to the West Coast. She left Paul behind, as he was now "getting strung out." Once in the West she called George, a good friend of Paul's, "to come over and hit me up." They began to live together. George had unlimited access to heroin: "For a couple of months it was like all you want, any time you want, you've got it, it's yours. So I was doing just thousands of dollars, for free." She used heroin several times a day. "I'd do a shot and my head would be between my knees and he'd say, 'Did you get high enough?' and I'd say, 'No, I need another shot' . . . I was drowning myself in dope." After three months, when George went away for the weekend and Dawn contracted what she thought was the flu, she realized she was addicted. "It freaked me out because I thought it couldn't happen to me . . . After that I started feeling like I was really going down the tubes real fast . . . going to hell on a sled. And so what I did was buy a plane ticket back to the East Coast, because I knew that the only thing there [in the West] for me was just to be in the mire of dope, and I was just caught in it." She resolved it would never happen to her again.

She returned to Boston and worked as a secretary for the next year and a half, laying plans for graduate school and "chipping" heroin on a once-a-week basis. She had contacted all of her old "dope crowd" friends and so had easy access, but her funds were limited. She established a Friday night using pattern to "reward" herself for having worked all week.

In early 1974 she began another heavy using period when she went to the West Coast for a visit and met her old boyfriend Paul, who was now on the West Coast, and several other friends who had become heroin addicts. She used the drug with them daily for one month but then had to make a choice between staying with Paul and returning East to complete her graduate school plans: "I knew that if I were back there [in the West] I would just get strung out . . . there was no motivation to stop using drugs, it was there, it was too easy." So she returned to enter graduate school in New York, where she stayed for two years. During this time she used hardly any drugs, and no opiates at all, even though she had "coincidentally" met a dope dealer.

In 1976, after completing graduate work, she returned to Boston and began a sporadic "chipping" pattern: heroin three times in January; Demerol ten times during the course of the summer; heroin again twice in the fall and about once a month after that.

Now Dawn is experiencing some conflict in regard to future opiate use. She still "loves the high," but she sees use as a tremendous risk to her new career. She feels strongly that heroin should be legalized in order to eliminate the risk and because, as she says, "you can function when you're high on heroin, you can do your job . . . I would not hesitate to drive, for instance, if I was stoned on heroin . . . as long as I wasn't too stoned."

Only three of Dawn's associates know of her opiate use, and all of them are also occasional users. She never gets high at home; her usual pattern is to go to someone else's house. She does not own her own works and never self-injects but is meticulous about cleaning the needles she shares. She will not buy more heroin than she can easily afford and is never high around "straight friends" or at work. She finds that the high state usually lasts for six hours, and she spends that time indoors talking and playing music. "You just talk a whole lot and you . . . fantasize a lot. You feel as though your dreams come true, and you start to think about them and little things don't bother you so much."

During the entire period of family conflict and heavy drug use, Dawn did extremely well scholastically and at work. She regards herself now as ambitious and potentially successful.

All three of these drug histories—Michael's, Jim's, and Dawn's—show a complex interrelationship between personality factors and social factors as determinants of the extent and quality of drug use.

It is clear that Michael, judged on personality grounds alone, is an unusually controlled person whose drug use would not be considered a problem if it were not for our current drug policy. It is also quite clear that without the influence of a peer group that approved of illicit marihuana use, provided reasonable assurance of its safety, and offered standards and procedures of appropriateness, Michael would not have used marihuana at all.

The other two cases, which are more complex, illustrate how hard it is to decide when an individual's drug use has crossed the line separating use from abuse and whether the change in either direction is going to be permanent. Both Jim and Dawn are committed to "high" life-styles and do not plan to give them up. Both have been physiologically addicted to heroin, which is generally considered the same thing as being in serious trouble. Yet at the time of our first interview Jim had been a controlled user for more than two years and on re-interview a year later seemed even more controlled than before. Dawn, whose last period of heavy use, once a day for a month on the West Coast, is more recent, will need a long-term follow-up before we can be sure that she has achieved genuine control.

Drug Abuse and Addiction

Though the terms "drug abuse" and "addiction" are used nearly interchange-ably by some today, historically the narrower concept of addiction has not always been regarded as drug abuse. Even "drug abuse" did not emerge as a problem until early in the twentieth century, when the nonmedical use of certain intoxicants began to evoke moral indignation and public concern and led to legal regulation.

The term "drug abuse" seems to have been applied first to the use of cocaine by Southern blacks, but as David F. Musto (1973) and John Helmer (1975) have pointed out, it originally reflected race and class prejudice against the black users rather than concern about the dangerous effects of cocaine. A little later the term was extended to the smoking of opium by Chinese Americans, and again it expressed fear of a despised minority. In this case, however, the importation of opium for smoking purposes was banned (1909), though its use in patent medicines continued to be permitted.

Not until the passage of the Harrison Narcotic Act in 1914 was the use of two more drugs—heroin and morphine—subsumed under the term "drug abuse." This act and the series of regulations and Supreme Court decisions interpreting it transformed the use of all unprescribed opiates from a bad habit into a criminal activity. Even physicians lost their right to prescribe opiates at will, and attempts to supply addicts legally with opium through medical clinics, which had begun in 1919, were all abandoned by 1924 (Musto 1973; Waldorf, Orlick & Reinarman 1974). Rural addicts who were unable to give up the drug moved to the coastal cities, where black markets sprang up and public animosity toward addiction developed.

Also in the early years of the twentieth century the meaning of the term "addiction" changed markedly. It had been used traditionally, at least since the Civil War, to mean "a habit, good or bad . . . more often the former" (Szasz 1975). Following the medical use of the opiates (particularly morphine) during the Civil War, addiction resulting from the nonmedical use of morphine became widespread. Popularly known as "the soldier's illness," addiction was regarded then either as a nonspecific illness or as evidence of character weakness, not as a form of degeneracy. Later, in the final years of the nineteenth century and the first decade of the twentieth, the use of patent medicines containing large amounts of opiates led to an even higher rate of addiction among the general population (higher than the rate in the late 1970s) (Lindesmith 1965). Yet the opiates were viewed as "God's own medicine," and although addiction was disapproved of, it was tolerated. "Morphinists," like the mother in Eugene O'Neill's autobiographical "Long Day's Journey into Night" (1956)—predominantly rural white women who in spite of their addiction managed to function in society—were viewed with pity rather than contempt (Brecher 1972). Nevertheless, their plight contributed to the passage of the Pure Food and Drug Act of 1906, which, though not excluding opiates from patent medicines, required that these drugs be identified on the label.

Between 1910 and 1920 the word "addiction" began to be applied to the culturally disapproved use of certain drugs, just as the term "drug abuse" is used today (National Commission on Marihuana and Drug Abuse 1973). Gradually, too, the word was given a more specific meaning. In 1912 Charles B. Towns described what he called the "addictive triad": increased craving, growing tolerance, and a withdrawal syndrome when the drug was withheld (Musto 1973). Today addiction is generally accepted as a scientific term that describes the inevitable *physiological dependence* that follows the continued and heavy use of substances (such as the opiates, barbiturates, or alcohol) that have certain pharmacological properties. Nevertheless, it is clear that the concept of addiction, like the concept of drug abuse, has long been approached in an unscientific or pseudoscientific way.

It is obvious, for example, that the original definition of the "addictive triad" rests on moral as well as medical opinion. Two of its three elements do not stand up to scientific analysis. First, it is impossible to define "increased craving" precisely, or to limit those notions to drug abuse. The very choice of the term "craving" indicates the subtle biases behind the definition: craving connotes weakness and a sense of desperation that may lead to antisocial and even criminal behavior. Second, for many years the concept of "growing tolerance" was accepted as a direct arithmetic progression: after someone had used a drug a certain number of times he or she would need a correspondingly greater amount of it to get the same effect. As a matter of fact, although all users definitely do experience an increasing physiological accommodation to the substance they use individuals differ so markedly in their capacity to deal with different amounts of substances without developing tolerance that it is difficult to understand how the complexity of this phenomenon has escaped detection by the scientific community. Have the observers perhaps been so carried away by their own moral convictions that they have not studied drug use objectively?

One reason for the prevalence of definitions of drug abuse that are neither logical nor scientific is the strength of Puritan moralism in American culture, which frowns on the pleasure and recreation provided by intoxicants. A recent editorial on drug abuse in the *American Journal of Psychiatry* epitomizes this cultural position. It calls for "an active effort to teach the individual and society how to enjoy and endure [life] without euphorants and escapants" (Cohen 1968). As Herbert Marcuse (1955) has pointed out, there is probably a rationale for this position—the generally accepted view that pleasure-seeking behavior, particularly if it threatens the cultural norm, must be rationed and controlled in an industrial society. Nevertheless, this view overlooks the fact that all known societies (with the possible exception of earlier Eskimo cultures) have used intoxicants for recreational purposes (Weil 1972) and that, certainly in our society, intoxicants offer many individuals the benefits of relaxation and greater social ease.

It is ironic indeed that this society set up a firm double standard of behavior in which the use of alcohol as a pleasure-producing, psychotropic drug is accepted while the use of any other intoxicant for that purpose is regarded as abusive. The fact that alcohol is psychotropic is easy to dismiss because more than 100 million social drinkers know from experience that an alcohol "high" can be controlled; abusive use, or alcoholism, is viewed as a disease that is caught by only the susceptible few. This illogical social attitude means that a single use of LSD or heroin is far more likely to be construed as drug abuse than is the heavy ingestion of alcohol (Jaffe 1975).

Our Puritan heritage is so deeply ingrained that even drinking is attended by a deep-seated ambivalence. In a study of the social setting in which drinking takes place, Rupert Wilkinson (1970) has given three examples of this ambivalence: the temperance movement, Prohibition, and the American adult's tendency to mention his drinking as though it were "naughty." Arthur Hellman, too, has called attention to the crazy-quilt pattern of American laws that regulate the dispensing and sale of alcoholic beverages, arguing that although they are unsupported by any principle of jurisprudence, they are condoned because they serve as a moral sop to the public belief that the "drinking evil" needs special handling (Hellman 1975). The idea that pleasure, or at least the kind of pleasure that leads to escape and euphoria, is potentially dangerous and must be rationed is imprinted in the American consciousness.

This Puritan attitude pervades the use of illicit intoxicants to an even greater degree, as shown by the ambivalence of many users of illicit drugs. On the one hand, most users of marihuana and the psychedelics contend that their drug use is acceptable and pleasurable and are defiant of society's definition of them as deviant (Gusfield 1972). But rather than repent of their deviance, as others might have done forty or even twenty years ago, they attack first the laws and then society itself. On the other hand as my study has revealed, even very moderate drug users also reflect Puritan attitudes and values by feeling guilty about their use. Some of my subjects claimed that they had used psychedelics such as LSD solely for "serious" purposes—that is, in order to gain personal or religious insight—and they expressed disdain for, and even labeled as abusers, their pleasure-seeking counterparts who wanted only to get "high" and enjoy their psychedelic experiences in a sensual way (Harding & Zinberg 1977). This attitude mirrored the disdain shown by society toward all drug users and toward pleasure-seeking behavior in general.

The superimposition of Puritan morality on scientific attempts to define drug abuse is also apparent in a recent disagreement in the scientific literature over the nature of addiction—specifically, the experience of acknowledged heroin addicts. From 1947 until recently, the accepted position was that taken by Alfred Lindesmith, who contended that during the initial phase of heroin use the user was totally infatuated with the drug's effects but that this pleasure phase usually passed after the onset of physiological addiction, when the addict became preoccupied with his struggle to stave off the dreaded symptoms of withdrawal (Lindesmith 1947). Lindesmith claimed that heroin users experienced little pleasure in the years of actual addiction and called for a recognition of addicts as socially and psychologically troubled or "sick."

In 1975 William E. McAuliffe and Robert A. Gordon disputed Lindesmith's conclusions in an article summarizing their survey findings. This article, which abounds with such words as "euphoria," "high," and "pleasure," and even compares the effect of the drug to a sexual orgasm, reports that long-term addicts actually get continuing pleasure from using heroin.

My findings, based on information gathered from many compulsive subjects, disagree sharply with both Lindesmith's and McAuliffe and Gordon's conclusions, as do those of Stanton Peele (1975). After prolonged heroin use my subjects did experience a "desirable" consciousness change characterized by increased emotional distance from both external stimuli and internal response, but it fell far short of euphoria. Some subjects described it as follows: "It is as if my skin is very thick but permeable"; and "It is like being wrapped in warm cotton batting." Many of them recognized that their preference for this consciousness change had little to do with warding off withdrawal sickness, although they were well aware of their excessive fear of withdrawal. Neither did their preference stem from a wish to feel "normal," because they knew that the ordinary self-aware state was an uncomfortable one for them. They tended to describe themselves in heaven-or-hell terms, not because that is what they felt but because they were incapable of explaining to a "straight" interviewer their complex relationships to the treasured drug.

The WHO Definitions of Drug Abuse

Researchers in the field of drug use tended initially to look at all styles of drug-taking behavior as drug abuse, that is, as physiologically addictive. Later, when it became apparent that not all substances were physically addictive, they turned to a new concept, that of psychological habituation. In 1957 the World Health Organization (WHO), through its Expert Committee on Addiction Producing Drugs, formulated official and detailed definitions of both physiological addiction and psychological habituation. By 1964, however, these two concepts had been found to be unsatisfactory, and a new WHO committee turned to a descriptive approach to abuse based on the type of "dependence" supposedly engendered by the various drugs. This approach, too, proved unsatisfactory. As Robert Apsler pointed out, "One cannot create precise definitions by relying on amorphous concepts for specifying the definitions. Often the definitions essentially state that something is bad without clarifying what the something is, without specifying the criteria on which the negative judgment is based, and without stating the assumptions from which the value is derived" (1975). Other investigators also criticized the attempts of the WHO committees, calling them ambiguous, confusing, and culture-bound (Fort 1969; Christie & Braun 1969; Freedman 1970; Young 1971; Goode 1972; National Commission on Marihuana and Drug Abuse 1973; Smart 1974). Unfortunately, because these definitions were formulated by the prestigious World Health Organization, they have continued to dominate the field.

Drug Addiction and Habituation, 1957. The 1957 WHO Committee defined addiction and habituation as follows:

> Drug addiction is a state of periodic or chronic intoxication produced by the repeated consumption of a drug (natural or synthetic). Its characteristics include: (i) an overpowering desire or need (compulsion) to continue taking the drug and to obtain it by any means; (ii) a tendency to increase the dose; (iii) a psychic (psychological) and generally a physical dependence on the effects of the drug; and (iv) detrimental effects on the individual and on society.

> Drug habituation (habit) is a condition resulting from the repeated con-

sumption of a drug. Its characteristics include: (i) a desire (but not a compulsion) to continue taking the drug for the sense of improved well-being which it engenders; (ii) little or no tendency to increase the dose; (iii) some degree of psychic dependence on the effect of the drug, but absence of physical dependence and hence of an abstinence syndrome [withdrawal]; and (iv) detrimental effects, if any, primarily on the individual.

Both of these definitions make use of the same four basic characteristics: desire, increase in dosage (development of tolerance), dependence, and detrimental effect. Habituation is presented as a less severe state than addiction, free of compulsive desire or craving, of increase in dosage, of physical dependence (and hence the withdrawal syndrome), and of detriment to society. But these four key terms cannot be accepted at face value. They need to be examined carefully and objectively.

Since the first characteristic, desire (related to habituation) or compulsion (related to addiction), is very difficult to separate from the third characteristic, psychic or physical dependence, they will be analyzed together. How can either physical or psychic dependence exist without a desire or compulsion? And conversely, is not the reason for a desire or compulsion the existence of psychic or physical dependence? This confusion in itself constitutes a major flaw in the WHO definitions.

While the concept of dependence seems to be more definite and therefore a better analytic tool than the concept of desire, it is very difficult to separate physical from psychic dependence. The presence of physical symptoms alone does not distinguish between these two types of dependence. Although, according to Fred Leavitt (1974), "physical dependence is defined as a state characterized by the appearance of physical symptoms when administration of a drug is suspended," psychiatrists and psychologists know that physical symptoms may also appear following the withdrawal of loved ones and other psychologically precious objects. Except at the furthest extreme it is virtually impossible to measure the degree to which psychological factors determine or interpret physical symptoms.

Moreover, "physical dependence" has proved to be a much less helpful concept than many experts on drug use originally expected. Its main advantage is that it is a physiological entity that can serve as a straightforward measure of addiction. It does not necessarily define drug abuse from a social and cultural standpoint, however. Obviously, the members of the WHO committee, who omitted any mention of alcohol, caffeine, and nicotine as drugs of dependence, were not thinking of the everyday beer or cocktail drinker, cigarette smoker, or coffee drinker, who more than likely is physically addicted, or of those individuals with hypertension who find their craving for salt irresistible, or of the ice cream "addicts" vividly described by John Pekkanen and Mathea Falco (1975). Nevertheless, a definition utilizing physical dependence as a measure of abuse could apply to substances and behaviors that lie far beyond the realm of illicit drugs.

The committee evidently assumed that physiological addiction was more overpowering than psychological habituation, although each member could have supplied many clinical examples showing the opposite. In their eyes, habituation was less inevitable and more susceptible to the elements of set and setting than addiction. Addiction was compulsive while habituation was the result of simple desire.

It is undoubtedly true that physiological addiction to an unavailable substance results in a painful syndrome, but it is debatable whether this is more painful than the suffering from an unfulfilled longing that involves no physiological attachment at all. Take, for example, the possibly tongue-in-cheek reference by John Kaplan (1970) to the numbers of people who are psychologically habituated to reading the Sunday New York Times. They have a habit that they enjoy; they look forward to reading the newspaper each week; they are disappointed and sometimes very upset if they cannot obtain it; they will put themselves and sometimes others to considerable inconvenience and expense in order to get it. For these habitués it is not the physiological but the psychological state that may eventually lead to desperation.

As for the power of drugs, the notion that the pharmacological properties of a drug, irrespective of set and setting, are the sole determinants of disturbed or violent behavior dies hard. There is considerable evidence to the contrary, however. The profound effect of set and setting was evident in the play, "The Concept," put on in 1967 by the residents of Daytop Village, a residential treatment center for hard-core addicts on Staten Island, New York. The play, based on real-life experiences, showed what could happen when an addict was cut off from his supply. At first, when he was in jail, he went through all the hell of the withdrawal syndrome: he screamed, begged, and suffered a variety of painful, overpowering physical symptoms. After being released and sent to Daytop for treatment he again received no drugs. When he began to complain about symptoms, he was simply handed a broom and told to shut up and go to work. And he did! The drug was the same in both situations, but because the settings differed, the experiences of withdrawal differed. The influence of set and setting on the withdrawal syndrome of heroin users was also demonstrated in Vietnam. Initially the enlisted men who were heavy users were given extensive hospital treatment for withdrawal, but later many of them were transferred to the outpatient department and simply given a little Compazine for stomach cramps.

The second characteristic cited in the WHO definitions, development of tolerance, which the committee members described in terms of "tendency to increase the dose," is even more ambiguous than the concepts of desire and dependence. This term implies that one must continue to use more of the substance in order to get the same effect and that without a period of abstinence the development of tolerance is irreversible. The concept of "getting the same effect" is very difficult to define or measure. Consider, for example, a heroin addict who has developed the habit of using his drug four or five times a day. He acquires a bit of cash, makes a good buy, and suddenly becomes a dealer. His habit increases rapidly, and in two weeks he is shooting up ten or twelve times a day. But soon he uses up his capital and loses his dealership. He is then back on the street copping, down to using the drug four or five times a day. Is he now getting the same effect he got before his period of heavy use? He doesn't know, nor does anyone else.

Had the WHO definition of tolerance been more solidly based on the pharmacological phenomenon of biological accommodation to drugs, it would have been a more useful measure of dependence. Such tolerance does, of course, develop in relation to doses of the opiates, alcohol, and the barbiturates. It is a very handy diagnostic sign of a drug habit and is used in the induction protocol of programs for methadone maintenance and drug detoxification (Blachly 1973; Gay, Senay & Newmeyer 1974). But tolerance should not be defined as a "tendency to increase the dose" when it really means the biological ability to withstand increased dosage. Some addicts enter treatment programs solely in the hope of bringing down their tolerances to manageable levels.

The question of tolerance also varies from one drug to another. Many people find that the first few times they try marihuana they can consume enormous quantities and experience little or no effect (Becker 1963; Zinberg & Weil 1970). Once they learn how to get high, however, they stabilize at a dose level that varies little from one individual to another. At some point, though, regular users complain that while they can get high just as readily, the high does not last as long as it once did. They also say that they must change their dope fairly often in order to continue to get high. These complaints sound like evidences of tolerance; since different strains of marihuana contain different combinations of cannabinoids and cannabinols, the user is probably not accustomed to the new strain. But that fact, if true, would indicate a very low level of cross-tolerance to a very similar drug, in itself a remarkable finding.

Regular users of marihuana develop control over their high and so can shorten its time span if they wish (Becker 1963; Zinberg, Jacobson & Harding 1975). But does this reduced time span result from a change in tolerance to the drug or from a change in the individual's psychological reaction to the drug effect? Certainly regular users experience their highs differently. The "giggles," for example, are almost exclusively part of the early use of the drug, when the incongruity between what Andrew Weil calls straight and stoned thinking seems uproariously funny (1972). Even the "munchies" (increased appetite following marihuana use) can be experienced differently by regular users. My study data, which agree with the findings of other researchers, show that once a user reaches a dose level that suits him, he tends to stick to it. None of our marihuana subjects evidenced an increase in use after a long period of regular consumption; on the contrary, several showed a decrease.

Neither did our users of psychedelics reveal a tendency toward increased dosage. After the first few pleasurable experiences, some users, especially those who had begun to use between 1963 and 1968, went through a period in which they took the drug several times a week for a year or two. But it is my impression that many users of psychedelics become so rapidly acclimated to the high-impact, consciousness-changing aspect of the experience that they begin to show still greater interest in the underlying speedy (amphetamine-like) effect of the drug. Today psychedelics tend to be used only occasionally—rarely more than six times a year. Like Dr. David E. Smith and the group at the Haight-Ashbury Free Medical Clinic, my staff and I did not find a single long-term heavy user of psychedelics (Smith 1975a). Our subjects, rather than showing a tendency to increase their dose, expressed a wish to continue use on a reduced or very occasional basis.

Users of barbiturates and other depressants do need larger and larger doses in order to get the desired effect, but only up to a certain point; for even if they develop tolerance to the high or sedative dose, they do not develop tolerance to the lethal dose, and continued increases will eventually produce a fatal overdose. As for the amphetamines, continued high doses eventually disrupt metabolic functioning so much that they too must be reduced. In fact, it is impossible for users of any of the drugs ordinarily associated with abuse to continue to increase their doses and get what they want from the drug or, indeed, survive. Clearly the phrase "tendency to increase the dose" is not a consistent or easily applicable mark of drug abuse.

The fourth characteristic listed in the WHO definitions—the concept of "detrimental effect" on the individual or on both the individual and society—is also inadequate. The specific definition of a detrimental effect must always be culturally determined. As John Clausen (1968) says, "A particular drug (e.g., marihuana) may be accepted as an appropriate adjunct to sociability in one society, used as an invaluable ingredient in religious contemplation in another, and banned by law as dangerous in a third." Even would-be scientific attempts to arrange certain drugs according to their goodness (benignness) or badness (harmfulness) are not free of this cultural determinism. Evaluations of current drug research that shows a specific illicit drug to be harmful have usually found that the drug is *associated* with detrimental effect rather than the *cause* of it. Claims have been made, for example, that marihuana causes brain damage, psychosis, the amotivational syndrome, birth defects, chromosome damage, reduction of sexual functioning, and/or interference with DNA metabolism and immune response. But according to a survey of research published in *Psychology Today* (Zinberg 1976) and a conference of experts sponsored by The Drug Abuse Council (Tinklenberg 1975), none of these charges has been proved (*Marijuana and Health* 1982).

This is not to say that some illicit drugs cannot and do not cause harm and even death. Indeed they do, but so do the licit drugs that are freely available for nonmedical use. Nicotine and alcohol are the most obvious examples; alcohol, in fact, is more likely than marihuana to produce the harmful effects of drug use usually ascribed to marihuana. Harm and death can also result from a response to nature or to the therapeutic use of drugs with or without a doctor's prescription, as in the case of allergic responses to animal bites or to an antibiotic. Nor is the abuse of illicit drugs described in the WHO definitions necessarily any more detrimental than the use of sugar or food additives.

Hearings sponsored by the FDA in 1977 on the efficacy and safety of over-the-counter medicinal preparations revealed that recommended dosages of many cold remedies, sleeping aids, and mood elevators were patently ineffective, but that larger doses, which did produce the desired effects, often had harmful side effects bordering on toxicity. Yet these drugs, some of them containing atropine, scopolamine, ephedrine, or potent antihistamines, remain on the druggists' shelves, a clear threat to the unwary consumer who believes the advertising he reads and has implicit faith in the government's watch-dog agencies (American Pharmaceutical Association 1967; Inglefinger 1977).

And finally, even in cases where a drug, licit or illicit, can be shown to be harmful to the individual, that harm is always related to a host of variables, such as dosage, chronicity of use, and health of the user. One of these variables, which is seldom recognized, is the psychological effect of the legal definition of abuse and of the socially accepted view of abuse. When most Americans hear the word "heroin," for example, they picture the typical junkie, but they are unaware that some of his symptoms are related to the illegality of his use (Young 1971; Goode 1973; Zinberg 1975). The WHO definition takes no account of the effect of these legal and social stigmas on the user.

The idea of a detrimental effect on society is even harder to elucidate. In sharp contrast to the WHO committee's view, one social theory holds that deviants perform a useful and necessary social function by defining the boundaries of social acceptability (Erikson 1964; 1966). Thus their behavior points the way to social change because the boundaries of acceptability gradually adjust to changing times and values; what is not accepted at one historical moment may be accepted at another. Smoking marihuana at an academic party would have been lunacy in the late 1960s, but ten years later it was hardly noticed. It is essential, however, to differentiate between the kind of value change that can be integrated into the social mores and the kind that cannot be so integrated. It is not realistic or constructive to label all currently illicit drug use (and no currently licit drug use) detrimental to society without first determining whether certain of these drugs or certain patterns of use can be successfully integrated into our social mores.

Drug Dependence, 1964. In 1964 a new committee of the World Health Organization made the concept of dependence the basis of its definition of drug abuse. After specifying dependence as "a state of psychic dependence or physical dependence, or both, on a drug, arising in a person following administration of that drug on a periodic or continued basis" (Eddy et al. 1965), the members wrote:

> The characteristics of such a state will vary with the agent involved, and these characteristics must always be made clear by designating the particular type of drug dependence in each specific case. . . . All of these drugs have one effect in common: they are capable of creating, in certain individuals, a particular state of mind that is termed "psychic dependence." In this situation, there is a feeling of satisfaction and psychic drive that requires periodic or continuous administration of the drug to produce pleasure or to avoid discomfort.

Unfortunately, this definition relies on the ambiguous concepts of psychic dependence and physical dependence that had been used in the earlier formulation. It also hints at the notion of desire or need in referring to the administration of the drug on a periodic or continuous basis. And in a later section of the definition (not quoted here), where some of the types of dependence are designated, the concept of harm or detriment to the individual and society reappears.

The old notion that dependence *must* result from the periodic administration of a drug has been utterly negated by my research study. Many of our users who had at one time used a drug regularly developed the capacity to keep the same drug on the shelf for weeks—and in the case of a psychedelic, for months or years—before they used it. They would have liked to use it, of course, but their ability to postpone use contradicted the assumption of dependent behavior.

And again, the inference that the use of illicit drugs is more addictive than the use of certain socially accepted substances is incorrect. The users of sugar and salt, caffeine, nicotine, and alcohol are no less controlled by their need for these substances than are the users of marihuana, LSD, and cocaine. The WHO committee, by ascribing the term "dependence" to the use of illicit substances considered pleasurable, was attaching a pejorative label to such use simply because it was illicit, not because these substances were unique in causing dependent behavior.

Further, the implication that greater problems arise from periodic or repeated use of intoxicants than from initial or nondependent use is not correct. The new or infrequent drinker of alcohol or user of barbiturates may have an automobile accident or engage in a brawl while under the influence of booze or drugs. If he cannot learn to use a substance adaptively, he is no less a problem because he is not dependent. In fact, most of the substances considered drugs of abuse (with the exception of alcohol and the barbiturates) are used with far greater control by regular, experienced users than by neophytes.

Finally, and worst of all, the 1964 WHO definition of drug abuse employs circular reasoning in an even more confusing way than the earlier definition. To quote Robert Apsler (1975), again "The definition of drug dependence . . . was developed in order to describe a particular form or pattern of drug use. Yet, when the question is asked, '*Why* are they using drugs all the time?' a common answer is, 'Because they are dependent on drugs.' In other words, the term drug dependence has become a cause; it is now often seen as an explanation of the pattern of drug use for which it was proposed as a definition."

Further Analysis of Drug Definitions, 1957 and 1964. The two WHO definitions (addiction and habituation, and then drug dependence), which sprang from the moralistic cultural concept of drug abuse, are not precise, objective, or medically supportable. This judgment, given after more than a decade of the so-called drug revolution—and after a great deal of study of the drug issue from every vantage point, including that of pharmacology, medicine, ethnology, sociology, and psychology—seems obvious. But the faults in the definitions could not have been so clear in 1956 and 1963, when the two WHO committees were at work. At that time drug users were a tiny group of repentant deviants; heroin addicts and even the marihuana-using "Bohemians" and musicians accepted the cultural view that they were doing something wrong. In that historical context, when little was known about most of the drugs and when myth and misconception were rampant, the committees' efforts to define a slippery topic in an objective way seemed reasonable both to their learned members and to the scientific community that was seeking guidance.

Nevertheless, from the perspective of the early 1980s, the WHO definitions as well as many other supposedly scientific expositions on drug abuse and dependence contain two disturbing flaws. First, instead of describing the harmful consequences of the psychoactive drugs the writers have dealt only with the causes or motivations behind drug use. Second, they tended to attack the users rather than the use of these drugs.

The first fault is clear in the description of amphetamine use given by the WHO committee in 1964: "The abuse of this class of drugs originates in and is perpetuated by the psychic drive to attain maximum euphoria: no physical dependence is created." Evidently the committee members, unable to point to physical dependence as an ill effect, decided to refer pejoratively to the reward of a socially proscribed "psychic drive"—that of achieving maximum euphoria.

When psychological motivation becomes the basis for judging the abuse potential of a substance, double standards can be set up and socioeconomic differences can be emphasized in a most specious fashion, as in a paper distributed by the American Medical Association (Gottlieb 1970):

> Drugs can represent both an attempt at personal adjustment, or a personal reaction to maladjustment. The dilettante-ish experimentation with drug-induced experience of the middle class, though fraught with dangers, still represents groping for meaningful personal adjustment. Having already experienced the impact of socialization through family, school, and peer groups, most will "return to the fold." In contrast, the urban poor resort to drugs more as an adaptation to maladjustment. This maladjustment stems from disturbed family relationships, poor school adjustment, and deprived if not hostile interactions with the dominant society.

Those concerned with motivational distinctions also refer to the cross-cultural use of drugs. The religious use of peyote by the Native American (Indian) Church, which is protected by statute, is the best known example. The same plant product—peyote "buttons"—is illegal for all but Indian users, and its principal active ingredient—mescaline—is illegal for all users. In this instance the user's motivation is employed to distinguish use from abuse: as long as pleasure or euphoria is not the sole object, limited use is approved. According to Richard E. Schultes (1972), "Aboriginal utilization of hallucinogens has a discrete, constructive, necessary purpose. It is religious. It is not frivolous or casual. Hallucinogens are not taken for the pleasure that they can afford—in fact, some afford no pleasurable sensations but are most definitely a trial to take" (see also De Rios & Smith 1976).

The second flaw in the WHO definitions and other scientific writings, that of attacking the user rather than the use of the psychoactive drugs, is more subtle but also more prevalent. According to the WHO committee, the frequent intravenous injection of cocaine "appeals to persons with psychopathic tendencies, which are often unmasked by the drug." Similarly, the hallucinogens "possess a particular attraction for certain psychologically and socially maladjusted persons who have difficulty in conforming to usual social norms. These include 'arty' people such as struggling writers, painters, and musicians; frustrated nonconformists; and curious, thrill-seeking adolescents and young adults" (Eddy et al. 1965). One gets the impression that if these drugs were not being used by these types of people, they would not be labeled drugs of abuse. Surely such personal denigrations of the users of drugs fall short of scientific judgment.

It must be remembered that each of the people attempting to describe addiction-dependency was trying to clarify the confusion introduced by previous definitions. Lindesmith's pioneering efforts to show the important psychological factors brought him considerable criticism at that time as an apologist for drug users, who were, of course, morally bad. The WHO efforts which I dissect so minutely represented the hard work of distinguished committees trying to introduce more order into a chaotic field of study. While in retrospect it seems possible to see the biases of previous workers in the field, I am sure that my own biases at this moment will be equally clear to scholars in the near future. Thus later in this chapter and in chapter 7 I warn against too broad definitions of these conditions and call for careful case histories that describe what is happening with as few labels as possible.

Medical and Legal Definitions of Abuse

WHO was probably the first medical organization to define the good use of drugs as medically prescribed use, and bad use, or abuse, as use that had not been medically prescribed. The *WHO Bulletin* of 1965 stated that "there is scarcely any agent which can be taken into the body to which some individuals will not get a reaction satisfactory or pleasurable to them, persuading them to continue its use even to the point of abuse—that is, to excessive or persistent use *beyond medical need*" (Eddy et al. 1965, emphasis added).

The following year the American Medical Association, through its Committee on Alcoholism and Addiction, also equated abuse with nonmedical use in a characteristic statement on the use of amphetamines:

> In this communication "use" refers to the proper place of stimulants in medical practice; "misuse" applies to the physician's role in initiating a potentially dangerous course of therapy; and *"abuse" refers to self-administration of these drugs without medical supervision* and particularly in large doses, that may lead to psychological dependency, tolerance and abnormal behavior (emphasis added).

In 1972 the American Psychiatric Association presented its definition of drug abuse, again based on the nonmedical nature of use:

> . . . as a general rule, we reserve the *term drug abuse to apply to the*

illegal, nonmedical use of a limited number of substances, most of them drugs, which have properties of altering the mental state in ways that are considered by social norms and defined by statute to be inappropriate, undesirable, harmful, threatening, or, at minimum, culture-alien (Glasscote et al. 1972, emphasis added).

And later in 1972 Edwin Lipinski reiterated the basic theme of all these definitions: "For the sake of clarity and at the risk of simplification, misuse [abuse] will be viewed as a nonmedical use of psychoactive drugs."

The term "nonmedical use" is complex; it has three possible connotations. First, it may refer to the use of a drug that has no recognized medical value. The expression "recognized medical value" is in itself a shifting and elusive concept. Before 1950 marihuana was listed in all the pharmacopoeias, was reputed to have many useful therapeutic properties, and was widely prescribed (Grinspoon 1971). For the next twenty-five years it was considered medically useless, but in the late 1970s it again seemed to be regaining recognition as an antiemetic and a reducer of ocular pressure (Sallan, Zinberg & Frei 1975; Hepler & Frank 1971). Second, the term "nonmedical use" may refer to the use for a nonmedical purpose of a drug having recognized medical value, such as the use of codeine to get "high" rather than as an analgesic or cough medicine. And third, "nonmedical use " may refer to the use of a drug without the supervision of a doctor or in contravention of a doctor's instructions. Reginald Smart (1974) has observed that according to this principle, drug abuse would include "all use of alcohol, tobacco, aspirin, etc. unless under 'professional advice.' This is so ridiculous it hardly requires comment." This third connotation has also prompted Thomas Szasz and others to remark that defining nonmedical use as drug abuse serves the economic and political interests of organized medicine (Szasz 1975).

The chief fault of the medical definition of drug abuse is that it claims to interpret completely and finally a type of behavior that lies outside the realm of medicine. At issue, of course, is the medical claim of hegemony over the use of most psychoactive substances, accompanied by a denial of this culture's natural interest in intoxication. Such a claim need not be challenged too strongly in relation to drugs with well-defined medical uses—stimulants, depressants, tranquilizers, and narcotics—even if these are also used for intoxication; but in relation to the psychedelics and marihuana, which have substantial social and personal significance as recreational agents but only questionable medical impact, the medical and scientific community is on shaky ground. Under current social policy, which encourages health professionals to bolster society's claim to the right to proscribe "hedonistic" behavior, a frantic "scientific" search is going on to discover any and all deleterious effects of the hallucinogens and marihuana. The result is that premature reports of unsubstantiated findings have reduced medical credibility with the very population under consideration—the drug users themselves. The restrictive concept that any nonmedical use of psychoactive substances is abusive has not only done much to sap users' faith in medical authority in this field but also raised grave doubts about the medical definition of abuse.

The legal definition of drug abuse—any recreational use of an illicit drug—is even less satisfactory than the medical definition. Whenever a defendant has challenged the drug laws in court, the prosecution has presented lengthy briefs supposedly proving the harm caused by the drugs and their potential for abuse. These contentions, however, rest on a number of misconceptions, chief among them the belief that the occasional use of certain drugs, such as heroin, without becoming addicted is impossible (National Commission on Marihuana and Drug Abuse 1973).

A long-standing problem has been the reluctance of legislators to seek scientific guidance during the formulation of drug legislation. For this reason cocaine, which is not a narcotic but a central nervous system stimulant, was defined as a "narcotic" by the 1914 Harrison Narcotic Act and has therefore been included in legislative efforts to stamp out recreational use of the opiates. During the 1937 hearings on the proposed Marihuana Tax Act only one medical witness was summoned, and he opposed the legislation (Grinspoon 1971). It looks as though medical and scientific testimony has been called for only when it has promised to support the contentions and fit the purposes of the politicians who draft the laws and of those who enforce them. But the legislative and judicial branches have not alone been at fault. Even before President Nixon's National Commission on Marihuana and Drug Abuse (the Shafer Commission) published its findings and recommended the decriminalization of the personal possession and nonprofit transfer of marihuana, Nixon stated that he would not accept these findings or allow the Attorney General to implement this recommendation.

Users' Definitions

Oddly enough, asking users what constitutes drug abuse sheds little light on the question. The alcoholic's denial of the problems caused by his habit is notorious: he either refuses or is unable to acknowledge that his drinking interferes with his health, personal relations, and ability to function. Similarly, many heavy users of drugs, particularly those in the depressant class, practice denial. Clinical reports describe individuals who stagger so badly that they can hardly walk and evidence marked nystagmus and slurred speech and yet insist that they do not use barbiturates excessively.

Denying or minimizing excessive use is not the only distortion practiced by users. Some nonaddicts claim to be addicted in order to get treatment at methadone clinics. Since these clinics are naturally reluctant to addict to methadone anyone who is not already physiologically dependent on an opiate, they must screen all applicants carefully. It is difficult to understand why certain individuals choose to pose as addicts, but the wish to join a deviant group and adopt its negative identity may be one reason (Gay, Senay & Newmeyer 1974). Again, some young users who wish to impress their peers and others may make exaggerated claims about their drug use and cling to these claims through intensive questioning. Some of these youngsters may even begin to believe their own stories despite the contrary evidence of laboratory tests or observers' reports.

As long as current social policy takes drug abuse and dependence as its point of departure, it will keep drug users on the defensive, forcing them not only to account for their use but to prove themselves nondependent. Those who wish to rationalize periods of compulsive use will continue to account for their dependence in terms of the drug rather than try to understand their own behavior (Zinberg 1975). Emphasizing the inevitability of dependence instead of recognizing it as a *possible* result of prolonged use always makes communication with users difficult because it suggests to them that they will not be understood. When the professional employs the concept of psychic dependence, the user must either respond with denial or accept the "abuser" label and become repentant. Those who give in to guilt and self-condemnation become incapable of making an objective assessment of the extent of their use or of its destructive results.

Guilt is not the only factor leading to such distortions. Other personality and cultural dispositions affect the accuracy of users' reports. A young man who is committed to the importance of the inner life and who finds himself yearning for one more joint may indulge in self-examination and even give an exaggerated report of his difficulties. Another young man who has a similar yearning but has been brought up to shun self-examination may plunge into troublesome behavior and resent having it called to his attention.

Of course, such tendencies to deny, minimize, exaggerate, or otherwise distort use are not confined to users of drugs; they may characterize those who engage in many other types of repetitious habitual behavior. Nevertheless, it is these tendencies that make the drug user's efforts to define drug abuse of little value.

"Use," Not "Abuse"

Drug abuse cannot be defined in the abstract; it must be determined on a case-by-case basis. This is the basis from which my staff and I proceeded in selecting and classifying subjects for our research on the controlled use of illicit drugs. In judging each case we had at our disposal two standards of measurement: *quantity* of use and *quality* of use. Quantity of use refers to the size and frequency of the dosage. Quality concerns how the drug is used or the conditions of use, which include the using pattern and the social setting (how much, when, where, and with whom the drug is used).

Quantity of consumption would seem to be the most useful measure of drug abuse, for any drug consumed to excess can cause serious problems. A drinker absorbing more than a quart of hard liquor a day can rarely function at work, keep up coherent social and personal relationships, or maintain health. Even here, however, there are exceptions—Winston Churchill, perhaps. Alcoholics Anonymous (A.A.), in its twelve-question pamphlet on drinking habits entitled *Is A.A. for You?*, asks such questions as, "Have you taken a morning drink during the past year?" "Have you missed time from work because of drinking?" and it defines four or more "yes" answers as evidence of a drinking problem (Alcoholics Anonymous 1954). Thus the symptoms of a user who passes (or flunks) this test must be related to quality as well as quantity of consumption. This is also true of the twenty-six-question checklist prepared by the National Council on Alcoholism (1975).

At extraordinary dose levels, quantity of use is generally a foolproof standard for differentiating use from abuse. A barbiturate user who has taken so much of his drug that he staggers sleepily, an amphetamine user so speedy that he never stops talking or moving, and a heroin user sticking the twelfth spike of the day into his body are all contravening the standards of acceptable behavior and must be classified as drug abusers. But once the extreme examples have been exhausted, sheer quantity may not be a comprehensive or practical measure of drug abuse. Further, the standard of quantity is not equally applicable to all types of drugs. What level of marihuana use should be defined as abusive? There is virtually no toxic dose, nor is marihuana physically addictive. In 1975 the *New England Journal of Medicine* described the case of a four-year-old girl who, after eating 1.5 g of hashish containing 150 mg of delta-9-tetrahydrocannabinol, became comatose, but recovered within twenty-four hours (Bro and Schou 1975). Heavy users of marihuana experience great difficulty in giving up the drug. Once they do give it up, however, they experience no great discomfort or psychic dependency and relatively little functional incapacity. Their relation to that drug appears to be more like that of the person who habitually takes a sleeping pill at night long after its sedative capacity is effective. The fear of sleeplessness and the symbolic nature of the pill-taking make it extremely hard to renounce. In attempting to classify our marihuana subjects, my research team and I had to consider carefully whether those who used the drug more than once a day, even though they gave no indication of compulsion, could be considered controlled. To be rigorous, we eliminated those who used the drug several times a day. But that did not help us classify those who used only once a day. Here we were forced to consider in addition each subject's quality of use in order to decide whether use or abuse was going on.

Quantity (including frequency) of use was a less difficult standard to apply to the low end of the scale than to the high end. When we had to determine the minimum quantity that would distinguish between occasional users and mere tasters or experimenters, we finally agreed on a frequency of more than once a month. But it was more difficult to decide on acceptable maximum use, as distinct from abuse, in terms of quantity alone. There we were obliged to adopt an admittedly subjective procedure—making the quality of use the major criterion.

A convincing example of the need to measure quality as well as quantity is the case of Dr. C., whose history was published in the January 1976 issue of the *American Journal of Psychiatry*. Dr. C. used four shots of morphine a day, five days a week, ten months of the year (Zinberg & Jacobson 1976). He abstained every weekend and also during his two months' vacation. His case had been presented earlier (1964) in the *New England Journal of Medicine* (Zinberg & Lewis 1964) and had been followed up continuously since then, including documented periods of hospitalization during which the subject received no drug and showed no withdrawal symptoms. From 1964 to 1975 Dr. C. had not developed tolerance or increased his dose. Yet when the later article had originally been submitted to *Science*, a referee of that distinguished arm of the American Association for the Advancement of Science had rejected it because "the title of the paper ["The Natural History of Chipping"] does not properly portray its contents. Dr. C. is addicted . . . [He is] an addict who 'maintains.'" This referee did not realize that in some cases of excess use, the quality of use may make for control.

Whenever my study team came across users who showed signs of physical dependency with impending withdrawal symptoms (unlike Dr. C.) or of very frequent and repetitive use, they classified such users as compulsive rather than controlled. Even these decisions, however, turned out to be far more complex than we had expected and required the application of the standard of quality as well as that of quantity. We found heroin users who exhibited some withdrawal symptoms and were not so controlled as Dr. C. but who nevertheless were extremely cautious about increasing their dose and took health-care measures. They were certainly not occasional users, but equally certainly they maintained certain controls successfully and were not interested in giving up heroin. We stuck to our rule and did not classify them as controlled users, but in that process we learned that compulsive use also encompasses many gradations.

Judgments about quality of use must take into account a complex set of factors. Here the social elements are often more important than the pharmacological. Making a regular practice of starting a long day of drinking early in the morning is quite different from occasionally ingesting a dose of LSD at the same time of day. The use of alcohol—a significant nervous system depressant—as a morning "eye-opener" is a clear indicator of trouble. This would also be true of LSD if its use were of the same compulsive nature; but if the morning dose of acid has been carefully planned and is to be followed by specific activities, usually carried out in a social framework, the quality of use will be radically different.

In the case of users of LSD and other psychedelics, drastic changes have occurred during the past decade in quality of use, changes that have made the experience less cataclysmic and thus have reduced the incidence of serious problems (see appendix C). By the early 1970s the admission of psychedelic users to mental health facilities for the treatment of acute or even long-term psychotic episodes following drug use, which had occurred frequently in the late 1960s and through 1970, had all but disappeared (Grinspoon 1974; McGlothlin 1974; Smith 1975). It is important to note that the quantity of psychedelic drug use did not decline until after 1973, according to the National Commission on Marihuana and Drug Abuse. In addition, since the established psychiatric resources were not always able to handle bad drug experiences successfully, the counterculture had begun to rely on its own experienced "personnel," ill-informed as they might be, to deal with bad trips. Many users, moreover, were willing simply to ride out a bad trip, knowing that the problem was a transient drug effect and not an indication of insanity. Even those among our subjects who had used the psychedelics heavily for some time did not usually show the interest in Eastern religious thought and a higher consciousness state that had been common a few years earlier. The new social setting, a qualitative element, seems to have been the predominant factor in that change.

Our finding that there is probably no long-term heavy use of psychedelics does not deny that users can react very badly to an acid trip, perhaps even to the point of having an acute upset. Nor does it deny that frequent acid trips over a short period of time can result in a changed outlook that may include intrinsic changes in personality. But there are subtle alterations—matters of conjecture or, more often, of values; for what a psychiatric or psychological examiner may call circumstantiality and ambivalence about reality testing may seem to the user to be an increased interest in abstraction and spirituality.

Another factor that makes it important to differentiate quality from quantity of use in the assessment of risk and the potential for harm is the vulnerability of inexperienced users. Certainly vulnerability to bad experiences from the drug is shown by the casualties among neophyte users of psychedelics in the 1960s. But, as noted earlier, neophyte users of alcohol, marihuana, barbiturates, and opiates may be more at risk for subjective deleterious responses, automobile accidents, damaging relationships, and generally making fools of themselves than more experienced users.

To summarize, drug abuse can be determined only on an individual basis. Only after examining each case and reporting in detail on a variety of factors relating to it can the investigator judge whether abuse has occurred. Therefore, instead of trying to formulate definitions of drug abuse, those working in the field would do well to make "drug use" their starting point and to report in detail whatever adverse effects of use they have observed. Then research could proceed in a more objective manner, and researchers, by comparing the case studies they have collected, would be able to determine whether they are talking about the same kind of drug use.

Dropping the term "drug abuse" is a necessary preliminary to understanding why and when people use drugs, how they use them, and above all, whether they can use them successfully—that is, in a controlled way. The descriptions of some users will clearly show their use to be excessive, but the histories of other users will reveal the same complexity that has characterized our own case studies. Getting rid of the ambiguity of one of the code words intended to indicate what society thinks is wrong about drug use will give investigators a chance to find and employ clear, precise, and realistic terms. With this clarity they can then study the whole range of phenomena included in the area of drug use and can undertake the task of developing and extending reasonable control over drug-taking behavior.

3

Research Methodology and Data

In 1972, when I began seeking financial support for research on controlled illicit drug use, the scarcity of previous research in the area was a liability rather than an asset. Although chances for funding were increased by the promise that my study would contribute new information about intoxicant use and misuse, there was virtually no direct evidence—other than Douglas H. Powell's study of twelve occasional heroin users (1973)—that cooperative and suitable subjects, particularly controlled users of the opiates, could be located efficiently or that they would be willing to reveal the details of their personal lives and illicit activities. Lack of tested approaches to this population raised the same kinds of difficult and fundamental questions that many other pilot and exploratory studies have had to contend with: How can controlled users be recruited? What kinds of information about controlled users are critical? What instruments or approaches should be used to collect data? Can it be reasonably expected that the data will be reliable and valid? In addition to these methodological uncertainties, it was likely that a project designed to consider the existence of controlled users would be heavily criticized by those who felt that this sort of study would hurt the cause of drug-abuse prevention.

Much credit is due The Drug Abuse Council (DAC) for its willingness to invest in this basic exploratory research despite the expected uncertainties and inefficiencies as well as the likelihood of public and professional disapproval. Initial funding by the DAC afforded the opportunity to test and refine research methods for the study of controlled use and to develop a clearer conceptual model of this style of use.

Methodology

The DAC study was exploratory and tentative. It had four rather modest goals: (1) developing appropriate means for locating controlled marihuana, psychedelic, and opiate users; (2) developing and applying means for gathering and, if possible, validating data from these users; (3) providing a description of the subjects, their personality structures, and their drug-using patterns; and (4) beginning to identify factors that might stabilize or destabilize controlled use.

The use of the term "controlled use" rather than "occasional use" in formulating these goals reflected my interest in understanding how controlled—that is, how successful and consistent—such occasional drug use could be, and thus how the potential harm of drug use could be minimized. Accordingly, several broad criteria for selecting subjects were developed to maximize the chance of finding subjects who were moderate and careful about their drug use. The most obvious requirement was that candidates should not be such frequent users that their use would interfere with family life, friendships, work or school, and health. The problem was to estimate what level of use might be reasonably expected to have adverse effects. Multiple daily use and daily use were ruled out immediately—not because it was certain that such use was always destructive but because, as Jaffe (1975) has pointed out, "the greater the involvement with drugs, the more likely adverse consequences." I also felt that whatever the behavioral evidence might be, there was little chance of convincing others that daily use, especially daily opiate use, could be controlled.

Although no further or more explicit cut-off points for frequency were established, the research team attempted to be conservative: we recruited subjects who had used once a week or less for at least one year prior to the initial interview. (Some candidates who had used more frequently slipped through our initial screening, however, and later we deliberately sought out more frequent users in an attempt to learn how useful frequency alone was as an indicator of control.)

In the DAC pilot project, the conditions for subject selection were rather general; they were also subject to periodic revision as interviews progressed and data were coded and analyzed. At all times the study was conceptualized as both qualitative and quantitative. Data were collected in such a way as to permit the construction of detailed case histories and the selection of excerpts from these histories that would give verisimilitude to the study and allow other researchers to compare our findings with their own experience. As the study progressed, data were coded, computerized, and statistically treated to determine quantitive significance.

In 1976 the accomplishment of the goals I had set for the pilot project led to the funding of my research by the National Institute on Drug Abuse (NIDA). Based on knowledge gained from the earlier project, the study team was able to settle on the following detailed, precise definitions of our subjects: "controlled," "marginal," and "compulsive."

Conditions for All Subjects
1. They must be at least eighteen years of age.
2. They must have no definite plans to move out of the Metropolitan Boston area within the next year.
3. They must first have used an opiate two or more years ago.
4. They must not have been in treatment for more than one month during the two years preceding their initial interview and cannot be in treatment at the time of the initial interview.

Conditions for Controlled Subjects
1. They must have used an opiate[1] at least *ten* times in each of the two years preceding admittance. If they did not fulfill this condition for *one* of the two years preceding admittance, they must have used an opiate within the last year and must also have met conditions 1, 2, 3, and 4 in at least two consecutive years of the preceding four.
2. In *each* of the two years preceding admittance they must not have had more than *three* periods of *four to fifteen* consecutive days of opiate use.
3. In those preceding two years the number of days of opiate use in any thirty-day period might have equaled but must not have exceeded the number of abstaining days.
4. In those preceding two years they must have been using all drugs (licit and illicit, except tobacco) in a controlled way.

Conditions for Marginal Subjects
1. They must have used an opiate at least *ten* times in each of the two years preceding admittance. If they did not fulfill this condition in *one* of the two years preceding admittance, then they must have used an opiate within the last year and must also have met conditions 1, 2, 3, 4, and 5 in at least two consecutive years of the preceding four.
2. In at least one of the preceding two years, they must have had at least *four* periods of *four to fifteen* consecutive days of opiate use; or at *any* time in those two years they must have had at least *one* thirty-day period in which the number of using days exceeded the number of abstaining days.
3. In *each* of the preceding two years, they must not have had more than *five* periods of *four to fifteen* consecutive days of opiate use. (Periods of more than fifteen consecutive days of opiate use were counted differently: see conditions 4 and 5.)

1. The term "opiate" is used here in order to simplify the criteria, but the same conditions were also applied to users of marihuana and psychedelics.

4. In each of those preceding two years, they must not have had more than *two* thirty-day periods in which the number of using days exceeded the number of abstaining days.
5. In *each* of those preceding two years, they must not have had more than *one* period of sixteen to thirty consecutive days of opiate use.

Conditions for Compulsive Subjects

1. They must have had at least *six* periods of *four to fifteen* consecutive days of opiate use in at least *one* of the two years preceding admittance.
2. If they did not fulfill condition 1 or 3, then in at least *one* of the two years preceding admittance they must have had at least *three* thirty-day periods in which the number of using days exceeded the number of abstaining days.
3. If they did not fulfill condition 1 or 2, then in at least *one* of the two years preceding admittance they must have had at least *two* periods of *sixteen to thirty* consecutive days of opiate use. (Thirty-one or more consecutive days of opiate use automatically made them compulsive users.)

All candidates recruited who did not meet one of these four sets of criteria were assigned to a fourth category, "other."

As these criteria indicate, the definition of "control" used in the NIDA study had none of the judgmental fuzziness that had characterized the DAC study. Instead, the question of how differences in current functioning (and other characteristics) related to level of use was determined empirically by comparing subjects who had been grouped by frequency of use alone.

Unlike the DAC pilot study, where, originally by accident and later by intention, some compulsive users of marihuana, psychedelics, and opiates had been recruited and interviewed (see table 1), the NIDA study had as its major research goal the comparison of controlled and compulsive opiate-using subjects. In order to achieve this goal, our limited resources were applied exclusively to opiate users, and further study of marihuana and psychedelic users was dropped. This decision was made partly because the notion that marihuana use could be controlled had become more widely accepted in the American culture, and partly because, even though the possibility of controlled psychedelic use was scarcely recognized, the research team had found no truly long-term compulsive psychedelic users among the six heavy users they had studied. It seemed, therefore, that in order to determine whether the use of any drug could be controlled, it would be best to focus on the opiates.

In sum, my investigation of the controlled use of illicit drugs shifted in 1976 from the use of general definitions to the use of more specific and objective definitions of drug-using categories, and from a concern with marihuana, psy-

TABLE 1. Size of subject groups by study project.

Subject types	DAC (N = 150)	NIDA (N = 99)	Combined sample (N = 153)
Controlled marihuana users	37	0	22
Compulsive marihuana users	12	0	0
Controlled psychedelic users	18	0	15
Compulsive psychedelic users	6	0	0
Controlled opiate users	41	41	61
Marginal opiate users	0	7	7
Compulsive opiate users	12	18	30
Others	24	11	35
Friends of users	0	22	0

chedelics, and opiates to a concentration on opiate use. Moreover, the study team and I began to make a selection of DAC and NIDA subjects that we called the Combined DAC-NIDA Analytical Sample. The statistical data cited throughout this book are drawn from this sample unless otherwise indicated. The numbers and types of subjects in the DAC project, the NIDA project, and the combined sample are presented in table 1, and the background characteristics of those in the combined sample are shown in table 2.

Candidates chosen for the sample were required to fulfill all the subject-selection criteria developed for the NIDA study. In the case of opiate users, the analytical sample combined those DAC subjects (twenty out of forty-one controlled opiate users and twelve compulsive users) who met the more stringent and objective conditions developed under the NIDA grant with forty-one controlled NIDA opiate users and eighteen compulsive NIDA opiate subjects. The DAC users of marihuana and psychedelics who met the NIDA definitions were also included in the sample, but the fifteen controlled marihuana users and the three controlled psychedelic subjects who did not meet these criteria were excluded from all of our statistical computations. The most common reason for excluding DAC subjects from the analytical sample was that they lacked the longer period of controlled use required by the NIDA guideline: at least two years as against the pilot project's one year.

The net effect of this procedure was, of course, to reduce the size of the analytical sample drastically. This reduction was unfortunate in a way, but I felt very strongly that the most conservative and demanding definitions of controlled and compulsive subjects—the cleanest sample—should be used to quantify the data. And even though the number of subjects used for quantita-

TABLE 2. Background characteristics of subjects in combined sample.

Background characteristics	Controlled marihuana subjects (N = 22)	Controlled psychedelic subjects (N = 15)	Controlled opiate subjects (N = 61)	Marginal opiate subjects (N = 7)	Compulsive opiate subjects (N = 30)
Age in years					
Range	18–49	19–70	18–45	23–29	20–42
Mean	30.1	30.1	25.9	25.7	25.9
Standard deviation	10.3	12.2	5.1	2.2	5.0
Sex					
Male	64%	80%	77%	57%	67%
Female	36%	20%	23%	43%	33%
Race					
White	100%	100%	82%	100%	83%
Nonwhite	0	0	18%	0	17%
Years of schooling					
Range	11–23	12–20	9–18	11–18	7–19
Mean	15.5	15.9	12.9	13.6	12.2
Standard deviation	3.3	2.3	2.0	2.8	2.7
Current marital status					
Married	18%	20%	20%	14%	17%
Single	82%	80%	80%	86%	83%
Socioeconomic class of family while growing up					
Upper-middle	9%[a]	40%	12%	14%	10%
Middle-middle	36%	27%	28%	0	20%
Lower-middle	27%	33%	37%	71%	37%
Lower	27%	0	23%	15%	33%

a. Percentage totals do not equal 100% owing to rounding errors.

tive analysis was limited, the project personnel conducted numerous screening interviews and held regular consultations with all sorts of users, addicts in treatment, and their families and friends, which supplied valuable information for the qualitative side of the project.

Since the analytical sample consists of controlled and compulsive opiate users drawn from two studies that, however similar, were conducted at different times, steps were taken to assess the comparability of these subjects. First, the controlled opiate subjects and the compulsive opiate subjects from both studies were compared on thirty-nine key variables chosen from several topic areas: demographic, personality, family history, history of drug use, current drug use, and past and present criminal activity. Results from thirty-nine t-tests and contingency tables (X^2) using those variables revealed remarkably few differences between DAC and NIDA subjects. Among controlled subjects, only five tests were significant at $p \le 0.10$; among compulsives, only three tests were significant at $p \le 0.10$. Since chance alone would dictate that approximately four of these thirty-nine tests would be significant at this level, it was considered that the groups were sufficiently similar to be combined for analysis. The lack of consistent trends (nonsignificant differences) between DAC and NIDA opiate users on conceptually related variables reinforced this conclusion.

It should be noted that the high degree of consistency between the two samples supports the generalizability of our findings to other samples defined and recruited in a similar manner. In effect, the NIDA study served as a replication of the DAC effort.

Obviously, choice of an 0.10 level of significance as the cutoff point in these comparisons increased the chances of our finding a difference between DAC and NIDA study subjects. However, since we set out to establish that no differences existed between groups, the selection of this significance level as opposed to the more common 0.05 reduced the chances of a Type II error and thus was an appropriate conservative choice (e.g., see Blalock 1979, pp. 160–61). This practice has been applied consistently to the analyses of data presented in this chapter.

CRITERIA FOR SUBJECT SELECTION. Research conducted by other investigators since about 1970 (see appendix C) has suggested that occasional illicit drug users, including occasional opiate users, may constitute a large portion of the drug-using population, but this research has revealed very little about the degree of control shown by such occasional users. Most studies have not addressed the way in which occasional use is patterned over time, the long-term stability of such use, the level of all other drug use, or various other questions related to control. In short, they tell little about the *quality* of drug use.

It was because of these shortcomings that my study team formulated the set of conditions listed earlier for selecting subjects for the Combined DAC-NIDA Analytical Sample. Each criterion was chosen for a specific reason. The requirement that all candidates should be at least eighteen years old grew out of our experience during the DAC study, when we had held informal interviews with twenty-one adolescents under eighteen in order to learn something about early using patterns. Drug use among this age group seemed too volatile to warrant the inclusion of younger subjects in either the final DAC sample or the NIDA sample. The purpose of requiring that subjects not have definite plans to move out of the Metropolitan Boston area during the year following their initial interview was, obviously, to maximize the chances for follow-up. The rule that subjects must have first used marihuana, psychedelics, or opiates two or more years before their first interview ensured some minimal stability in the patterns of use under study. The requirement that subjects could not have been enrolled in a treatment program for more than one month during the two years preceding the initial interview, and that they could not be in such a program at the time of the initial interview, ensured that all subjects were active drug users in the community.

Since most of the people we interviewed had had experience with more than one drug, the research team had to decide whether to treat each such multiple user as a marihuana-, psychedelic-, or opiate-using subject. Obviously, it would have been possible to put those who had used all three types of drugs into all three categories. But we decided instead to assign each subject to only one category according to whether marihuana, a psychedelic, or an opiate was his or her drug of choice. This decision represented a departure from those studies—and there have been many of them—that have considered the subject's drug of choice to be irrelevant. In my view, to have studied how well someone controlled a particular drug that he did not like very much would have been very much like studying moderate ice cream users while including some subjects who did not care for ice cream but did have a taste for candy.

In constructing the precise conditions for selecting and assigning subjects to the controlled, marginal, or compulsive categories, five issues were given special consideration.

First, pattern of use over time was weighted more heavily than the total number of days of use. For example, in the two years preceding their initial interview, controlled users might have used opiates on as few as 20 occasions or on as many as 365 occasions, but they were not permitted to have had more than three instances of from four to fifteen consecutive days of opiate use. (In fact, as will be discussed later, no controlled users approached the upper limit of 365 days of use.) By contrast, compulsive subjects were required to have had a number of long periods of consecutive daily use. Marginal subjects fell between these extremes, oscillating between periods of frequent use, infrequent use, and abstinence.

Second, in assigning opiate users to one of the three categories, we regarded the likelihood of physiological addiction, which was correlated with consecutive daily usage, as more important than the total number of using days. The research team wanted to ensure that those designated as controlled users had not been physiologically dependent on opiates for at least two years. Since the development of clear physiological dependence requires about two weeks of consecutive daily use (Jaffe 1975), the sample of controlled users was limited to those whose daily using sprees were of no more than fifteen days' duration. At the same time, the criteria allowed for some restricted spree use because we had found that the pilot project subjects who had managed their use of opiates quite well and had avoided adverse consequences had been able to indulge in a few short periods of consecutive daily use. For example, several subjects who ordinarily used once a week or less had increased use to every day or almost every day during a vacation or under some other special set of circumstances and had then returned to their usual pattern of less frequent use. As it turned out, our controlled subjects' sprees tended to be much shorter (four to five days) than the allowed maximum of fifteen days. The research team's leniency in regard to length of sprees and total number of days of use permitted in a two-year period reflected my own sense that we would probably have difficulty in locating very many carefully controlled opiate users.

Third, all controlled and marginal subjects were required to have used their drug at least ten times in each of the two years preceding the initial interview (with some modifications if the subject met the other relevant conditions for at least the four preceding years). One purpose of this rule was to ensure that use had been regular enough to test the subjects' ability to maintain some level of control. In effect, it eliminated the major group of experimental or minimal users that has often been included in studies of occasional use and that probably accounted for the large numbers of users treated in the surveys discussed in appendix C. The other purpose of the rule was to ensure that subjects were recent or active users.

The fourth issue relating to subject selection—a much more complicated matter—was the level of other drug use. Those assigned to the category of controlled subjects were required to have been in control of all the drugs they used (except tobacco) for at least two years preceding the initial interview. Because my study probed the general issue of control over intoxicant use, it was important, for example, to avoid counting as controlled opiate users those who were able to keep their opiate use within prescribed bounds but who were coincidentally abusing barbiturates or alcohol or some other drug. Therefore, daily but moderate consumption of alcohol was deemed acceptable, but daily use of any other licit drug (except tobacco) or of any illicit drug disqualified a candidate from assignment to a controlled category. Although I believe that daily tobacco use is risk-laden and abusive, to have required controlled users to be less than daily users of tobacco would have eliminated many otherwise suitable candidates. As it turned out, 83% of controlled opiate users, 59% of controlled marihuana users, and 53% of controlled psychedelic users in the combined sample were daily tobacco users.

The question remained, however, whether less than daily use of a large number of drugs might not still constitute overall abuse. What about including as a controlled subject a once-a-week heroin user who made use of marihuana once every other day and of barbiturates every third day, and who always had a drink before dinner? The possible permutations of different drugs and schedules of use made this problem especially difficult. Since, in any case, we could not gather data about all drug use in sufficient detail to make these distinctions, we opted to add the following requirement concerning use of other drugs: if either the candidate or the interviewer felt that total or overall drug use (including even less than daily use) interfered with the candidate's ability to meet ordinary social obligations, he or she was rejected as a controlled subject. This refinement had the disadvantage of being more subjective than our other criteria, but in practice it enabled a rough judgment to be made relatively easily. When in doubt, we elected to err on the conservative side and not to assign a questionable subject to the controlled category. In fact, most controlled subjects did not use a great many other drugs very often, and as will be indicated in discussing the validity of the data, there was good reason to expect that the subjects' own estimation of the effects of drug use on their ability to function would be accurate. In the end, only seven candidates whose opiate use was controlled were rejected for the combined DAC-NIDA sample because their use of other drugs interfered with their functioning, although each of the other drugs in question was used on a less than daily basis.

The average frequency of use, by the controlled opiate subjects in the combined sample, of seven types of other drugs during the year preceding initial interview is shown in table 3. It is striking that at least 41.7% of these subjects completely refrained from using five types of drugs (including "other"): psychedelics, amphetamines, barbiturates, cocaine, and such "other" drugs as inhalants and PCP. Moreover, when such subjects did take nonopiates, their consumption was generally quite moderate. About 36% of the sample used alcohol on at least a daily basis. About 46% were coded as "daily" marihuana users, but in this one case the definition of the word "daily" was limited to use once every *other* day because all the controlled subjects used at that lower frequency. None of the controlled subjects used any of the other five drug types more often than once a week. In summary, the average frequency of nonopiate drug use among controlled subjects was low enough to support the statement that their use of all drugs was controlled.

The fifth issue relating to selection of subjects concerned an additional category designated as "other." If a subject simply did not fit the basic conditions required of all subjects, he was omitted from the sample, but a subject who did meet these general conditions but failed to meet the specific conditions for either the controlled, marginal, or compulsive category was classified as

TABLE 3. Frequency of use of nonopiate drugs by sixty-one controlled opiate subjects.

Current frequency	Alcohol	Marihuana	Psychedelics	Amphetamines	Barbiturates	Cocaine	Other
			Percentage of subjects[a] using seven drug types				
Multiple daily[b]	6.8	0	0	0	0	0	0
Daily[c]	28.8	45.8	0	0	0	0	0
Twice a week	44.1	20.3	0	1.6	1.7	5.0	3.3
One to three times a month	10.2	13.6	4.9	0	10.0	16.7	0
Sporadic (less than once a month)	8.5	16.9	23.0	21.3	30.0	36.7	1.7
Not using	1.6	3.4	72.1	77.0	58.3	41.7	95.0

a. For up to two cases per drug type, specific frequency data were not available beyond the fact that use occurred less often than every day.
b. Two or more occasions of use per day.
c. Once per day, or once every other day in the case of marihuana.

"other" (see table 1). Most "other" subjects fell into two major subgroups: (1) those who would have been classified as controlled except for the compulsive use of one other drug, almost always marihuana; and (2) those whose pattern of use was not accommodated by the criteria. For example, one subject had used opiates for some eight years and had used them fourteen times during the year preceding the initial interview, but he had abstained for four years before that. Although he was clearly a moderate user, his current pattern had not been continued for the two years preceding the interview that we required as evidence of stability of use. Data on "others" provided us with valuable qualitative information about the range in patterns of drug use that fell outside the criteria we had selected to define controlled, marginal, and compulsive users.

The following six cases illustrate the types of using patterns we assigned to the three major subject categories.

1. Arthur, a "controlled user," was a forty-year-old white male who had been married for sixteen years and was the father of three children. He had lived in his own home in a middle-class suburb for twelve years. He had been steadily employed as a union carpenter and had been with the same construction firm for five years. During the ten years prior to the first interview, Arthur had used heroin on weekends. For the first five years of use he occasionally injected during the week but midweek use had not occurred during the previous five years.

2. Greg, a "controlled user," was a twenty-seven-year-old white male, a full-time undergraduate student in special education, participating in a work-study program. He came from a middle-class Irish background and lived at the time of the interview with a woman student. He had used heroin two or three times per month for three years before the interview but had shifted his pattern a year before the interview to four times a month, with occasional three-day periods of use. He also had had two four-day using sprees within the previous year.

3. Max, a "marginal user," was a twenty-seven-year-old white male from a lower-middle-class background who had completed high school only. He lived with three roommates in an apartment building he owned. He had been a trucker but was training on the job as a luncheon chef. For two years prior to interview he had used heroin about four times a month, either once or twice a week. During the year prior to interview he had used heroin daily (while dealing) for one month.

4. Bert, a "marginal user," was a twenty-nine-year-old white male from a lower-class background, unemployed at time of interview. During a year-long period of prescribed opiate use, which had ended a year and a half before he was interviewed, he had exaggerated his complaints of pain from an eye problem in order to obtain Dilaudid, which he had

used nonmedically on an average of three times per week. In a few instances he had used for three or four days in a row, and once or twice he had used for more than half the days in a month. Following that period of use, he had "cut back" to the pattern of nonmedical use he described on interview: three times a week on a strict schedule ("just weekends and in the middle of the week; you can't get addicted that way"). If this pattern of use had continued for six additional months, he could have been reclassified as a "controlled user."

5. Phil, a "compulsive user," was a twenty-two-year-old white male from a lower-class background who lived with his divorced mother and two siblings. He had left school after the ninth grade but had later obtained a general equivalency certificate. At the time of interview he was un-employed but had held a series of short-term jobs, mainly as a factory worker, since his return from military service. Two years before his first interview he had been using Dilaudid and about twenty Percodan daily, which he had got by breaking into drugstores. His periods of daily use were frequent and usually lasted for about three weeks ("until the supply ran out"). Following some months in jail, he had used heroin and Dilaudid approximately twice a week during the year before his interview.

6. Bob, a "compulsive user," was a twenty-six-year-old white male who lived alone, a college graduate with a degree in psychology. Following separation from his wife and child three years before interview, he had worked sporadically at part-time jobs. Dealing drugs had become his major source of income. He had used heroin at least three or four times per week since beginning use thirty months before interview and had had many periods of daily use lasting as long as two weeks.

LOCATING SUBJECTS. With limited funding and without the benefit of hard data from previous research regarding the number and characteristics of controlled or even occasional illicit drug-takers, it was not possible to draw a random, or representative, sample for study. The only possibility was for sub-jects to self-select into the study, and this method resulted in uncertainty about the degree to which they were representative of all controlled, compulsive, or marginal users. Priority was placed on the recruitment of controlled users. I expected that some compulsive and marginal subjects would be recruited in the process of seeking controlled subjects, and that if more subjects were needed and time permitted, at least the compulsives would be relatively easy to locate.

Five recruitment techniques were used in both the DAC and NIDA studies.

1. The researchers described the project to friends and colleagues who had some professional or personal contact with drug users, asking them to spread the word about the research and to refer to us anyone who might possibly be considered a moderate marihuana, psychedelic, or heroin user.

2. Brief descriptions of the research, including notices to be posted soliciting subjects, were sent at several times to more than eighty high schools, universities, drug-treatment programs, and counseling and other social service agencies in the Boston area. Follow-up telephone conversations took place with representatives of many agencies, either in response to their questions about the project or in order to encourage their cooperation. Some agencies expressed concern about confidentiality, about the possibility that the research would interfere with a therapeutic relationship, or about whether the research should be done at all, but almost all of them were willing to help by posting a "wanted" notice.

3. Following Powell's example (1973), advertisements soliciting subjects were placed periodically in area newspapers. The ads took several forms. For example:

   Drug Research Subjects Wanted for a study of nonaddicted, nonmedical occasional opiate use. Subjects with controlled semi-regular use of heroin, morphine, Demerol, Dilaudid, codeine, Percodan, etc. needed for paid, fully confidential interview. Call Mon.–Fri., 10–4, (phone number).

4. Subjects who went through the interview process were asked to refer other drug users who might be interested in participating. Very occasionally, subjects who claimed to know a lot of other users (particularly opiate users) were offered a bounty of $5 for everyone they referred who proved to be suitable for interview. Most interviewees, however, seemed willing to refer friends without financial incentives simply because they had enjoyed the interview and had decided the research did not pose a threat to confidentiality. This snowball technique was a particularly fruitful source of subjects.

5. Early in the DAC study some interviewees told us about fellow drug users who would have been likely candidates but were not willing to talk to the researchers. In order to reach this more reticent group, we decided after several months to train some of our own subjects for recruiting and interviewing. Eventually eight of these indigenous data gatherers were employed for varying lengths of time and were paid $15 or $20 for each interview they conducted.

We learned a good deal about tracking down suitable candidates from our experience in recruiting subjects.

First, as was expected in view of the more deviant status of opiate users, it was more difficult to contact and arrange interviews for controlled users of opiates than for compulsive opiate users or for any type of marihuana or psychedelic users. Without exception, controlled opiate users expressed much more concern about confidentiality than did any of the others. All of the controlled subjects were well aware of the illegality of what they were doing, but the controlled users of opiates were also aware of the extreme sense of deviance associated with their use; yet they lacked both the indifference regarding social acceptance shown by the marihuana and psychedelic users and the sullen disregard for consequences shown by the compulsive opiate users.

Second, again as expected, most of the people who contacted the research staff or whom indigenous data gatherers asked for approval to interview were not suitable candidates. Figures for a two-year period indicated that 70% had been rejected during screening discussions.

Third, with opiate users in particular, much time was required to secure a single viable interview, not counting the time spent on the interview itself. Researchers and indigenous data gathers spent an estimated ten hours on recruitment for each viable interview with an opiate user. Dealing with ineligible candidates and broken appointments accounted for most of this extra time.

Fourth, the most fruitful means of securing interviews involved personal contact between a candidate and someone who could provide reassurance about the nature of the study. Seventy-seven percent of marihuana subjects, 67% of psychedelic subjects, and 42% of opiate subjects were recruited through referral by another subject, through a friend of the research team, or by an indigenous data gatherer.

Fifth, the use of indigenous data gatherers to recruit subjects was generally successful. Although considerable time was invested by the research team in training and supervising these special interviewers, they in turn were able to recruit many subjects who would not have been willing to be interviewed by the research staff, and the quality of their interviews was quite good. Four indigenous data gatherers proved so capable and successful that their participation was extended to other areas of the project, such as interpretation of case material and selection of excerpts. The primary drawback to using indigenous data gatherers was the loss of follow-up data, to be discussed in a later section.

MEANS OF GATHERING DATA. At first contact with a potential subject (usually by telephone) my staff or indigenous data gatherers described the purposes of the research, the procedures for safeguarding confidentiality, the content of the interview, and the payment. Before making arrangements for an interview they also administered a brief series of screening questions, covering age, sex, current major activities, all drugs currently used, drug treatment history, frequency of use for selected drugs, any past or present problems associated with drug use, and the candidate's future availability. Because candidates did not know the details of the selection criteria, it was very difficult for them to deceive the research staff deliberately about their eligibility, and consequently our rejection rate was high.

Although interviews could be arranged for any time of the day or week and could be conducted either at the research offices at The Cambridge Hospital or at some other location such as the subject's home, most took place during normal business hours, and virtually all were held at the hospital. The screening procedure was repeated before beginning the interview.

The extent to which we were able to reassure candidates about confidentiality obviously had a critical effect on recruitment and on the quality of the interview itself. Nine procedures were used to safeguard the interviewees' identity.

1. No subject's name or any other identifying information was available to anyone outside the research proejct.

2. Interviews were tape-recorded and transcribed, and these records were assigned code numbers. A list of matching code numbers with identifying information for follow-up purposes was held by a party living outside the United States who was in no way formally connected with the proejct, making it virtually impossible for this information to be subpoenaed. (Later, after receiving assurances from law-enforcement personnel that they would not subpoena records, we transferred identifying information into a local safe-deposit vault.)

3. Identifying information on subjects interviewed by indigenous data gatherers was known only to those data gatherers.

4. Subjects were told that they could decline to answer any question without explaining why.

5. They were shown how to operate the tape-recorder and invited to shut it off at any time if they wished to discuss something "off the record" or if they wanted a moment to decide whether to reveal certain information.

6. Subjects were instructed to alter the names and other identifying information concerning other people whom they might discuss.

7. At the close of the interview, subjects were given the opportunity to review and erase any part of the tape.

8. In writing up cases, care was taken to alter certain information so that a reader who knew the subject could not identify him. (Several subjects were asked to read their case histories, and all were satisfied that they

could not be identified even though a fair sense of the events and characteristics of their lives had been retained.)

9. No information provided by one subject was told to another subject, even when the two were closely related and knew that both interviews had been conducted.

Procedures for protecting confidentiality were explained to each participant at the beginning and close of the interview, and each received a written statement of these safeguards signed by the interviewer. Having subjects sign a written statement of informed consent for participation in the research would simply have increased their risks; therefore, consent was given orally, and a statement noting this was signed by the interviewer and placed on file.

Because so little was known about controlled users, it seemed likely that a lengthy, semi-structured interview would be the most appropriate instrument for collecting data. In the interest of economy, however, some experimental interviews based on a shorter, structured questionnaire were conducted early in the pilot study with various drug-takers. These experimental interviews proved to be inadequate. Responses were minimal; the reasons for choosing between alternatives remained unexplained; sufficient information for assessment of personality was not obtained; and later the subjects described the experience as an unpleasant chore. Soon a semi-structured interview was developed that elicited certain fixed information from all subjects but allowed them to respond on their own terms rather than requiring them to choose between fixed alternatives, and that also permitted them to tell stories and shift topics as they wished. This approach demanded skillful interviewers and complicated the reduction of the data for statistical analysis. But this type of interview, which included questions designed to elicit information that would help us decide on the personality structure of the applicant, the degree of emotional difficulty, and the degree of coherent, stable emotional functioning, allowed us to pursue important psychological and social issues as they arose. In addition, it proved tolerable for the subjects.

The initial semi-structured interview covered seven major areas:

1. Basic demographic information (age, sex, race, social class, education, employment)
2. Family history
3. History of licit and illicit drug use
4. Current social circumstances, including relationship to work, school, family, mate or spouse, and friends
5. Details of drug-using situations and attitudes toward use
6. Interviewer's assessment of general psychological state
7. Opinions regarding drug laws and regulations, drug education, drug

culture, and related issues. (The interview schedule appears in appendix A.)

The content of the interview was altered at several points during the study as our contact with subjects suggested new areas that deserved attention and as criticism and recommendations were received from indigenous data gatherers. Making these changes did not necessarily mean that questions asked of one subject were not asked of another, because additions could be incorporated into a follow-up interview as needed. (The basic follow-up or reinterview schedule appears in appendix B.) Individualized questions were added for subjects whenever topics raised in the initial interview required further clarification. Usually these questions were devised during our biweekly research conferences when subjects were discussed and personality assessments made.

Initial interviews generally lasted for two hours, although some were much longer. Follow-up interviews were somewhat shorter. Subjects were paid at least $10 for each interview; they might be paid up to $20 if the interviewer felt that the larger amount would help secure an interview (usually a reinterview) or, more rarely, as reimbursement for travel expenses.

FOLLOW-UP. At the initial screening and at the beginning of the interview, subjects were made aware of our interest in follow-up, but recontact information was not solicited until the close of the interview. This practice developed because some qualified candidates had refused to come in for an interview when full identification for the purpose of follow-up was made a precondition. But after discussing confidentiality face-to-face with the research staff and after having experienced the interview, 97% of all subjects were willing to provide us with some means of contacting them. Recontact information might consist of a phone number or address or of similar information for another person, sometimes a parent, who would know where the subject could be reached even if he or she had moved to a new location. Subjects were advised (1) that if the interviewer reached someone else when trying to contact them by phone, the research would be described as an opinion survey and no reference to drug use would be made; and (2) that recontact letters would omit any reference to drug use. To assist the follow-up process each subject was given a business card with the name, telephone number, and address of the interviewer and was encouraged to call if he or she changed locations or wanted to schedule a reinterview or to ask further questions about the research.

In addition to letters and phone calls to subjects or second parties, follow-up efforts included advertisements in area newspapers soliciting reinterviews with subjects who could not be contacted. On average, three attempts were made to arrange a follow-up interview for each subject, excluding those for whom no recontact information was available and those who initiated their own follow-up; but as many as eleven attempts were made in some cases.

Follow-ups occurred approximately twelve to twenty-four months after the initial interview. The follow-up rate for all subjects was 47%; the breakdown by categories was as follows:

Controlled marihuana subjects	27%
Controlled psychedelic subjects	40%
Controlled opiate subjects	61%
Marginal opiate subjects	71%
Compulsive opiate subjects	33%

No subject who was recontacted refused a follow-up interview. Failure to follow up was largely due to subjects' relocation (72% of the opiate users) and the lack of recontact information (28% of the opiate users). Some subjects refused to provide recontact information to the research staff, although most of them initiated follow-up themselves. The major responsibility for lack of recontact information rested with the indigenous data gatherers, whose follow-up rate in relation to all subjects was only 31%, which sharply reduced the percentage of follow-up for the entire study. The failure of a few of them to follow subjects had to do with changes in their own life situations, such as separation or divorce and relocation.

The Data

VALIDITY. In some public discussions of this research, questions about the validity of the data (especially those on controlled opiate users) have been raised. These questions have been put in such a way as to suggest that no such users existed or could exist and that these subjects must have deceived the research team about the level of their drug use and other critical issues. One commentator even criticized the project staff for not performing urinanalyses on controlled users to verify that they were not addicted, adding that if such subjects had had nothing to hide they would have been willing to cooperate in that manner. While questions about the validity of any research data are always appropriate, the presumption that many drug users distort the accounts of their use is not entirely reasonable.

A number of validity studies that have been conducted with drug- or alcohol-using respondents who appear to have had good cause for concealing sensitive information have shown that data from such individuals tend to be both reliable and valid. Studies of alcohol users, for example, have supported the validity of adolescent surveys (Single, Kandel & Johnson 1975), of self-reports of life-history data from alcoholics in voluntary treatment (Sobell &

Sobell 1975), and even of self-reports of alcohol-related arrests (Sobell, Sobell & Samuels 1974). Validity studies concerned primarily with drug use have produced similar results. This is true of house-to-house surveys of psychotropic prescription-drug use (Parry, Balter & Cisin 1971), studies of a range of illicit drug use (Whitehead & Smart 1972; Amsel et al. 1976), and more particularly, studies involving illicit narcotics use (Ball 1967; Maddux, Williams & Lehman 1969; Stephens 1972; Maddux & Desmond 1975; Bonito, Nurco & Shaffer 1976; Robins 1979).

There are, it seems, few exceptions to these findings of high reliability and validity. When Newman et al. (1976) found discrepancies among multiple self-reports of age of first use of narcotics, they were able to give two plausible explanations for the discrepancies: first, subjects may have been motivated to overstate the length of their drug use in order to enhance their chances of admittance to a drug-treatment program; and second, both the subjects and the staff who did the interviewing seemed to attach little importance to the age of first use. Another apparent exception to findings of high reliability is a study by Chambers and Taylor (1973), who found that only one-third of methadone patients accurately reported their ongoing illicit drug use. But as Maddux and Desmond (1975) have pointed out, "Some patients probably denied their drug use because they feared disapproval or adverse action from the program staff."

In my project, rapport with subjects was excellent. Most subjects felt free to discuss even the most intimate aspects of their lives, and the interviewers were generally satisfied that subjects were truthful. Several factors accounted for this rapport. (1) Staff were not related to a treatment program. (2) Staff approximated the age range of subjects and therefore were probably perceived as trustworthy or sympathetic. In fact, many subjects supposed that the staff members themselves used illicit drugs. (3) The atmosphere of the interview was casual and the time allotted was sufficient to allow for "off the record" conversations before, during, and after the interview. (4) The various steps taken to assure confidentiality helped place the subjects at ease. (5) All the interviewers were trained to ask for the same information about important aspects of attitudes and actions concerning drug use and to pursue contradictions when found. (6) Interviewers were also trained to ask about and pick up nuances of psychological functioning,

Even though the staff and I had good reason to believe that the information we collected would be valid, we employed several techniques to test the veracity of subjects' statements.

First, the interviews were structured so that selected topics were raised more than once in slightly different ways at widely spaced intervals. Inconsistent responses could thus be detected at the time of the interviews and attempts made to resolve any discrepancies.

Second, follow-ups provided another opportunity to identify inconsistencies. A set of core questions, most of which concerned drug use, was repeated at follow-up. Therefore, if a subject initially distorted his report of his relationship with his wife or the manner in which he used barbiturates, the same distortions would have had to occur during a follow-up interview held twelve to twenty-four months later in order to escape detection by the researchers. Follow-up interviews also provided an opportunity to enhance personality assessment, to learn more about the nicities of drug use, and to pursue other specific issues raised in the initial interview that the research team felt needed clarification or verification.

Third, the subjects who were recruited by other subjects provided opportunities to cross-check data. Thirty-four percent of all subjects in the combined sample were socially connected in some way to at least one other subject from the three samples. Among controlled opiate users, about whom the greatest skepticism exists, the percentage of subjects related to another interviewee was 43%. The rule on confidentiality, stating that no subject would be told what another had said, proved important with respect to this validity check.

For example, one controlled opiate subject, Mary, reported that she was concerned about her mate's somewhat increased level of opiate use and strongly suspected he was not being honest about using the drug with other people. When her mate, Sam, was interviewed, he discussed using with other people and his attempts to keep this a secret from Mary. Both subjects were followed up approximately one year later. A detailed analysis of initial and follow-up data revealed that fifty-eight topics had been discussed by both subjects or reviewed at follow-up. Corroboration occurred on fifty-five of these items. Areas of agreement included demographic information, current activities, drug-using history, current drug use, drug-using practices, and criminal activities. In addition to Sam's hidden opiate use, agreement occurred in many other areas where the reported behavior might have been regarded negatively (for example, dealing, fleeing a warrant for arrest, receiving welfare payments while working, contracting hepatitis). The three areas of disagreement were comparatively minor and centered around the circumstances of Sam and Mary's first use of heroin together. Mary reported that she had first used heroin with her sister and brother-in-law and that Sam had not participated because he feared the drug. At her next try, she said, Sam had joined the group and had fainted immediately after injection because of his fear of needles. Sam did not report that Mary had first used without him or that he had fainted (although he did note that he had become nauseous). The disparity in their reports was not only minor but came about through Sam's omitting material rather than by direct contradiction.

Because indigenous data gatherers had continuing personal contacts with the subjects they had interviewed, they had many informal opportunities to check the validity of the data they collected. Our own continuing relationships with these data gatherers also provided us with a host of opportunities to test data about them. Indigenous data gatherers served in effect as intensive case studies.

During the NIDA study, testing the validity of data was further formalized by actively recruiting a "friend" or collateral for each subject interviewer. Subjects were asked to send in close friends who had known about their drug use for at least two years. (No restrictions were placed on the friends' drug use.) This request was explained by telling subjects that we wished to learn more about how the attitude of people they knew might have been affected by the subjects' drug use.

One or more friends were recruited for each of seventeen NIDA opiate users. Interviews with friends were shorter than those with the subjects themselves, concentrating on the friends' perceptions of the subjects' drug use and other behavior. Comparison of a friend and a subject could be made across a large and variable number of topics. (One analysis involving a controlled opiate user yielded twenty-six topics on which information was available concerning both parties.) Although data from friends sometimes slightly altered our understanding and interpretation of a subject's statements, instances of contradiction that would have necessitated a change in coding of the data were so rare and minor that after twenty-two interviews the procedure of recruiting friends was abandoned. For example, in the analysis of the controlled opiate user just mentioned, disagreement between the user and the friend occurred on only one of the twenty-six topics. This disagreement concerned whether the subject and friend had been using opiates together once every three or four months, as the subject reported, or once every two or three months, as the friend reported.

Overall, the application of these procedures confirmed our sense that subjects were truthful. When we acted upon our original plan to discard interviews whose validity had been brought into question, only three interviews for the DAC and NIDA studies together had to be rejected. In each instance the interviewer had expressed concern about validity before the problem was officially confirmed by examining friends' interviews or by identifying inconsistencies between the subject's initial and follow-up interviews.

Perhaps the most striking feature of the interviews was the subjects' willingness and at times eagerness to discuss their personal relationships, drug use, criminality, sexual behavior, and other matters that might have caused them embarrassment in another context. Subjects apparently felt well protected and rarely exercised their option to reject a question or turn off the tape recorder. In fact, deleting from tapes any identifying information that might have incriminated a host of people became something of a chore for the research staff. The team and I speculated that many subjects had used the interviews to relieve themselves of much information that they could not readily share with others. The chief problem was not to "get at the truth" but to place reasonable limits on this type of confessional behavior so that the interview did not evolve into a therapeutic encounter.

DATA REDUCTION. Most of the time spent on this project was devoted to reducing the vast amounts of information—literally thousands of pages of transcript—into manageable form for analysis and then carrying out that analysis. Data reduction took three forms: case-history analysis, excerpting, and coding.

To begin with, case notes were prepared from the transcripts and tapes for presentation to other staff. Attendance at case presentations varied, but it often included an indigenous data gatherer who contributed direct experience with the drug, and with drug users, to the discussions. Periodically, an interested outsider was invited to participate in order to help identify biases among the staff. Notes on the sometimes heated discussions of cases were made a part of the subject file, and from these notes and the transcripts, case histories (like those appearing in chapters 1 and 2) were drafted and revised by other staff.

Next, after the transcripts had been carefully reviewed, material was excerpted that seemed to represent the point of view of a number of subjects, suggested some new perspective, or encapsulated the subject's overall current and past personality functioning. Excerpts such as those appearing in chapters 4 and 5 were circulated among staff and indigenous data gatherers for comment. In this way the richness of the original material was preserved, and both the variety and the commonalities among subjects, including their attitudes, were identified.

Finally, working from transcripts and tapes (as needed), the staff coded each subject's initial and follow-up interviews separately for computer analysis. Since coding required translating the subject's language into a set of exclusive, fixed categories, it was inevitably subjective. (The cases and excerpts presented in this book are intended in part to provide access to untransformed material.) At least the coders, who included both indigenous data gatherers and staff, proved consistent in their judgments. The first few attempts by a new coder were checked for agreement and accuracy by more experienced staff members. In addition, during the project, twenty cases that had been coded were selected at random and assigned to another staff member or indigenous data gatherer for coding. The second coder did not know that someone else had already coded the cases and thus had no motive for taking special care in preparing them. With more than 200 items to be coded per interview, there was disagreement on fewer than 2% of the items.

The style of analysis employed on the project was mixed, incorporating both an individual, case-history, qualitative approach and a more selective, quantitative, statistical approach. Each method included a subjective element and provided a different, though not necessarily contradictory, picture of control over drug use. The statistical overview presented later in this chapter is intended to restore in some degree the general trends and distribution of differences that are obscured by the case-history approach.

STABILITY OF CONTROLLED USE. The most critical question facing the research staff concerned the stability of occasional, nonaddictive opiate use. Can controlled use be a lasting pattern, or must it be considered simply a brief, transitional stage preceding either heavier involvement or total discontinuance of use? We discovered that such use can be a lasting phenomenon (table 4). Some of the controlled users in our combined analytical sample had had stable patterns for as long as eight, nine, or even fifteen years. The mean period of current controlled use during the study was 4.5 years. Moreover, although the criteria for controlled use permitted a large number of occasions of use, most subjects were infrequent (less than weekly) users. In the year preceding their initial interview, only 26% had had any spree use. During the same period 23% had used opiates less than once per month on average, 36% had been monthly users, and 41% had been weekly users.

That our controlled subjects had maintained moderate use for an average of 4.5 years showed without question that controlled use can be stable. Controlled subjects were at least as stable in their use as compulsive subjects were; no significant difference was found between these groups in the duration of their current using styles as displayed in table 4: $t(89) = -0.85$, $p = 0.40$.

Unfortunately, data on marginal subjects were not amenable to statistical analysis because only seven of the users in our sample fell into that category. But data on their frequency of opiate use and using sprees in the twelve-month period preceding the initial interview show that while this group was by no means so intensive in the use of opiates as were compulsive subjects, its members did not demonstrate the consistent restraint and careful manner of use that characterized controlled users. The very existence of marginal users, however, makes a strong case for a continuum of opiate-using styles; as the detailed case histories indicate, assessing the level of abuse for this intermediate group was difficult (Zinberg et al. 1978).

Nevertheless, one who accepts the traditional view that opiate users must progress from experimental to moderate use and then on to increasing involvement with opiates and finally to addiction might still argue that our subjects simply had not reached the point in an opiate-using career where compulsive use develops (Robins 1979). But our findings do not support this view. Since there was no significant difference ($t[89] = 0.51$, $p = 0.62$) between the lengths

TABLE 4. Current opiate use in the combined sample.

Variable	Controlled subjects (N = 61)	Marginal subjects (N = 7)	Compulsive subjects (N = 30)
Duration of current style of use (months)			
Range	24–180	24–72	24–174
Mean	53.4	38.6	59.5
Standard deviation	31.7	34.5	39.3
Average frequency of use in previous twelve months			
Multiple daily	0	0	23%
Daily	0	0	23%
Twice a week	41%	57%	47%
One to three times a month	36%	14%	3%
Sporadic (less than once a month)	23%	29%	3%
Using sprees[a] in previous twelve months			
None	75%	43%	46%
Sprees only	6%	14%	0
Sprees plus other use	20%	43%	54%
Length of using career (years)			
Range	2–20	6–11	2–15
Mean	7.2	8.4	6.8
Standard deviation	3.2	8.3	3.4

a. Four to fifteen consecutive days of use.

of the total using careers of the controlled subjects and the compulsive subjects, it can be concluded that the two groups had had equal opportunity to become compulsive. Moreover, the length of the total using careers of the controlled subjects—a mean of 7.2 years—suggests that they had already had ample opportunity to progress to compulsive use.

The notion that opiate users always advance through stages of increasing drug use is also contradicted by the following facts about the careers of our compulsive subjects. About half (47%) of them had never had a substantial period of infrequent use; they had been compulsive users every year of their using careers. Only 23% of them had had any years of controlled use. Further, the average duration of that small percentage's longest period of controlled use (1.3 years) was significantly less than the current period of control in the sample of controlled users (4.1 years), measured in years of using career: $t(55.3) = -7.07$, $p < 0.001$. Thus, it appears that only a few long-term compulsive users passed through an early stage of controlled use, and those who did so tended not to remain in that stage for long.

Another question—whether any of our controlled users had a past history of compulsive use—is relevant to the issue of the stability of controlled use. Twenty-nine (48%) of the controlled subjects had had one or more such periods during their using careers. It might be argued, therefore, that their current period of controlled use represented only a temporary remission from compulsive use or a tapering off along the way to becoming abstinent. Again, however, the data strongly suggest that these subjects' current controlled using style was a highly significant segment of their using career. For example, their current period of controlled use (mean = 3.5 years) was significantly longer than the average duration of their longest periods of compulsive opiate use (mean = 1.6 years): $t(28) = 4.62$, $p < 0.001$. And their current period of controlled use also represented 45% of their total using careers, which included periods not only of compulsive use but of other opiate-using styles as well.

Although there was no way to foretell whether all our controlled subjects would eventually progress to more intensive use (Robins 1979), this seemed unlikely. Follow-up data available for 60% of the controlled subjects show that 49% had maintained their using pattern and 27% had reduced use to levels below those required for them to be considered controlled users. (Of these, 24% had become abstinent.) Another 11% had maintained their controlled pattern of opiate use but had begun using other drugs too heavily for us to consider them controlled subjects. Only 13% (5 subjects) had increased their opiate use sufficiently to enter either the marginal (8%) or the compulsive (5%) category. Of the two subjects who became compulsive users, one had had a significant period of dependency on heroin and the other a period of dependency on barbiturates before becoming controlled; and one of these had returned to controlled use at the time of reinterview. Even if all these subjects should eventually become addicts, their period of controlled use would form a long and distinctive segment of their using careers. At the time of initial interview, their current period of controlled use represented 60% of their opiate-using careers.

CRITICAL DIFFERENCES BETWEEN CONTROLLED AND COMPULSIVE OPIATE USERS. Although the criteria for admission to this study resulted in the creation of subject groups with quite different patterns of use, I wondered initially whether these groupings would prove to be significant and distinct in terms of both the quality and the consequences of their drug use. As it turned out, comparisons made between the controlled and the compulsive opiate subjects did reveal several differences that were closely related to the commonplace distinctions made between drug users and drug abusers.

A highly significant difference was found between controlled and compulsive subjects in the ability to keep opiates on hand without using them: 59% of controlled subjects as against only 17% of compulsive users were able to deter use when opiates were immediately available: $X_c^2(1) = 11.798$, $p = 0.001$. (Here and elsewhere, subscript $_c$ in X_c^2 indicates use of Yates Corrected Chi Square.) Controlled users also had significantly lower peak frequencies of opiate consumption during their using careers than compulsive users: $X^2(4) = 33.678$, $p <$ 0.001. Only 23% of controlled subjects, compared with 87% of compulsives, had ever used opiates more than once per day. This difference was not simply an artifact of the criteria used to define the subject groups, for these criteria placed no restrictions on frequency of use prior to the two-year period preceding subjects' initial interviews, and within this two-year period controlled users were permitted to have had brief periods of spree use. In addition, a notable difference, which was partially an artifact of the subject criteria, existed between the two groups in terms of whether they had ever used a nonopiate drug compulsively: $X_c^2(1) = 4.337$, $p < 0.04$. As expected, far fewer controlled subjects (59%) than compulsive subjects (83%) had such a history.

These examples indicate that controlled users were more moderate about drug use than compulsives and, as might be expected, that they also suffered fewer negative consequences. Fewer, although not significantly fewer, controlled subjects than compulsive subjects—36% as against 45%—had had any adverse reactions from opiates, and when they had had such reactions they had responded differently. After a negative experience controlled subjects were likely to take new precautions or to suspend use, while compulsives were more likely to maintain their old pattern: $X^2(1) = 3.970$, $p < 0.05$. Controlled subjects were significantly less likely to have been treated for drug use (41% as opposed to 77% of compulsive users: $X_c^2[1] -8.892$, $p = 0.003$). In addition, the controlled subjects were treated less often; only 36% had been treated more than once, compared with 61% of the compulsives: $t(28.7) = -2.86$, $p = 0.008$.

Another relevant finding related to current functioning and especially to employment. A significantly greater number of controlled users (37%) than compulsives (10%)—$X_c^2(1) = 6.267$, $p = 0.01$—worked full-time. And a similar though not significant trend existed in relation to part-time employment, with 44% of controlled opiate users employed part-time versus 27% of compulsives. Self-related performance at work showed the same expected difference between the two groups, with 71% of the controlled subjects "doing well" as compared with 62% of the compulsives. Finally, more controlled subjects (55%) than compulsives (39%) reported that they liked their work.

No definite causal relationship between drug use and the ability to work is implied by these findings; differences in work performance between the two groups may have been due to a variety of factors. At the same time, there does not seem to have been a relationship between compulsives' relatively poorer performance and a lack of social opportunity, as indicated by variables relating to social background. There was no difference between controlled and compulsive users in terms of the reported socioeconomic status of their family while they were growing up ($X^2[3] = 1.361$, $p = 0.71$). There was no difference in the total number of school years they completed ($t[44.1] = 1.29$, $p = 0.21$). Insofar as these factors affected future employment, controlled and compulsive subjects might have been expected to do equally well in their work life.

Besides the variables already discussed, many other variables—some associated with availability of and experience with opiates, some with set (personality), and some with setting—were examined in an effort to pinpoint other critical differences between controlled and compulsive opiate users.

DRUG VARIABLES. Since the availability—or, rather, nonavailability—of drugs is viewed by many policymakers as the most crucial factor in reducing use, the apparent moderation of our controlled users would be less striking if it could be shown to have resulted from a lack of opportunity to use opiates rather than from individual restraint. Yet our analysis of variables relevant to the question of opportunity to obtain drugs showed no significant differences between controlled and compulsive subjects. The variables considered included: (1) current ease of obtaining opiates ($X^2[2] = 4.495$, $p = 0.14$); (2) number of sources for obtaining opiates ($t[89] = -.71$, $p = 0.48$); (3) current dealing of any drugs ($X_c^2[1] = 0.0$, $p = 1.00$); (4) current dealing of opiates ($X_c^2[1] = 0.10$, $p = 0.92$); (5) number of drug types currently used ($t[40.5] = 0.98$, $p = 0.32$); (6) number of drug types ever used ($t[46.9] = 0.88$, $p = 0.39$; (7) history of significant reduction or discontinuance of opiate use due to its unavailability ($X_c^2[1] = 0.058$, $p = 0.81$); and (8) history of significant increase in opiate use due to availability ($X_c^2[1] = 1.508$, $p = 0.23$). In short, in terms of access to opiates, the controlled and compulsive subjects were equally at risk in relation to losing or gaining control over their drug use. These negative findings are among the most important results of our research because questions about availability are crucial to any theory of controlled use as well as to the development of public policy toward drug use.

A corollary finding concerned the method used to administer opiates. Analysis of several relevant variables did not support the view that compulsive users inject opiates and controlled users do not. There were no significant differences between these groups as to whether they currently injected opiates ($X_c^2[1] = 0.903$, $p = 0.342$), whether they injected heroin ($X_c^2[1] = 0.536$, $p = 0.46$), or whether they had ever injected opiates ($X_c^2[1] = 0.352$, $p = 0.55$). In fact, for all three variables the direction of difference was the opposite of what might have been expected, showing that a greater proportion of controlled subjects than compulsives actually injected the drugs.

It was also assumed for the purpose of analysis that controlled users tended to use "softer" opiates, such as Percodan or codeine, for which addiction would develop more slowly, and that compulsives tended to use "hard" opiates like heroin, morphine, or Dilaudid. Again, however, the data did not support the supposition. When controlled and compulsive users were compared as to whether they were using or had ever used seven different opiates, all but two of the fourteen comparisons proved not significant at $p \geq 0.10$. The two differences turned out to be artifacts resulting from the use of methadone by subjects who had been in methadone treatment programs. And when the type of opiate was dichotomized into "hard" (heroin, morphine, Dilaudid, methadone) and "soft" (codeine, Percodan), no significant differences were found between controlled and compulsive subjects in relation to the following relevant variables: whether they were using "hard" opiates ($X_c^2[1] = 0.012$, $p = 0.91$); whether they were using "soft" opiates ($X_c^2[1] = 0.000$, $p = 1.0$); whether they had ever tried a "hard" opiate ($X_c^2[1] = 0.000$, $p = 1.0$); and whether they had ever tried a "soft" opiate ($X_c^2[1] = 0.000$, $p = 1.0$).

Finally, with reference to drug variables, analysis showed no significant differences between controlled and compulsive users over a wide range of variables relating to the circumstances of early opiate use. These variables included: (1) whether first opiate use had occurred alone or with others ($X_c^2[1] = 0.000$, $p = 1.0$); (2) positive versus negative or equivocal reaction to first use ($X_c^2[1] = 0.033$, $p = 0.86$); (3) age at first use ($t[43.9] = -.37$, $p = 0.71$); (4) age when opiates were first purchased ($t[42.5] = -0.70$, $p = 0.49$); (5) number of tries before a "high" was achieved ($t[83] = 0.72$, $p = 0.48$); and (6) number of other drugs used prior to or concurrently with first opiate use ($t[89] = -0.04$, $p = 0.97$).

All these findings overturn, or at least are inconsistent with, arguments that are sometimes used to explain why it is that controlled opiate users exist, arguments that flow from current prohibitionistic policy. Neither availability of opiates, method of administration, type of opiate used, nor early experience with opiates served to distinguish our controlled subjects from our compulsive subjects.

SET VARIABLES. Five personality scales were used in this study: (1) passive versus active; (2) intimacy versus isolation; (3) rebelliousness versus conformity; (4) awareness of affect versus distance from affect; and (5) distortion of reality versus acceptance of reality. Each personality scale was scored from one to six points on the basis of material taken from each subject's interview. The results of all opiate subjects in the combined sample, displayed in table 5, indicate that the direction of association was as expected. Three results were significant at $p \leq 0.03$, indicating that the compulsives were more passive, more distanced from affect, and more distortive of reality than the controlled subjects.

Other findings on personality dealt with variables that have frequently

TABLE 5. Direction of association on personality scales for all opiate subjects
in combined sample.

| Scale dimension | t-test | | | Direction of association |
	d.f.	t	p	
Passive vs. active	(89)	2.16	0.03	Compulsives more passive
Intimacy vs. isolation	(89)	−1.20	0.23	Compulsives more isolated
Rebelliousness vs. conformity	(89)	1.28	0.20	Compulsives more rebellious
Awareness of affect vs. distanced from affect	(89)	−2.86	0.01	Compulsives more distanced
Distortion of reality vs. acceptance of reality	(89)	4.32	0.001	Compulsives more distorting of reality

been taken as indications of early personality deficits, such as criminal and
delinquent behavior and unusually difficult family background. The tests administered
showed no significant differences between controlled and compulsive
users at age eighteen or younger in relation to the following factors: (1)
catastrophic family difficulty, such as death of parent or parental divorce
($X_c^2[1] = 0.454$, $p = 0.50$); (2) significant violence in family ($X_c^2[1] = 0.242$, $p = 0.62$); (3) parental discipline, whether strict, moderate, or lax ($X_c^2[2] = 1.73$,
$p = 0.42$); (4) history of trouble in elementary school and through high school
($X_c^2[1] = 0.954$, $p = 0.33$); (5) relationship to father while growing up ($X_c^2[1] = 2.798$, $p = 0.25$); and (6) alcohol- or drug-abusing parent ($X_c^2[1] = 0.324$, $p = 0.57$).

In addition, as has been noted in relation to the work performance of
subjects, there had been no significant difference in social class between controlled
and compulsive users when they were growing up. Two variables relating
to the quality of early life did, however, distinguish one group from the
other. First, controlled users were significantly more likely than compulsives to
rate their relationship to mother while growing up as "close" rather than "distant"
or "equivocal" ($X_c^2[2] = 6.061$, $p = 0.05$). Second, controlled users were
more likely than compulsives to evaluate family cohesiveness while they were
growing up as "close" rather than "moderately close" or "distant" ($X_c^2[2] = 5.461$, $p = 0.07$).

Although there were differences between controlled and compulsive users
on the personality scales, differences did not appear on most of the dimensions
that are usually associated with preexisting personality disorders. Of course,
the obvious difference between the two groups was that one was actively

2. Chapter 6 considers the influence of active addiction on personality and offers a general
typology of the personality of the active addict and the emotional responses that develop as a result
of this experience.

TABLE 6. Motives for opiate use.

Type of motive	Controlled subjects (%)	Compulsive subjects (%)	X_c^2	p
To get a rush	23	37	1.273	0.26
To escape	41	70	5.662	0.02
To take risks	3	13	1.870	0.17
To alleviate depression	21	80	26.327	<0.001
To enjoy the high	85	73	1.762	0.28
To socialize	46	17	6.225	0.01
To use for recreation	57	23	8.058	0.01
To use for relaxation	54	43	0.551	0.46

addicted while the other was not.[2] To be actively addicted means, in practice, to be much more in touch with those affects that are associated with drug use than with any other affects, and therefore to be at odds with the general perceptions of external reality. Seen in this context, it is particularly interesting that the personality variables on which the two groups differed were early closeness to mother and to family, for even currently the compulsive users, unlike the controlled subjects, were on poor terms with their families. In addition, compulsives' histories revealed that they felt considerable bitterness because their families had rejected them. Although we had no quantitative data to show that the sensed lack of closeness between compulsive users and their mothers and families was retrospective falsification, our interviewers formed the subjective impression that some distortion might early have taken place.

One area related to the set or personality of our subjects in which obvious differences existed between controlled and compulsive users had to do with their motives for opiate use. On the basis of comments made throughout the interviews, subjects were coded in regard to their current motives for opiate use, and multiple responses were accommodated. The data in table 6 reveal a striking pattern of difference between the two groups. Without exception, more compulsive than controlled subjects claimed the first four motives for drug use: "rush," "escape," "risk-taking," and "alleviation of depression." The differences between the groups in relation to the second and fourth motive were significant at $p \leq 0.02$. The first four motives might be conceptualized as indicating that the compulsives were using for "unhealthy" reasons. For the second set of motives—"likes the high," "social use," "recreation," and "relaxation"—which might be conceptualized as social or celebratory use, the pattern of responses was reversed. In every case more controlled than compulsive subjects held these "healthy" motives, and two of the four were significant ($p = 0.01$). This divergence in motives between groups was also found when subjects were coded as to their primary motive for use. Significantly more compulsive subjects (72%) than controlled subjects (22%) designated an unhealthy primary motive; and significantly more controlled (78%) than compulsive subjects (28%) revealed a celebratory or social motive ($X_c^2[1] = 18.256$, $p < 0.001$).

These findings appear to lend support to the view that compulsive use represents a kind of self-medication, an attempt to soothe a painful internal state. There is good reason to suppose, however, that in the case of our compulsive subjects this was at least as much a consequence of the setting—the isolation and environmental stress resulting from addiction—as it was indicative of a longstanding personality disorder that predated the addiction. And it must also be remembered that the motives described by our subjects applied to their current use, not to the outset of either opiate use or compulsive use.

Our controlled subjects' choice of motives, which could have been as readily ascribed to social drinking as to opiate use, underscored again how different recreational or occasional use of opiates is from addictive use. This difference was also reflected in the results obtained for a variable that reported subjects' assessment of the importance of opiate use in the context of their primary motive for use. Only 20% of controlled subjects as against 73% of compulsives felt that opiates were extremely important to them ($X^2[2] = 24.859$, $p < 0.001$).

The analyses of set variables produced mixed results. There were differences between the groups on the personality scales and motives for current opiate use; however, few differences were found for variables dealing with the quality of early life. As the next section reveals, setting variables differentiate between controlled and compulsive users more sharply.

SETTING VARIABLES. Friendship patterns and peer group activities played a major role in influencing both controlled and compulsive using styles. Probably the most important difference between controlled and compulsive subjects was that controlled users tended to have more friends and associates ($X^2[3] = 11.426$, $p = 0.01$). Not one controlled subject was a "loner," whereas 11% of compulsives classified themselves as such. Moreover, 68% of controlled subjects, compared with 37% of compulsives, had "various groups of friends." This result was supported by findings concerning the historical impact of opiate use on friendship patterns. There was no significant difference between groups in regard to the question whether opiate use had had an impact on friendships or it had been associated with a change in type of friends. But an inspection of responses coded "other" revealed that while 17% of compulsive subjects had become loners after beginning to use drugs, not one controlled subject had become so. Seven percent of controlled users did speak about an overall reduction in the number of their friends, but in every case this had resulted from their voluntary severance of relations with persons who were, or had become, more intensive users. Compulsives not only suffered a drastic reduction in friends, but those who were loners claimed to be so because former friends had dropped them.

In addition to the number of friends, there were also important differences between controlled and compulsive subjects in regard to types of friends. Findings were significant for the following three variables: (1) how many controlled opiate users the subject knew ($X^2[3] = 13.641$, $p = 0.003$); (2) how many compulsive opiate users the subject knew ($X^2[3] = 15.189$, $p = 0.01$); and (3) how many illicit drug users who did not use opiates the subject knew ($X^2[2] = 7.093$, $p = 0.07$).

The first two variables, which are related to style of use, were based on the hypothesis that the way an individual uses drugs is influenced by the way his or her associates use them. Controlled subjects tended to know more controlled users than did compulsive subjects: 88% of controlled users knew "many" or "some" controlled users in contrast to the compulsive subjects, only 56% of whom knew controlled users. Also, 30% of controlled subjects, compared with 11% of compulsive subjects, knew no compulsive users.

Responses to the third variable, which deals with relationships to users of nonopiate illicit drugs, indicated that controlled subjects tended to know more such users. Seventy percent of controlled subjects as compared with 44% of compulsive subjects knew "many" of them. This result was consistent with the expectation that controlled users would maintain a wider range of social connections than compulsive users. The same idea was buttressed by the fact that 62% of controlled subjects as against 54% of compulsive subjects knew "many" or "some" people who did not use any illicit drug. This result, however, was not significant: $X^2(2) = 1.371$, $p = 0.50$. Evidently, controlled subjects' maintenance of a wider network of social connections—a larger peer group—provided them with valuable feedback and reinforcement for moderate use, while compulsive subjects, who tended to know more compulsive users and fewer controlled users and who also tended to be loners, seemed to be cut off from the limiting influence of more moderate drug-takers.

The question of peer group influence on using style was pursued further by obtaining results for two additional variables: (1) how often opiate use occurred with controlled opiate users ($X^2[3] = 21.417$, $p < 0.001$), and (2) how often opiate use occurred with compulsive opiate users ($X^2[3] = 11.400$, $p = 0.01$). Here a strong, consistent relationship emerged. For example, 67% of controlled subjects as against 23% of compulsive subjects "always" or "usually" used opiates with controlled users. But only one controlled subject "always" used opiates in the company of compulsives, compared with 14% of compulsive subjects.

Another piece of evidence related to peer group concerned the possible influence of a mate on the subject's style of opiate use. For several variables, including the following, no significant results were obtained: (1) whether mate used opiates ($X_c^2[1] = 0.000$, $p = 1.00$); (2) mate's awareness of subject's opiate use ($X_c^2 = 0.145$, $p = 0.71$); (3) mate's feelings regarding subject's opiate use ($X^2[3] = 2.419$, $p = 0.49$); and (4) whether mate used illicit drugs other than opiates ($X_c^2[1] = 0.000$, $p = 1.00$).

There was, however, a strong and expected association between the mate's style of using opiates and the subject's style of use (Fisher's Exact = 0.117). Of those controlled subjects' mates who used opiates 91% were occasional users as against 58% of compulsive subjects' mates who were users. A similar result was obtained for the mate's style of use of nonopiate drugs. For example, whereas no controlled subjects' mates were compulsive users of other drugs, 25% of compulsive subjects' mates used other drugs compulsively ($X_c^2[1] = 3.325$, $p = 0.07$).

These results roughly paralleled the results for friends. In both instances, regular contact or exposure to other people with a particular opiate-using style appeared to be associated with the subject's having that style of use. It is interesting that mates' feelings about subjects' opiate use were not significant. Evidently the critical matter was what the mate did, not what he or she wished the subject to do.

Still another aspect of peer influence to be investigated was a subject's usual company or companion for drug use. The coding items for this variable were analyzed independently: (1) alone, (2) with mate or spouse, (3) with various friends, (4) with one circle of friends, (5) with several using groups, and (6) indiscriminately. Results for the first five items were not significant ($p \geq 0.10$), but the results for "indiscriminately" were ($X_c^2[1] = 11.465$, $p = 0.001$). Only one controlled subject was indiscriminate about his using companions as against 27% of compulsives.

The general result for these items corroborates the importance of the earlier findings: the companions' style of drug use was more important than who the companions were. The positive finding for the coding item "indiscriminately" implied that not making a choice about using companions was more important than the kinds of companions one chose. Moreover, this finding suggested that making choices about *how* to use drugs—specifically, using them in compliance with certain social sanctions and rituals—might be an important component in control.

The assumption (developed from our qualitative case-history approach to the interview material) that social sanctions and rituals could be important factors in distinguishing between controlled and compulsive use was borne out by the statistical findings regarding rules for opiate use. Controlled users were generally much more cautious about the way they used opiates (Harding &

TABLE 7. Rules for opiate use.

Rule	Controlled subjects (%)	Compulsive subjects (%)	X_c^2 (1)	p
Never use in a strange place	18	13	0.206	0.65
Never use with strangers	31	27	0.038	0.84
"Snort" only	13	0	2.833	0.09
Special schedule for use (e.g., after work only)	34	20	1.374	0.24
Plan in advance for use	30	0	9.254	0.002
Don't share "works"[a]	26	27	0.000	1.0
Clean up surroundings before use	23	17	0.176	0.68
Never use alone	26	10	2.299	0.13
"Copping" rules (e.g., know your source personally)	53	20	7.428	0.01
Budget funds for drug use	48	23	3.968	0.05

a. Responses to this rule were corrected by including only those who were currently inject-ing opiates.

Zinberg 1977; Zinberg, Harding & Winkeller 1981). With one exception (that of not sharing "works"), controlled subjects were always more likely than com-pulsives to adopt a variety of rules to minimize the risks of use (table 7). For the following rules, tests showed these differences to be significant at $p < 0.10$: refusing to inject opiates, "snorting" only, planning for use, exercising caution when "copping," and budgeting money to be spent for opiates. On average, controlled users also had a significantly greater number of these and other rules for use than did compulsives ($t[89] = 3.53., p = 0.001$).

The ten specific rules for use that appeared in the coding were supple-mented by a category designated "other," which was used to record mis-cellaneous rules. The results for "other" followed the trend of the specific rules and confirmed our hypothesis that because the use of opiates, and particularly heroin, is so widely disapproved, each user or using group must develop social sanctions and rituals ad hoc. This lack of opportunity for culturally based learn-ing about controlled opiate use means that rules tend to be idiosyncratic. Ninety percent of controlled subjects and 50% of compulsives followed "other" rules. Of these, only thirteen were cited by more than one subject, and the remaining twenty-one rules were idiosyncratic. Examples of "other" rules were "Don't mix drugs," "Don't use for depression," and "Don't use if you're driving."

Another aspect of the social setting that is believed to be crucial in deter-ring many people from using drugs, fear of consequences, showed no significance in differentiating between controlled and compulsive users, as the responses to the following five items indicated.

1. Subject knows someone who died or overdosed as a result of opiate use: *no* significant difference ($X_c^2[1] = 0.989$, $p = 0.32$).
2. Subject knows someone who had a serious adverse reaction to opiate use: *no* significant difference ($X_c^2[1] = 2.013$, $p = 0.16$). As might be expected, however, more compulsives than controlled users (*77% versus 58%*) had known someone who had reacted adversely.
3. Subject knows someone in legal trouble with nonopiate illicit drugs: *no* significant difference ($X_c^2[1] = 0.2412$, $p = 0.62$).
4. Subject knows someone in legal trouble as a result of opiate use. This result approached significance at $X_c^2(1) = 2.719$, $p = 0.11$; but it was the compulsives (97%), not the controlled users (81%), who knew someone in legal trouble and might have been expected to fear legal involvement.
5. Finally, no significant differences appeared in responses to the question whether subjects had *ever* discontinued or significantly reduced their opiate use as a result of either health concerns ($X_c^2[1] = 0.0844$, $p = 0.77$) or fear of dependence ($X_c^2[1] = 1.308$, $p = 0.25$).

These data supported the view that there was no difference between the groups in the way they viewed the consequences of their use. The discovery that compulsive users were not significantly deterred by fear of consequences came as no surprise: such users were unlikely to fear becoming compulsive because they already were compulsive and thus had committed themselves to a way of life heavy with risk. But it would have been easy to assume that fear of consequences might keep controlled users from becoming compulsive. Although some subjects told anecdotes indicating the importance of a critical incident, such as the overdose death of a friend, these instances were rare and sometimes seemed overdramatized. Clearly fear of consequences of punishment had little power to control drug use.

All of these findings, whether negative or positive, showed a high degree of association between our subjects' style of opiate use and the two broad types of setting variables: the using style of friends and mates and the rules for use. Moreover, the nature of the associations coincided with the basic theoretical position that had grown out of our qualitative analysis of individual subjects. Setting variables were found to be a major, if not the primary, element in determining degree of control. Indeed, when the set and the setting variables were considered in combination, they were much more useful in differentiating between drug use and drug abuse than was the drug variable, which proved to be of little or no significance in our qualitative analysis.

4

Research Findings: The Beginnings and Effects of Drug Use

NUMEROUS QUESTIONS ARISE WHEN CONSIDERING ILLICIT DRUG USE. How do people begin to use marihuana, the psychedelics, or the opiates? How do they get the drugs, use them, and pay for them? What, generally, are the effects of use? How do these effects impact on the user's psyche, on his close relationships, on his capacity to work and function socially? And, above all, how does he manage—if he does—to use the drug reasonably and in a controlled fashion?

The preceding chapter has offered quantitative answers to these questions. This chapter and the next approach them qualitatively by letting the users speak for themselves. They consist mainly of excerpts from interviews in which the interviewers (I) have asked the respondents (R) a variety of questions about their use of illicit drugs. A few of the responses have been edited in order to clarify the meaning, and in all of them proper names have been changed. For the users of all three types of drugs the questions focus on the following general topics: (1) beginning use (in the case of the psychedelics, the history of early use); (2) effects of use; and (3) social sanctions and rituals that helped to control use. Unless otherwise stated, all excerpts apply to *controlled* users. This chapter deals with the first two topics. Chapter 5 presents findings on rituals and sanctions.

Marihuana

The following excerpts illustrate the types of responses given by our marihuana subjects to interviewers' questions about how they began to use the drug, how it affected them generally, and specifically how it affected their work and personal relationships.

BEGINNING USE. One of the many confirmations of the representative nature of our analytical sample came from our subjects' descriptions of beginning use. Twenty-five years after the publication of Howard S. Becker's "Becoming a Marihuana User" (1953), these users reaffirmed his observations and upheld ours. Despite the enormous estimated increase in marihuana use since Becker's day—since then about 57 million have used—the beginning users expressed great apprehension about this first step. They were not immune to the general public's concerns about what the drug might do to them (that is, the possibility of addiction or derangement) or unaware of and unconcerned about its illicitness, as the following exchange reveals:

I: How did you feel about marihuana prior to using it?
R: I was scared.
I: In any particular form?
R: I didn't really know what it was; I had just heard everyone talking about it, and I had heard that smoke was so bad and this and that, and how people that have family problems do it. But I didn't want anyone to think I was shocked, because then they'd think I was an old grandmother, and I wasn't. But I was really scared for a while.
I: When did your fears begin diminishing?
R: Probably when I smoked myself.

The beginning user looked for a guide to show him what to do and how to do it correctly—and safely. In this search the neophyte tended to overestimate greatly his more experienced peers' understanding of the drug. Most younger users, too, consistently overestimated the extent of others' use. And my staff and I found, as Becker had found earlier, that most beginning users did not get "high" the first time, often to their discomfiture.

R: The first time I tried it? It was in my sophomore year of high school and a friend—oh, no, my brother—gave me my first joint. He didn't want to either. I had to force it out of him.
I: How did you go about that?
R: Well, I knew that he smoked, and I'd wanted to try it, but I didn't know where to look, and I didn't know anything. And he didn't want to give it to me because then he said it would come back that he was the one who turned me on. He really didn't want to give it to me, but finally he did. I said that I'd get it somewhere else if he didn't give it to me, so he just gave it to me, and I smoked with a friend—well, not even such a good friend—I don't even think we got off. No, I'm sure we didn't: I remember now. But I didn't want to seem completely stupid to him, so I just kind of acted like I knew what I was talking about.

Usually the first experience did not bring much pleasure:

I: Do you remember enjoying it?

R: No, I didn't like it. I mean, I don't know if I got high or not, but to me it didn't taste so hot.

Nonsmokers often had a particularly difficult time.

I: On how many occasions did you use marihuana before you experienced a high?

R: Uh, probably ten or twelve times, and I felt as if the reason was that I didn't really know what the smoking was all about. As I said, I have no experience with cigarettes, and inhaling was a foreign issue to me. If I did it, it hurt. And that's why I didn't get off—'cause I didn't know what smoking was about.

Another nonsmoker's patience was finally rewarded:

I: You said that it was about six or seven times before you did get high?

R: Oh, it was more than that. About fifty times.

I: How come you kept smoking it?

R: I dunno—I just did. I don't really know why I did.

I: But the *first* time you actually got the high was when you were trying hashish?

R: Yeah—well, I had smoked hash before, but all of a sudden it just hit me.

It was our impression that the last user, in spite of his determination to get high, had had considerable unconscious anxiety about the whole process, and that his tenacious assault upon his fears was characteristic of his personality structure and general behavior. Others worked through their anxiety in different ways, again in consonance with their personality structure and behavior in situations other than drug use. One cautious and methodical young man put it this way:

R: There were a couple of people in my dorm who were using it, and they offered me some, and I didn't get off on it the first few times.

I: Had they offered it to you before the time you accepted?

R: Not directly. It had been passed around in situations where I'd been, but I would just let it go by, and it hadn't been in any sense forced on me, it was just there and then I finally wanted to pick it up. Curiosity really.

Another young woman whose everyday life was characterized by keeping herself within a middle ground, neither too loose nor too tight, said in answer to the question, "Can you remember the circumstances of your first use?"

R: Yeah, very well. I was with some friends, and someone came in, a friend of the people I was seeing. I didn't know him, and everyone was smoking—I knew they smoked, but I was very skeptical. I was very conservative about it, and I still didn't really know what it was all about. I still thought that it was dangerous. I wasn't really persuaded to smoke, I just watched everybody. I saw nobody going mad or anything; they all were laughing and having a good time. So I said well, OK. I smoked and I got high. I liked the high and I smoked.

The popularity of marihuana can act as a deterrent to beginning use for those of an independent spirit who automatically on personality grounds resist becoming passive followers. This was true of more of our subjects than we had anticipated, particularly those whose resistance was buttressed by social factors.

R: I was initiated into drugs, into marihuana, by my brother; I always had a sort of negative attitude toward drugs when I was in high school. Some of my friends smoked grass. And they said, "Come on, get involved in it." They were really "hippie" types [laugh]. When I say that, it's a nonderogatory term; but it was pseudo-hippie. That was in 1969 when the peace movement was very active. They were together with a purple light bulb and glasses and a poster on the wall, and they were really into the "drug culture," sitting around in a circle, "right on," things like that, so I had a negative attitude toward it because I just thought it was so plastic. I think there was also a certain part of my Catholic upbringing that was involved, with its "Don't do anything." I don't know if that's true or not, but I think that definitely influenced me, so I just didn't want to get involved in it. Then when I finally did, it was in a totally different situation, and I enjoyed it. I got involved with my girlfriend, at that time, in a more real sort of situation.

Although several subjects reported minor anxiety attacks when first experiencing intoxication, these passed quickly. The only user who reported a serious disaster from his first experience presented it as a joke:

I: How old were you? How did it happen?
R: I know that when I was in high school I smoked pot a couple of times, but I don't have any clear recollection of that. I didn't get stoned. The first time after that I was working in this car dealership in Boston, and this guy I used to work with said to me one day during lunch, "Do you want to go out and smoke a couple of joints on the roof?" And I said, "Yeah, sure." And about three days later we did it again, and I lost my job because I got so blown away. I was moving a car from the roof down,

they had a ramp that you had to drive down. Well, I just couldn't control my faculties. I was bringing this car down from the body shop to the waiting customer, and I took up two poles on the way down. And I completely wiped out the passenger side that had just been replaced. Well, the hubcap got down slightly before I did [laugh]. I came down there and he said, "Pick up your check," and that was that. That was the first time, other than the couple of days before when I got stoned; there really wasn't much to it—you know, the first time.

It was clear to the interviewer that this subject was well aware of the danger of a drug experience that resulted in such loss of control. His response also bore out the fact that beginning users have the most acute difficulties with control, particularly when driving. Experienced users may have driving problems too, but they tend to be of a different sort, similar to those of alcohol users—problems of risk-taking and overestimation of control rather than of lack of awareness.

Most parents have great difficulty in sharing their children's marihuana use (see chapter 1). Joining in an illicit activity is hard enough, but the reversal of the usual relationship between the experienced parent-teacher and the inexperienced child-learner may be extremely complex, especially because the intoxication experience often results in loss of control and even helplessness. Here is an excellent description of that confounding situation.

R: My mother smoked marihuana one time. I–my brother and I—had three joints and we knew she wanted to try it. So I said, "Ma, I got some now; do you wanna try it?" And she said, "What?" And I said, "Some grass." And she did try it and she hadda do it before her husband got home. And he'd have been home in about two and a half hours, so it took us about fifteen or twenty minutes to smoke, and she said she didn't get high. But then she went into her room, and when I opened the door to see what she was up to, she was reading a book upside down—not reading at all, just pretending to do something so she could just be alone and feel what it felt like to be stoned on marihuana. And then I closed the door because she asked me to get out, and then she put the TV on, and I heard the TV on, so I went back in. I was really interested to know how she'd react. So she had been watchin' television for about ten minutes and the picture was all blurred, it wasn't even there—so she didn't really care to watch television or read. She just wanted to laugh and be alone, so I did leave her alone after that, and my brother and I could hear her, in the parlor, laughing. I thought that was good. But she never did it with us again. I believe she's done it, y'know, after that. I mean, with her girlfriends, because I know her girlfriends do it. They're older women, and they ask me for joints once in a while.

GENERAL EFFECTS OF MARIHUANA USE. The overwhelming majority of our sample reported positive effects from marihuana, though few were as ecstatic as this user:

I: Did you enjoy it the first time you used it?
R: I loved it, I loved it, I loved it.
I: When did you next try it?
R: Next weekend, I loved it. I have ever since.

All but two of our subjects (and they will be described later) insisted that they had always been in control of their marihuana use. For example:

R: There was no time I ever had to need a high, or, y'know, just do something daily because it had to be done. I'd get high if I wanted to, then the next few hours I'd light up a joint. You know, it's under control. It's never a need or urge that I have to satisfy. Yeah, tried speed, tried acid, never got too involved for the reason that it's too exhausting—and I just don't like doing things that are gonna tie me up and knock me down.

Most of our subjects were special-occasion users. Regardless of their specific frequency of use, these subjects indicated that smoking marihuana was associated with certain activities. They insisted that the change in perception when intoxicated heightened their enjoyment of these activities.

I: Are there any activities that the use of marihuana makes easier for you?
R: Living my life [laugh]. I think that most of the things I do that make me feel good, I would just as soon do stoned as straight. I mean, if I'm in some kind of athletic stuff—occasionally I get together with some friends and play touch football—that's just as much fun or more fun stoned. Chess is definitely more fun stoned. In fact, that's one of the reasons I got into chess. There's a puerile element to most games that I just don't get off on, or else it's really rigid. I'll play hearts sometimes, and I enjoy hearts, but it's a very cerebral sort of enterprise, it really is. But chess, once you know the rules and a couple of openings and stuff, chess is largely intuitive. And that's what getting stoned is about. It's opening the third eye, just sort of increasing that capacity, and that's why I like to play chess stoned. So I guess, in general, things that involve intuition are most fun stoned.

Perhaps the most frequent effect reported was the increased enjoyment of eating, the well-known "munchies."

I: What do you particularly like about marihuana, the marihuana high?
R: You know, everything is much more enjoyable, stuff like that. Eat a hell of a lot more, get the munchies all the time. I don't really know. Kills a lot of time.

Many planned their use around this activity:

I: Do you ever smoke marihuana before dinner?
R: Once in a while. If I'm going out to a restaurant and I really want to chow down and get my money's worth, I'll smoke a couple of "jays" before I go out. And that way I know I'm going to get my money's worth.

Another frequent report was that the changed perception enhanced users' enjoyment of sexual activity.

R: I find that sex is better when I'm stoned.
I: How come? What's the difference?
R: Well, because I can do more things with grass. I can, well, when I'm straight there's just too much goin' on, you know, in my head. If I wanted to kiss a girl while I was straight, there'd be too much going on in my head for me to really get into the kiss, whereas with grass I can get into the kiss much more easily. I can really *feel* the kiss, the energy in the mouth, and that's all I feel. Like a blending of energies . . . more into body feelings rather than thinking, "Well, am I doing this right, will she like this, will I like this?" Everything just happens naturally, and you are only in that experience, not in another and not in your head. You can even feel what the other person is feeling, I mean in her body. You can feel with your body when her body is close to orgasm and then you begin to feel it too. There's something like a merging of feelings, body feelings, and every touch, every movement, is like magnified a hundred times. Touches even on the hands or even toes become intense. The only problem is that usually after such an intense experience I just want to fall asleep. But that's OK, too. There's this sense of timelessness. Nothing exists but this moment.

This description of enhanced enjoyment, which was echoed in one form or another by most subjects, seemed to the interviewers to be accurate. But some other reports of pleasurable experiences seemed to indicate that the users were having difficulties.

For example: "I think I use it in three ways. Be a big shot. Next I use it for hiding myself; if I've got a problem, I cut it out right then and there. And the third thing is enjoying myself. Going out for a ride and smoking marihuana and laughing and stuff. You know, you go down the corner of Boston Common and run a while, or get high and run track or something; that's all it is. That's what I do for enjoyment. Something to hide away from." In other areas of his life this young man showed a tendency to self-consciousness that resulted in defensiveness and a fear of exposure. This tendency seemed to be enhanced by his marihuana use, controlled though it was.

Another example of drug use reported as pleasurable was even more alarming:

> R: It's easier to go to school stoned. It's just easier to space out the classes more. You're just less conscious of the busywork and the bullshit. You just sit there and leave your body there if you want. I used to go to math class at two o'clock, my last class, and just fall asleep. I'd never done that before, sleep in the afternoon or sleep in public or sleep in school, and I'd just go in there, fall asleep, and when I heard the bell, I'd wake up, and instantly I'd be awake. It was as if I was in alpha, meditating. Oh, that freaked me out, 'cause I'd sleep through the class, but I'd wake up instantly at the bell, I mean wide awake, more awake than when I came into the class. And I'm just able to daydream in that class. Draw pictures. And I'm also more able to listen to the teacher. If I want to tune into the teacher and it's noisy and I'm stoned, I become a better receptor.

The last report seemed alarming not just to the research team but to other subjects as well. One user expressed his general concern as follows:

> R: I think that [it's dangerous] for people getting involved with drugs, especially young people beginning high school. I know that when I talk to my brother [and his friends], they tell me some pretty incredible things about drug abuse in high school. When I went to high school I was a fairly serious student, but they say that the majority of kids that go to school go to school stoned in the morning. That's like being an alcoholic. And I know you cannot go to school stoned and learn as much as you would have if you weren't. It's just sort of a way to avoid the unpleasantness of school. But it really is a type of escape. I believe that. As far as hard drugs are concerned, in high schools it's just too tempting for kids to become involved in this totally new experience, in a way, and [they] give it more credit than it's really worth. You can read so many articles about pro-drug attitudes—that there is truly something beyond the physical aspect of it—that these kids will try it and it's great

and they get really into it. And all of a sudden it's a new way to become socially involved with different people, which isn't what those kids need. The same thing with grass, I guess. All of a sudden there's a key, and they're involved in it, and it just can take away a lot.

Only a few of our subjects (41%) expressed overt difficulties with marihuana use, and most of them tended to blame the drug's illicitness rather than the drug itself.

I: Have you ever had any difficulties or adverse experiences with marihuana?

R: Only when I'm high or if I try to smoke in a public place like on the street. If I'm alone or with friends at somebody's house it's OK, but I get really, really nervous to be outside with it, even when I'm with friends. My friends don't seem to mind, but me, every time I see a police car or someone looks at me funny, I think they know I'm high or I'm carrying something and I get really paranoid. If I'm high on alcohol, I never get those feelings. I can even be staggering around a little or talking funny, but I never worry about it, I just enjoy it. But the fact that you're not supposed to possess grass or use it makes me afraid that someone is going to do something about it—like a cop.

The fear of being caught by the police falls into the same category:

R: Yeah, I've gone places with him in my car. I'll go some place and there will be roaches all over the car. Or I'm afraid someone will open the glove compartment and there will be an ounce of pot in there or something.

In addition, many of our younger subjects were afraid of being caught by their parents:

R: I came home one day and I'd just done a dope deal or something, and I left a few ounces of pot hanging around on the top of my bureau 'cause I just went out to the store to get something and I didn't figure he'd be back, and I left the door open and he came in and saw it . . . "Oh, what's this?" Well, I said, "It's not mine," 'cause it wasn't, 'cause I'd sold it [laughs] . . . And he said, "Well, what are you doing with it?" and I said, "Just holding it for somebody." "You're holding it for somebody?" he said, and I said, "Yeah, he'll be here in twenty minutes to pick it up." And sure enough in twenty minutes they came and picked it up . . . so I solved that one. So after that he just said, "Do you use that stuff?" and I said, "Well, yeah, I've tried it." "Do you use it a lot?" I said, "No." I didn't use it a lot . . . and I didn't see that much wrong with it anyway . . . and a few other times that we've talked about it, he told me that he used to smoke. I don't know if he used to use it, but he smoked it from time to time when he was younger. He used to live in Texas and I guess there are places where it was just growing! So he didn't think it was all that horrible. At that point I'm sure that the reason he felt that way about me using it was because it was an illegal drug and it could put me in jail. But I know how he feels now: he feels that it's a really stupid law.

The worst effect of marihuana use described by 4 (18%) users was a highly agitated state, usually defined as becoming "paranoid."

    I: Did you ever have any adverse or unpleasant experiences with marihuana?

    R: Yeah, I've become extremely paranoid at times, yeah. I was riding my motorcycle.

    I: Did that stop you from using it?

    R: No, I realized it was me, the same way as I had bad experiences on MDA. I realized it was me it was coming from, not the drug.

Two reported giving up marihuana for a brief time after such experiences. However, two other subjects wanted to continue use and tried to figure out under what conditions they could do so without experiencing the feared reaction.

    R: I don't know if it's physiological or mental, but I can't do grass a lot and enjoy it because it gets me nervous, and I don't like being nervous. And it was hard for me to admit that. We have a group here, and I finally laid it on them, one time when I got high and I was really, really uptight. I was sitting there and I was almost at the point of I don't know what . . . I was getting really upset at telling them this 'cause I had never told them that I get paranoid . . . I find it much easier to control hallucinogens than it is to control grass. Grass is almost always guaranteed to get me uptight. If it got where I enjoyed it, I would do it as much as I felt like doing it. 'Cause I see where people have it as a very large part of their lives, but yet it doesn't rule them; people I know who are therapists, they'll get high excessively, but yet still are doing viable things and enjoying it. I feel sort of bad that I can't do it that much, but I just have to live with it. But I would say that if I could get things straight, I'd probably smoke a little bit more. It is enjoyable when you do enjoy it. I've really dug it at times.

In a sense such subjects use this reaction as a further mechanism, albeit a shaky and dangerous one, to promote control.

EFFECT OF USE ON WORK AND RELATIONSHIPS. With the marked exception of the young man who lost his job in the garage, as well as of some students whose schoolwork was affected, our subjects denied that marihuana had had any definite influence on their work life. They also did not feel that it had influenced their relationships with people negatively. (This response was in sharp contrast to that of our opiate-using subjects.) The most common effect reported was a bonding of friendships. Subjects contended that the experience of using together enhanced a feeling of closeness and solidarity:

R: We all worked together in this drug-counseling place. And, of course, because of our jobs we weren't supposed to use drugs, but of course we did. Soft drugs. We were all really different types and I think there would have been a lot more abrasiveness in our work together if we hadn't had this experience of coming together and getting stoned together. We even used to do it after hours in the counseling office! But it's like, well, grass breaks down your own defenses, so you can see through the defenses of other people. You can see, well, something like the core of their being. So that if Jim talks too much to people on the hotline or if Alice grabs all the phone calls before anyone else can get a chance to, well, you don't get so angry at them because you know you've had these times when you were high and relaxed together. And all those annoying personal habits either weren't there or just didn't bother you as much.

R: It's like you can develop a real sense of trust with people you get stoned with. Everybody gets a little whacked out, things are really funny that usually aren't, people's associations get really loose, but if you're high, too, you can understand them. I thing that you need the same sort of trust to get really high with people that they say you need for an LSD trip. And if you get a little anxious or paranoid, there's always someone there to say something funny or tell you it's OK. I mean, it's the kind of experience that whatever you say or do is OK. I don't find that to be true in other situations. I feel closer to people I've gotten stoned with than to people I haven't.

Users often claimed that the drug itself produced this closeness. The research team, however, believed that it resulted from the sharing of an illicit and pleasurable experience, which gave the sense of being on the inside of something special and naughty that was not shared by the straight world.

R: I remember we used to feel really superior to people who weren't high or who had never smoked. We felt we understood things that they didn't. Well, it was a sort of religious trip we were into and we felt that when we were stoned we were close to God or the life source or whatever you want to call it, and people who were pot virgins never experienced that. Well, maybe they did; I mean, you read all these things about Indian yogis and whatnots who are high all the time. But we felt we got a glimpse of that experience when we were high and we could return to it whenever we wanted to, by smoking. No struggles, you know. No renunciation, no chanting, just light up a "jay"!

Marihuana use certainly provided a special topic of conversation. It made the user feel like a member of a club.

R: I talked about drug use a lot with some friends, maybe because most of them get high, you know, that's why. If I hung around with friends who didn't take drugs, I wouldn't talk about it, but most of the people I know do use drugs.

On the other hand, marihuana use was not approved by all groups. Many of our subjects reported estrangement from old friends who did not use, because the users feared criticism and disapproval:

R: I began using with new friends because none of my other friends would want to smoke.
I: Did you ever ask your friends if they wanted to try?
R: No, not really, because I knew what they'd answer. I don't think I wanted so many of them to know.
I: Why?
R: Because they'd probably be disappointed in me.
I: You mean, be disappointed that you'd be different or changed?
R: Not so much that I'd be different, but I'd be taking drugs, and they'd say, "You don't need that, you can be happy without it."

Another issue mentioned by at least 23% of our subjects was dealing (selling drugs). Most experienced users deal at one time or another. Usually this is not for profit (although many try to get a free ounce or so for themselves out of it) but for convenience and solidarity. If someone can make a good buy in the world of marihuana users, he is expected to let his friends in on the transaction. He thus becomes a dealer. Being a dealer, he can also make new acquaintances and develop a certain prestige:

I: You would just deal marihuana with your friends?
R: Yeah. Occasionally I'd deal to an outside person, but mainly with friends. It was exciting.
I: Dealing for profit, or dealing to cover costs, or . . .
R: Dealing for kicks. I mean, for the excitement, and the macho, and the

ego. I was the dealer and my name was known nationally. I was so proud when I met some girl for the first time and became really close, and after a while she said, "I've heard of you," and that was really an ego thing.

Psychedelics

The psychedelics differ from marihuana (and also from the opiates) in combining three different characteristics: they are nonaddictive; they are high-impact drugs; and users quickly develop a tolerance to them.

All of our clinical evidence supports a fact that has now become well known: few individuals continue heavy (frequent) use of psychedelic drugs over a prolonged period of time (Becker 1967; McGlothlin & Arnold 1971; Bunce 1982); in fact, no such users appeared in the reported sample. Of the controlled psychedelic subjects, 56% reported daily or weekly use as their highest frequency. The mean length of most intensive use for these subjects was only 13.78 weeks (S.D. = 14.14, range = 1–52), compared with 86.46 weeks (S.D. = 107.06, range = 4.5–364) for controlled marihuana users and 48.11 weeks (S.D. = 56.46, range = 1–260) for controlled opiate users. Some of our subjects, however, referred to transitory periods of heavy use as a kind of "addiction."

I: How about in terms of yourself, have you ever been drug-dependent or drug-addicted?

R: Yes. I was, maybe, drug-addicted. I guess there was a sort of psychological dependency. When I was in high school, I was tripping on acid two or three times a week. That was when I was about sixteen.

I: How long did that go on?

R: The heavy part of it went on for two or three months.

This self-definition of "addiction" was based not on any physiological or even psychological assessment of dependency but rather on an assessment of subjective feeling. Psychedelic use is an experience with an astonishingly high impact, whether positive or negative:

R: We prepared for our first acid trip.

I: What did you do?

R: Well, first of all, I trusted him to be my guide, sort of. I had read that you needed a guide, a guru, in case anything bad happened. Well, we were in love, and he had tripped a few times, and he had never had any bad experiences, he said.

I: What did you do?

R: We went to his house in the country. We ate bee pollen before we dropped the acid tabs.

I: Bee pollen?

R: Yeah. I didn't know, but Joe said that acid eats up the B vitamins in your system, and bee pollen would protect us from that.

I: I see.

R: We spent some time together first, getting close to each other. We braided each other's hair. We took a blanket and walked about a mile into the woods, to a very sunny spot surrounded by rocks and trees. Oh, this acid, one of Joe's friends had already tried it and he said it was very gentle, good for a first trip. He said the trip would last a few hours, so we dropped it in the late morning so we could enjoy it in the afternoon and come down that night in the country house where no one else would be around. And we didn't have to work the next day, so I wasn't worried about getting too . . .

I: What happened?

R: Oh, it was lovely, just lovely. At first, for about an hour, nothing happened, and I thought, Oh, this isn't working, maybe something's wrong with me. But then I noticed how beautiful and how sort of real the rays of sunlight on the rocks were. It was like I'd never seen sunlight before. It looked like rays of butterscotch. And the little animals, grasshoppers and squirrels and birds, came out, and it was like they weren't afraid of us because we were so at peace, and they knew we wouldn't hurt them. I felt at one with nature. It's something I've looked for since then but have never experienced again. And we looked into each other's eyes and we were friends and we weren't afraid and we made love, there on the blanket in the woods.

The negative experiences were equally intense:

I: What were your bad trips like?

R: Very paranoid, just got very paranoid, and I wouldn't go near anybody, and I'd feel freaked out by everybody, and I would think something was happening which wasn't. At one point, I thought—I was at this party and I was tripping and I had a bad trip—I thought I was supposed to fight all these people. It was, it was a really bad trip.

Not only is it impossible to sustain such levels of stimulation, but the experience soon becomes repetitious (Zinberg, Jacobson & Harding 1975). In addition, tolerance develops quickly, which adds to the user's assessment of himself as becoming addicted.

R: I developed a very high tolerance to psychedelics at that point because I was using them so frequently, and to such a degree where I could, you know, like right now, I think if I took half a tab of acid, I'd go way up

> there. It would take me maybe five or six, and one time I took twenty
> tabs.

Once they had built up tolerance, our subjects found they could control the
effects of tripping in order to deal with commonplace circumstances. Until
then, however, none of them, in contrast to the users or marihuana and the
opiates, could conceive of working or carrying out other general activities while
using the drug.

EARLY PSYCHEDELIC USE. Before 1960 the psychedelics had been used
experimentally as an adjunct to psychotherapy, as a treatment for alcoholism,
and as a method of sensitizing therapists to the nuances of psychological disrup-
tion. Such experiments had gone on for years without causing undue anxiety,
but of course they had been carried out in medical and other highly controlled
settings that almost automatically provided defined limits. A great change
occurred in the early 1960s when Timothy Leary, with his "tune in, turn on,
and drop out" slogan, touched off more general consumption of these drugs.
Their use spread with amazing rapidity, especially among students, for they
promised a great religious experience, a sense of oneness with the universe,
and insight into oneself. At the same time, of course, they threatened to bring a
freak-out, a bad trip, a lasting psychosis, or a genuinely irreversible personality
change.

Because our project was based in Cambridge and the Greater Boston area,
where Timothy Leary had launched his "crusade," we interviewed several
users who had known Leary and begun their psychedelic use with him. Excerpts from their responses to our questions will illustrate the nature of use in
the Leary era as well as the continuing influence of that era and the subsequent
development of different ways of thinking about use.

Even the earliest users, in the throes of joining a social crusade with
spiritual and political overtones, were searching for evidence to counter the
general public's fears about psychedelics, fears that the users loudly decried.

> R: Of course, I had some hesitation about taking it at that time, but I soon
> became aware of the fact that there was little basis to my fear. Right in
> this house I had Tim Leary come in and one of the experts down at
> Harvard Medical School—experts in this field—who was interested to
> see what the drugs did to chromosomes. He persuaded me to invite
> Leary here to have his and our chromosomes tested, and out of the four
> of us who gave our blood for this purpose, on a kind of blind basis, the
> only one who showed any abnormal number of breakages in the chro-
> mosomes was the only one who had never taken any of these drugs. My
> friends, when I told them this story, they said, "Oh, we ought to

promote LSD as something that improves your chromosomes, 'cause Tim's were the best of all."

Another characteristic of the early use of psychedelics, which was far less evident with marihuana and hardly existed with the opiates, was the development of an ideological position. Users of psychedelics were not simply smoking a joint, they were becoming part of the enlightenment. This view of use came at least in part from Leary and his influential outpourings.

I: Before you tried hallucinogens, what did you know about them?

R: Well, all I knew was what I'd read about them, and I took a very dim view of it. It seemed to me silly to think that a drug could touch off a religious experience, and this is what Tim Leary was telling us. He told us about his convicts that he was giving it to, and he said they were talking like medieval mystics, and this made me a little skeptical. But here I was supposed to be a big expert in the field of psychology of religion, and here were claims about it, and I felt that I shouldn't come to premature conclusions without taking it myself, and that was my chief motivation.

These strong ideological convictions helped the individual overcome his anxiety about us and face up to the "straight" society's disbelief that such a drug experience could be interesting and even important.

R: I'd read in the papers about acid—and in magazines and stuff like that, usually *Life* magazine—and about how people's chromosomes were being this and that. There was some pretty scary publicity about it. It struck me that people were probably fooling around with their fundamental chemistry, you know. And this particular guy did it, and then told me about it, and it didn't seem to me that he was changed. In fact, he seemed better. It was very important to him. It was probably the most important thing in his life, by a long shot. And since he was that close a friend, I was open to him.

There is little doubt that Lester Grinspoon and James Bakalar (1979) were right when they noted that the early users of psychedelic drugs were frustrated by the public's failure to take seriously their positive feelings about the inner change that resulted from the drug experience. One of our subjects stated it as follows:

R: Oh, yes, yes, I did enjoy my first trip. Even though it was an ordeal in ways, and I can't imagine anybody wanting to take a trip on LSD without a good reason for it, any more than I can imagine going to the dentist for fun. But it was not only good things for me that were valuable, it gave me insight into the value of the drug. In thinking about this school situation during the trip, it occurred to me that if the president of the institution could give LSD to all of his faculty, his problems would be over. But, when the trip was over, suddenly I realized that something had happened to my animosity. My hostility had about 90% drained away, and I haven't stayed awake a minute since then, worrying about that situation. So that was maybe the high point of the trip.

The fervent anti-drug propaganda of the 1960s that was aimed at discouraging use of LSD was not particularly successful. The dire warnings that LSD caused physical damage (which turned out not to be true) and the made-up stories about users being blinded by staring at the sun did not always frighten potential users.

I: Had you read about LSD prior to using it?

R: Several times, yeah. From all kinds of viewpoints. I'd read a lot of bullshit. I'd heard about these people blinded by it watching the sun, and heard that was all bullshit. The chromosome thing turned out to be pretty much bullshit. And I'd read a lot of Tim Leary who seems to have—I don't really agree with all of his things, but at the time his kind of movement that he was the head of was pretty important to me. It was more all-encompassing than the resistance movement, which only seemed to be extremely political. I was kind of getting disenchanted with just changing the system. I thought changing consciousness had something to do with it. I was really getting into Leary's philosophy.

Users were affected by anti-drug propaganda, but instead of being turned away from the psychedelics they tended to idealize their use.

R: I feel I owe a tremendous debt to LSD. Um, I think that it helped to sensitize me to certain things about myself, once I was ready to be sensitized. It's sort of a chicken-and-egg thing; that is, I suppose that some of what happened to me would have happened if I'd been straight, but I really think that there's something about drug use, intelligent drug use, that leads to the necessity to face up to certain parts of oneself, or myself, with greater clarity and greater force than might have been true otherwise. It's the whole question of being jived, and the whole question of putting on airs and of pretending to be other than what one is. It's just much, much harder to pretend when there are psychedelics involved than when not.

Instead of recognizing that use was an interesting experience that some people might like but most would not risk, the users themselves became committed and active proselytizers.

> R: I was more advanced in drug use than the rest of the group. I was out of the group, like. I used to get a high sensation about it. They'd say, "What are you using that shit for?" Weirdos. And I'd say, "Shut up, you don't know what you're missing." So I got a few people to get high, and they did psychedelics with me, mostly mescaline, and they liked it, really liked it.

Besides idealizing psychedelics, many users became extremely moralistic about their use.

> I: I vaguely remember your mentioning before that acid for you meant deciding to do some thinking work, as opposed to just getting high and having a good time. Is that fairly common?
>
> R: Yeah, it is for a lot of people I know. I mean, it's hard to get high and have a good time on acid. It really is hard. It's strenuous work.

> R: I very rarely pleasure-trip. I usually do psychedelics when I have something I want to work out. Sometimes I pleasure-trip. It's a definite aid to my personal growth. I probably trip once or twice a month. Prior to tripping, I do needs assessment. What's my need in relation to the drug? I want to make sure it's a good reason if—I don't do psychedelics when I feel I need to escape because that's when I know I won't have a good trip. To make sure if I need a recovery period, like if I'm going to have time or not, I'm very . . . Sometimes I'm affronted by my sense of responsibility, and it bothers me [laugh]. But, yeah, I'm very careful that there's enough time to do it right, and I'm not going to interrupt the pleasure of that trip. I usually get off late afternoon, you know, to experience that change into night. I'm basically a night person. I like tripping at night. I never trip alone.
>
> I: Is there anyone in particular whom you'll trip with?
>
> R: Not constantly. There are certain people that I have, that I know, that I trip with, but not necessarily one in particular or two in particular. But it's always a constant set of people that I trip with.
>
> I: How large is that?
>
> R: Probably ten people.

Words such as "sacred" and "sacrament" were prevalent in the drug culture.

> R: I wouldn't use in the city or with people whose vibes I wasn't sure

about, with people whom I got bad vibes with. To me LSD is almost a
sacred thing; you should take it in a natural setting, somewhere where
you're with the earth.

Many actually tried to organize a church. They extolled the psychotherapeutic
value of the experience in cataclysmic terms.

R: I totally freaked out on LSD. But to me it was the best thing that ever
happened.

I: What do you mean?

R: It seemed like the therapy that John Lennon went through with Janoff,
whatever they call that. It seemed like the process of bringing you back
to your childhood, bringing you back to your instincts. It took Janoff
two years to pull that off with his questions and answers. It took me two
hours getting high off that LSD. My whole existence was wiped out. I
didn't know my name. Most of this, what I'm telling you now, is from
accounts of what people tell me because I was unconscious of it. I took
this LSD when I was inside the city area, and the energy was built up.
And it was those hang-ups I mentioned to you before—my parents and
my sexual hang-up—and I totally erupted in this guy's room. Just
vomiting and throwing things and screaming, and they took me outside
and walked me through the snow. I remember I thought I was Jesus
Christ expounding to all the people. I really was yelling a bunch of
nonsense. I'd no idea what I was yelling, and I came back to my room
and I tried to rape this girl. People stopped me, but I saw this girl and I
said, "Do you want to ball me?" And I grabbed her. Then when I was
coming down, I saw that it was my paranoia with my parents and my
frustration over being a virgin that brought it all on. Also, I realized
what an ego trip I was on and realized that I was living in an illusion that
I was not even aware of. I really thought—the way that I woke up from
that acid—I never felt worse in my life.

Because these therapeutic expectations were highly exaggerated, many users
were disappointed in the results of their drug use.

R: Um, it was preplanned in that I had been reading about some other
people's psychedelic experiences and how they had gotten into really
heavy places, like getting back to the moment when they were born,
that sort of thing. And I thought, wow, I'd really like to trip and try to
concentrate on getting back to the moment when I was born. Of course,
what happened was that the trip brought nothing like that whatsoever,
but that was kind of the impetus behind it. And I first realized that by
reading something, it was possible to get somewhere more important
on psychedelics than I realized before.

I: And so you were really setting out to do some work on this?

R: Yeah.

The crash from excessive expectations often led to painful and rather hollow mouthings of a religious nature. The decision to turn to Eastern religions and mysticism came partly from these disappointments. Partly, too, that decision was the outgrowth of the drug experience itself. The sense of a genuinely alternate state of consciousness—an awareness that perceptions, both external and internal, can change—raised questions about the unvarying nature of the usual state of consciousness and everyday reality (Zinberg 1974). I believe that the campaign against use of these drugs deprived users, for a time at least, of the opportunity to work through their drug experiences and to integrate them socially and psychologically with their usual consciousness experiences. Thus forced out of their everyday environment (Zinberg 1981; Zinberg and Harding 1982) by their drug experience and by the culture's response, they turned to obscure and sometimes bizarre philosophical or religious ideas.

I: What's the main thing you recall about it? What happened?

R: Well, generally, the first trip was one of the most unusual—it lodged me into maybe a black, sinister side. I really got into the black arts.

I: So you were into magic?

R: Well, after that I was convinced of something.

Obviously, this type of experience only increased the alienation between users and the straight society.

There also were important political overtones. As Kenneth Keniston (1969) and others have shown, the drug-using groups initially were apolitical. And certainly the straightforward political young people who in the early 1960s were struggling for civil rights and improved health care in Mississippi and Alabama were anti-drug and contemptuous of drug users. But in consonance with the old maxim, "The enemy of my enemy is my friend," the drug revolutionaries as well as the civil liberties revolutionaries soon began to see the reigning cultural outlook as narrow, repressive, and destructive.

R: I think there are now many fewer people taking acid—that the relationships are much more carefully worked out about acid. It used to be that a whole corridor of students, you know, in a dormitory, just would take it on the spur of the moment. When I first came to teach here, that was around 1969–1970, things like that would happen. There would be campus riots here, tear gas, and the police, and the kids would be tripping their brains out. I know that people wouldn't do that any more. They are too wise.

It would be going too far to say that "make love not war" came solely from lysergic acid and a few other chemicals, but the use of psychedelics had ideological significance in the anti-war movement. It could be argued, and probably correctly, that the drug-using part of that movement was the fringe, the alienated, and not the core movers and workers. Yet drug use was important in that it espoused in an ideological sense the fighting of repression. For many of our psychedelic subjects, too, aggressive political activity, which contrasted sharply with their earlier drug stance, seemed to compensate for the feeling of disappointment over the psychedelic experience.

> I: When you were tripping, can you recall any really good moments or experiences that you had? Anything stand out in your mind?
>
> R: Let's see. Well—not really. Tripping I always got the attitude, is this all there is?
>
> I: It was never a monumental thing?
>
> R: Yeah. I always expected so much more from it. But it made me aware of myself and of other people who were using it. I watched those other people who were using it and saw that the answer wasn't just to sit around and hallucinate in your head and then decry Kent State and Cambodia on the one hand, but then just give up on the other hand. I saw that wasn't the answer. There were bad, horrible things going on. These were bad men, evil men, who were running the country and lying and cheating the people. I had to do something about it. At the same time, I developed an intense dislike for these "peace" people who were always loaded.
>
> I: You said you felt you had to do something about it. Did you?
>
> R: Yeah, yeah. I joined the campus SDS. I occupied buildings. I got my head busted. All those things.

EFFECTS OF THE DRUG. The effects of psychedelics on our using subjects were remarkably consistent, whether positive or negative. Certainly the patterns of the drug's effects were far more consistent than was the case with either marihuana, opiates, or alcohol. The first important effect mentioned again and again by our subjects was the influence on relationships, a kind of powerful bonding among people who tripped together.

> R: I asked my friend about his first trip, and he said that none of the people really knew each other; they had heard of each other and had met at cocktail parties, but that's all. And at the end of the trip, they knew each other [laugh] extremely well. So I imagine that through that, through acid, I will get to know some of these people better. If they'd be willing to try it, I think that's one way people could get to know me quickly.

Most of our subjects experienced this bonding and sense of personal closeness. Many reiterated that psychedelic use had had a profound influence on their interpersonal relationships. A sense of openness about themselves enabled people who used together to relax certain critical faculties. The shared experience seemed to establish a feeling of kinship, as reported earlier by Zinberg (1974) and by Grinspoon and Bakalar (1979).

I: What happened during the trip?

R: We talked. I had never talked so openly about myself before in my life. And it was easy. I didn't feel, you know, like hiding anything about myself, or that what I was was so terrible. Then he told me about himself, and I could understand him and feel close and think everything he thought was bad about himself was really OK, just like it was with me.

Sometimes the shared experience included more than openness; it appeared also as a special type of kinship shared by those who had done something daring, dangerous, and illicit.

R: I was with a pretty stable group of friends. We all got high pretty regularly [laugh]. And there weren't any tensions, like this was a group I felt comfortable with and part of. In eleventh grade I started getting into acid pretty heavily, toward the end of the fall and into the winter. By wintertime I was tripping like a couple of times a week. On some levels, none of my friends were very bright. School was essentially a very weird situation for me in terms of—I was like an honor-type student, on the one hand, and had nothing to do with the other honor-type students who were super-straights. The people I hung around with, some of them were bright but didn't use it; some of them just "hung out."

I: So there was a real disjunction between your school life and your friends? The friends you hung around with outside of school? How did you feel?

R: I felt good. I liked the idea of the contrast that I had. It was a small school, and I was possibly the brightest person in that school, but at the same time, I didn't work at being in school.

This was particularly true of the younger group, who tended to talk a great deal to one another about their shared experience: Who had done it? When? With whom? Was it good acid?

I: In thinking about your group of friends, do some people more than others seem interested in using LSD?

R: Sure.

I: The acid group?

R: Yeah.

I: If so, how do they show it?

R: They talk about it: "Let's trip together"; they describe their trip experiences in detail. I'm amazed at the amount of time that I will spend
talking about trips with people. "Last time I tripped, this and this
happened. I saw this and that . . ." "Yeah, yeah, the last time I
tripped, this and that happened to me . . ." That's a pretty frequent
conversation.

This apparently repetitious conversation also seemed to buttress sanctions and
rituals. The secret-society aspect of use led many of our subjects to adopt odd
times and odd places for tripping.

R: We weren't supposed to, 'cause it was a formal school trip, right? And,
you know, about a third of the school tripped, and, you know, it was
really, it was incredible, the way people got along.

I: How did the principal and the teachers handle it?

R: Well, they thought it was a really good weekend, right? 'Cause here
were all these people who were—they didn't see us all day 'cause they
were out walking and stuff. And then they'd come back after a day of
tripping and we were still tripping, you know, sitting around talking at
night, sitting around the fire.

I: Did they ever find out?

R: Probably, but nothing's ever been said.

R: Uh, I—every once in a while I'd stop working, maybe for a weekend or
something, or for a Friday and a Saturday, and every Sunday there was
a whole bunch of us that got together in church and did acid.

I: Just before church, or in church?

R: No, it was like in the afternoon, you know, when nobody was in the
church; we'd just go in and sit down and talk and stuff.

I: And do acid?

R: Yeah.

Once the users had learned to control the effects of the drug, they often
took special pleasure in going into the world to test the impact of their different
vision and its effect on their interactions with other people.

I: Was the second experience you had similar to or different from the first
one?

R: It was similar in that it was taken with the same friends. This one was at night, and at one time we did go into the town and buy something. And I learned about how to come down enough to, like, go and buy something at a store, and stuff like that. I learned, like, how to control myself and not be paranoid.

I: How did you learn that?

R: Uh, it's a group thing. Like, you're gonna—someone tells you that you can do it and you do it. You just come down when you have to. Just pull out, because acid isn't like a body drug. It's a head drug. And if you learn to know it, you can pull yourself out of the mood.

R: There was often a secret pleasure in going into the world and experiencing it. You know, how it was out there. Let me look at them with my eyes open, for maybe the first time. I wanted them to see me too, to know what I'm like when the hostility is drained away.

Users' relationships with their parents made this testing of interactions extremely problematical. One young man who did not wish to be discovered by his parents admittedly took a great risk when he tripped in the next room:

R: My parents were in the other room. Most of my previous drug use at my earlier ages was done in my own room with the door closed. And usually with a light burning very dimly. I did most of my tripping there, at night.

The dilemma of how to continue use when their children were present was often expressed by our older subjects:

I: How much is too much acid in your opinion?

R: In a given dose, you mean?

I: No, in usage.

R: Well, I can only speak for myself. I would say that for me, I come back to my rules about using it. I like to use it with, like, one person or a small group of people that are very carefully picked out, in a careful situation where I'm not going to be confronted with tasks that I won't be able to do. Like, I won't use it during the university term when I'm teaching, or when I have to prepare something. And also the kids. The kids, by the way, don't like it. My daughter very specifically says she doesn't want me to be tripping. At least not in her presence. And that's the arrangement. That's an important restraint on me, by the way. She says, "Daddy, I don't want to be around you when you're tripping. You act funny, and I'm afraid that the car is going to crash and you're going to be arrested by the police." She sees this on TV, as a matter of fact. So I said, "OK, that's the deal." And since they live with me half the time

> and with their mother the other half, they're frequently here. It means
> I have to arrange it specifically. It's usually Saturday night.

Obviously this subject's efforts to establish and maintain the social sanctions
and rituals that would allow the trip to be successful would have been interfered
with by concern about his children and certainly by conflict with them.

The second major drug effect often mentioned by our subjects was a sense
of personal revelation that might be experienced either as physical sensation
(sexuality or sensuality, including eating) or as personal insight (philosophical
or spiritual understanding of oneself and the universe).

> R: What happened was that I got much more interested in talking with
> people I was with and in walking around outside. Again it was winter
> and there was snow on the ground, and it was quite pretty. Again, I was
> making reflections on visual things, but beginning somewhere inside
> my head to see that there was a heavier dimension to all this than I had
> realized before—just, you know, the first revelation.

The reports on physical sensation, and especially sexual and sensual interests, varied considerably more than was the case with marihuana users.
Many subjects reported enhanced sensuality after use of psychedelics:

> R: Everything looked so good. I could just look at the sea and feel it on my
> skin and in my bones. Touching it was ecstasy. Sensations were
> exquisite.

But some reported decreased interest in direct sexual experiences.

> R: I was too into myself to want to touch him. He looked beautiful and I
> wanted to look at him. But not anything as rough as sex. He said the
> same thing. He really loved me and sometimes he would want me, but
> right now he didn't think he could even get it up.

Several men reported difficulty in achieving erections, and several women
remained dry and unresponsive physically, despite great waves of sensuality
and longing. However, an occasional subject transcended that barrier and
reported:

> R: A merging. I couldn't tell which of us was which. I was in her body and
> she in mine. It was incredible and when I finally came, it was like no
> orgasm I ever had before. It was my whole body.

Inasmuch as psychedelic drugs, which are chemically related to the
amphetamines, are appetite suppressants, subjects did not report the delight in
eating that characterized our marihuana users. But they often reported great

pleasure in simply tasting small quantities of a special substance, particularly after a long period of tripping.

I: What else do you remember about the trip?

R: Well, we had been on the beach for hours, lolling around, talking, enjoying ourselves. Once in a while, somebody wondered whether, you know, we should have something to eat or drink, and I couldn't even imagine it. Then somebody, he was very energetic all day, got up and went into the house and brought back boysenberry sherbet. It was Häagen-Dazs, and I took one mouthful. It was absolutely delicious. I thought it was the best thing I had ever tasted in my life. I could taste every nuance of the flavor and also felt, really felt, the texture as I never had before in my life. I took one more taste, but that was all. It was perfect, but it was enough.

The sense of personal revelation or illumination was not limited to physical sensations but might take the form of personal insight, either in regard to oneself or, in a philosophical-spiritual-religious sense, to the universe. This was not a static response but one that changed as the user gained more experience with the drug.

R: When I trip now, I think about what's going on in my personal life rather than thinking about communicating with a godhead or something like that. There is less of a psychedelic thing to it, and more of a personal thing to it. I don't know if that's going to be a permanent change, I don't really know.

These illuminating effects of psychedelic use were consistent with the individual's personality structure and with what was going on in his or her emotional life at the time. For example, subjects who in their usual state of consciousness tended to deal with conflict by turning passive concerns into some active form would respond, while tripping, in the same general way. Somaticizers somaticized; cerebral types cerebrated; and so on.

I: What's the biggest mistake you've made about drugs?

R: Being too overconfident. In the two or three trips that I've had, I guess I consider that that's where my mistakes were. That I felt getting high would improve the quality of whatever was going down. I could have realized it if I had just stopped to think about it; it was a situation that could only be hurt by tripping. The mistakes I've made in terms of drugs are the mistakes I've made in general, in terms of not slowing down to think about what's really going on.

R: It used to be that I would wait for things to happen, for someone to come to me. Which is sort of a paranoid model. From the way I grew up, I waited for things to happen to me. I became aware of that sort of pattern through LSD use. For some people, it takes them months of therapy to figure that kind of thing out. The acid thing just [snaps fingers] put me right at that place of understanding the pattern. So, in a sense, even though I was probably crying for half the trip, it was not so much fear or anxiety as just settling into a lot of it. It was the same kind of crying people do in marathons in therapy. They are crying, but it's kind of a relief, almost, to be crying. It's kind of a "I'm comfortable with myself" kind of crying. And I'm back in touch with that pain, which is to say a real experience that I had cut myself off from. I think of acid experiences, tripping, and therapy a lot in the same way. It's probably why in the first six months of this year I didn't do any acid much. 'Cause my therapy was the same thing, more or less.

The importance of set does not mean that a personality problem or difficulty bred bad trips per se. As H. L. Barr et al. (1972) discovered, there are typologies of reactions to psychedelic drugs, and the severe reactions do not necessarily follow personality disturbance. Some of Barr's most disturbed subjects handled the experience well, while some of those with the best-balanced personality structure had trouble. Our findings completely substantiated that conclusion. Set was a crucial factor, but the trip experience was more closely related to some aspect of the setting (for example, to personal relationships) and to social sanctions and rituals than to personality difficulties.

I: Did you ever have any adverse or unpleasant experiences with hallucinogens?

R: Yes, many.

I: Yes?

R: Well, I particularly had a single experience, a bad, horrible experience with MDA, which is the kind of thing that just works on the emotional kind of realm. But at that point I was going through a kind of crisis dealing with my parents, and the parents were the internalized parents. That lasted for about thirteen hours. It was the most horrible experience I've ever gone through.

I: Did that stop you from using it?

R: No.

Most of the experiences reported in this section concerning subjects who had bad trips were idiosyncratic, based on specific set issues, and often the users had shown bad judgment through inexperience or by not following the accepted sanctions and rituals. Such mistakes became less common as our subjects continued to use psychedelic drugs. My conviction that heavy psychedelic use is unlikely to persist grew out of our subjects' reports of their long-term experiences, which showed the shifting nature of the drug's effects. Many said that their anxiety over tripping increased rather than decreased, although this did not necessarily cause them to give up use: 61% indicated that they would like to continue very occasional use, while 94% reported that they had reduced use from their beginning level.

R: I don't know, maybe I'm wrong, and maybe any acid I would do would give me the same good high as before. But I don't get it; I'm afraid, and to me it's not worth risking it because eventually, if I keep taking more and more drugs, eventually I'm gonna get a bad trip and I'll get bummed out, and I don't want that to happen, and that's why I don't do that much.

I: Do you plan, at any point in the future, either immediate or long range, to trip again?

R: I'm not planning it, but I suppose, under certain circumstances, I would. I always said after I tripped the first time that I didn't want to trip again unless, like, I was again with a guy that I really like—unless I was going out with someone and I really enjoyed and trusted him, and then I'd wanna trip with him.

Our subjects' previous concerns about the bad health effects of the drug seemed more overwhelming as they continued use. For many, the experience simply became more and more negative.

R: I started having bad trips, and I just stopped. Plus my tolerance was getting rather heavy. It took two or three to get off, to trip. I just stopped.

What had previously seemed like personal insight leading to a gentler and more accepting view of the world also changed.

I: Why did you stop psychedelic use?

R: I was getting too screwed up. I was getting in a real kind of trip where I was feeling, you know, kind of superior. And I've noticed that a lot with people who do a lotta acid. They get into a kind of real trip that they're better than other people. And I was just doing that too much. I dunno, just kinda know-it-all and everything. I can't really explain it—just knowing it all and stuff of that nature. I realized it mostly this summer, 'cause when my friend lived right behind me, there was a house and a buncha acid freaks lived there, and, you know, I could really see it in them, exactly.

In this case, the subject was aware that the "insight" had turned sour. In several other cases, the subject's representation of his evolved view of the world, which he himself experienced as insightful and accepting, seemed to the interviewer to be condescending, pretentious, and alienated, lacking an awareness of how that subject might be seen by others.

R: There's a real difference in the way you look at the world if you've had the experience of tripping.

I: What do you mean by that?

R: It's, uh, well, you get sort of a more objective sense of what's going on in the world. Things happen, but they don't affect you as much. Things that used to bother you, maybe, you can sometimes see that they're really funny, or, well, sort of temporary. Like, this, too, will pass. People who don't trip don't understand that.

I: Why not?

R: It's like you get a sense of the larger picture of things. People who don't trip are too tied up in themselves to see anything beyond their own petty little troubles and problems.

I: Were you like that at one time?

R: Yes.

Moreover, on successive follow-up interviews more than half of our subjects had another consistent reaction: they began to find the drug experience isolating in an intellectual sense and increasingly less interesting. Some of these users had given ecstatic accounts of their early trips, and many had never had trouble with bad trips. Most, in fact, had never experienced a bad trip.

R: There are things that I like to do that some of these acid people don't do, which is writing and thinking about politics, and talking about things, and things like that. I tend to encourage people to be more like that, to do that. I miss the people that can talk about a lot of these things.

R: I want to communicate sufficiently that there is less of a special quality to being high than there used to be. That it is something that feels good, and it keeps me in touch, and I place great value on getting stoned in some circumstances. But I don't have a sort of revelatory kind of feeling about tripping that I used to—sort of a closer-to-God kind of feeling. And now things are more mundane, I guess.

Ultimately, most subjects seemed to agree with the following user's summation of his experience.

R: Finally, I realized it was simply boring, yes, boring, boring. Who would have believed it? It was so good at first, so good. How I wish I could feel like those first times again! That was glorious. Now it's repetitious. It takes such a long time, too. I've already thought those thoughts and seen what the drug has to show me, and it isn't much fun doing it over and seeing it over. It's such a shame, but that's how it is.

I: Is that just *your* reaction?

R: No, my friends feel the same. We talk about it once in a while, how great it is. And sometimes we talk about trying it again, maybe after a long time. And then it will be more like it was. But the last time I did it, it was just boring.

Opiates

The decision to use any of the three illicit drugs in this study—marihuana, the psychedelics, or the opiates—inevitably results in some degree of anxiety for the user. This anxiety may arise for physiological, psychological, or social reasons—that is, in connection with the drug variable, the set variable, or the setting variable.

The decision to use marihuana is accompanied by a relatively low level of concern. Since its use has become socially normative within certain age groups, there is little psychological or social anxiety, although in certain states there is still fear of engaging in an illegal activity. The greatest worry, especially among beginners, arises from the recent attention given to the health hazards that may follow marihuana use.

The decision to use a psychedelic brings greater anxiety because of the drug's greater promise of pleasure or pain. Nevertheless, the concern about psychedelics—and this is also true of marihuana—is ameliorated by two facts, one physiological and the other social. First, there is little risk of quick addiction; and second, although society does not openly approve of these drugs, it does not automatically associate them with deviance, criminality, and potential degradation, as is the case with the opiates.

The decision to use an opiate is filled with anxiety on all three counts. In regard to the psychological or personality factor, people who decide to take such risks come from that small fraction of the population that is skewed toward embracing danger or resisting self-care. Further, the experience of addiction diminishes personality differences and makes all compulsive users seem very much alike (Zinberg 1975). Thus it is not surprising that many investigators have regarded the personality factor as dominant in the decision to use an opiate as an intoxicant. Yet the social factor—the setting variable—should not be disregarded. The importance of setting showed up most strikingly among our controlled opiate users, who, with the exception of those few who had an unusually well-developed system of internal checks, could not have remained controlled on the basis of personality factors alone. Instead, their ability to continue moderate use depended to a significant degree on social sanctions and rituals, as well as other social supports. At the same time, however, they felt the anxiety engendered by society's association of opiate use with degradation, deviance, and criminality.

Unless otherwise indicated, the excerpts that follow were drawn from interviews with some of the sixty-one controlled opiate users in our combined analytical sample. A few (so indicated) were taken from interviews with some of the thirty compulsive users at the same time. A few more (so indicated) were extracted from interviews with the "significant others" of certain controlled subjects whose statements we wanted to verify. Because these "others" were personally close to the users, they were familiar with opiate use, and many of them had tried it.

It is frequently assumed that everyone who tries using an opiate, particularly heroin, is overwhelmingly positive about the experience. This is a misconception. The responses of the controlled users in our combined sample seemed to the research team to be far more positive than those of a random sample of the general population of users would have been, even though these subjects had had bad experiences as well as good. This positive reaction from controlled subjects, as well as from most of the compulsive opiate users in the sample, can be easily explained. All of them had chosen to use opiates on a more or less regular basis, that is, to become regular users. Hence their enjoyment of the experience must have canceled out their sense of fear and risk. With the "significant others" the situation was quite different. Although many of them had tried heroin or another opiate, most had not reacted positively to the experience and therefore had not continued to use. The responses of some members of this group are included in order to correct the impression that everyone who tried the drug enjoyed it—a conclusion that would otherwise be inevitable because of the predominance of regular users in the sample.

BEGINNING USE. All the subjects in our combined sample shared the fear of the general public that any use of heroin would lead to addiction, and their beginning use was characterized by that overwhelming concern:

I: Had you heard anything about heroin before you started using it?
R: Yeah, I guess, you know, that it was addicting and it was terrible and this and that, but I'd also heard that you're not going to become a junkie by doing it once. But I'd talked with people who said that there are certain people who because of their body chemistry can have one drink or do heroin once and then become an alcoholic or a junkie.

I: How did you start using?

R: I found out that my sister and brother-in-law had been using it. Not all the time, but just every now and then.

I: Did they ask you to use?

R: No, they were waiting. I was asking them about it. Yeah, I wanted to try it. Well, finally she would say, "You should try it sometime," and I'd say, "Well, when are you going to *get* it for me?" Well, so they taught me how to. Finally, all three of us went off to get it. My boyfriend didn't want to do it the first time. (But he doesn't do it a lot). We went off to this guy's house and bought some heroin and brought it home and tried it. And I thought it was *great*. My sister's husband did it for me, showed me how to use it. But they said, "Y'gotta watch out for this stuff, y'know. It's great, but it's true, it *is* addicting." So I ended up using it like them. Every now and then.

Even if the subject had known a controlled user very well and believed what he had said about the experience, this was still not enough to remove the fear of becoming addicted:

R: Well, after all, she was a nurse. And I knew she'd been doing heroin off and on for years, and I knew she wouldn't bullshit me. She just wanted me to be with her and enjoy it. All the same, I kept thinking everything I've heard all these years can't be all bullshit. So I was scared, real scared. But I said, what the hell, she's to be trusted and I let her fix me.

Generally, however, the social factor, that is, reassurance from close associates, helped the beginner overcome his or her anxiety.

I: Did you have any apprehension or anxiety before you first used it?

R: Yeah, I wanted to do it. I was scared until my friend would say, "No, I don't want you to learn how to do that without me."

Beginning heroin users often dealt with their concerns in the same way that many people deal with other concerns, by trying to outwit themselves. The next user, who had been very much interested in heroin but too frightened to go ahead, had hoped to avoid his fear by spontaneity—by not allowing himself time to think.

R: I really had no intention to do it [heroin]. And a friend of mine was going to try it for the first time, so I said, "All right, I'll meet you down here and we'll do a half-bag each." So I met him that night, we did it, and I don't know, we just got sick all night.

It would not be unreasonable to assume that this user's negative reaction came in part from the anxiety he was trying to avoid.

Several subjects found it easier to begin if they didn't have to make the decision to go out and buy the drug. When it was provided for them, there seemed to be less onus and therefore somewhat less anxiety.

I: The first time you used heroin, how did you get it?

R: These people I was running around with—I was at a party with Jane— they had some. In fact, I didn't purchase it myself. They didn't even ask me to chip in with them to get it. They offered me some.

A combination of reassurance, spontaneity (false in this case), and being offered the drug by a friend characterized one couple's initial use.

R: It wasn't something I considered I'd ever really get into. It was just like a surprise came along, that kind of thing. This guy that was a mutual friend of ours lived with this whole crowd of people that had been using it for years and years, and he had an on-and-off access to stuff. He said, "Did you ever try junk?" I said we hadn't, and he started telling me he was shooting it like once a week or something. And I knew other people who did it. And he said, "Oh, let's get some," and I said, "Great." So those people came over to shoot up with some dope.

I: When did you next use?

R: About a month later.

Many of our subjects began heroin use by snorting the drug. Those who injected it usually started by injecting it under the skin ("skin-popping"). If it was injected into a vein, someone else did it for them. Having someone do it for them was quite different from doing it for themselves.

R: The biggest thing about heroin, one of the biggest things I found about it, is there's a big psychological trip in shooting it. You know. And that's something that you sort of have to come to deal with in your own way. You either feel comfortable with it or you don't do it. The first couple of times I remember what I went through, but I'm still standing here.

I: How long did it take you to learn?

R: I knew how to do it after the first time, but it was a matter of—I couldn't get to that point. I'd really thought I could do it, you know. I'd get to the point where I had cooked the stuff all up and I'd tie myself off, and I'd get it all up into the thing there and everything. I'd just get ready. The needle had just touched my vein, and that would be it—I couldn't do it. And so probably the first three or four times after that, maybe five times, somebody had to get me off. But then one day I thought, "Oh, this is crazy. If I'm staking my life every time I do this, wondering what's in this sack, you know, and then letting somebody else, I should have the guts to do it myself. If I had the guts to do it in the first place, I should be able to do it myself." So I just sat down, tied myself off, and did it. And that was that.

Our subjects' concern about intravenous injection was realistic because most of the severe complications accompanying heroin use have come not from the drug itself but from this mode of ingestion. Anxiety about injection was so great that even people who had used heroin several times would not begin (quite correctly, in my opinion) to self-inject unless an experienced person was present.

I: How long did it take before you learned to shoot yourself up?

R: Quite a while. I think it took me about three months. And even the first time I did it, I didn't want to do it. I didn't like the idea.

I: Did one of your friends show you how?

R: Yeah. He was around when I tried it myself. He was right there to make sure I didn't do anything wrong.

A few eager beginners moved from snorting to injecting far more quickly.

I: And what about heroin? When did you start that?

R: Well, I started that about ten to fifteen years ago.

I: Tell me about it.

R: Well, my friends talked to me about it. I wanted to try it for quite a while, because some friends used it. And they were into it for quite a while, and I wanted to do it but I was afraid to do it. So we sat down and we talked for a while about it and they talked me into just trying it. And I really liked it, an awful lot, right from the beginning.

I: What was the first way you used it? Did you shoot it or snort it?

R: Uh, well, it's funny 'cause I snorted it, and after a while I felt so good that I wanted to shoot some and I shot some in the same night.

I: Did you get sick from it?

R: No, I didn't get sick at all, which was amazing because everyone else seemed to be getting sick, you know. And ever since then I've liked it so much that I haven't wanted to stop it, you know. I mean, not that I have a habit or anything, just that I really like it. Weekends—jeez, I look forward to that every weekend.

But whatever the manner of ingestion, the desire for social support and interaction predominated with almost every beginning user.

R: A friend where I worked used to take heroin on weekends—a weekend chipper—and he turned me on to it. We worked in a very hectic situation there, would get really tensed up. And so he began to describe to me how relaxed this drug could make you feel. After a while, I asked him to show me how to use it. It was very inexpensive then in the good old days. He turned me on to it and I would get high a little bit with him, but my main friend was this girlfriend of mine. I turned her on to it and I would get high with her most of the time. Snorting, just snorting.

I: What can you remember about the first time?

R: Oh, the first time was wonderful. It made me feel very warm and it was like, it just took all the tension away. I had to go meet some people to go to the movies after that, I remember, and I remember waiting for them in the lobby of the movie theater and just, you know, feeling unafraid of anything. Not that I can remember feeling afraid of anything before, but all of a sudden I was very unafraid. Nothing could harm me. So I liked the feeling. Felt very open and very calm and very invulnerable and very peaceful and nice. I really loved it. Interesting thing is if I don't do it for three or four weeks I just forget about it, forget what it's like to be high and don't need it. Or if I do use it, I can feel when things get out of hand, and basically I don't enjoy it that way.

Interestingly, neither the extent of social support nor the extent of the user's initial positive response necessarily indicated the degree of his or her eventual attachment to the drug. Initial reactions differed, but positive responses like those of the preceding and following subjects were common.

I: How old were you when you first used?

R: About eighteen. And then I met this guy at school who was into opiates, who was shooting smack at the time. And we talked about it. We were friends, he was kind of in my circle of friends. And I asked him to get me some, to get me some morphine, and I skin-popped it. And I loved it. Lots of fun, got loaded on it. I remember I took it the first time with this girl who was just a friend of mine. And, ah, she was a very laid-back kind of person and I'm kind of two-faced. I like being active and, on the other hand, I like to spend a lot of my time just relaxing. And I, I loved this drug. Just lay there and didn't get bored, just felt comfortable. I felt very comfortable with her. The first time I took morphine, I knew that I liked the drug, and that it was very compatible to my psyche.

By contrast, some responses were far more qualified:

I: What was your first use like?

R: Well, I wanted to, it made me feel good in a way. It gave me some kind of release. See, I was pretty tense at the time, and it was a very pleasant kind of thing, although I got sick, see, 'cause it takes getting used to. I went through that period with heroin, just as I went through the same period with tobacco.

And sometimes unpleasant effects were reported as major elements during initial use.

R: I liked it, but I got sick. I was always running to the bathroom and throwing up, but it was like, "Oh, I feel great," and all of a sudden I'd feel, "Oh, I'm sick," and I'd go to the bathroom. It'd be over in two seconds, and I'd be back again. But I don't throw up any more.

This subject needed perseverance and a strong desire for the drug in order to continue use after being sick.

For many other subjects perseverance was required in another way because, to our surprise, not everyone experienced the drug's effects immediately. Despite heroin's reputation for great power, some beginning users of opiates, just like beginning users of marihuana, had to learn to get high.

I: Did you get off the first time?
R: No, didn't feel anything. At first I didn't, you know, understand the high, because at first you want to go to sleep and something like that. But I gradually got to understand the high.
I: How long did it take before you understood the high?
R: Well, I guess it must've been about two or three times, 'cause the first time I tried it, it was like there was nothing there. All I was doing was just itching. But then, one time I tried it and it seemed like I could feel a little something, like my body just got off and relaxed.

It is, of course, hard to untangle the influence of the drug from the effects of set and setting. Nevertheless, the kind of social group that was involved in the initiatory process clearly made a difference. In fact, the greatest concerns of controlled users seemed to stem from their relationships with compulsive users. Hence, despite the next subject's later conviction that she could avoid addiction, being initiated by a former addict appeared to affect her initial response.

R: It was after he got out of treatment. We've become very good friends, and rather than living at home, he was living with me. And, uh, it was something that I had toyed with, experimenting with heroin, thinking that once I had experienced it, I could share a degree of empathy.
I: What was first use like?
R: I think I did too much. Because I couldn't do anything but lie very still. If I tried to stand, I would get extremely nauseated and very dizzy. It was an unpleasant sensation to do anything but lie very, very still. And

looking back on it I think that some of them must have been very concerned about me because every few minutes they would speak to me so as to get a response and make sure I was still there.

I: How did it feel when you were lying there?

R: It was pleasurable, but there was a certain amount of—I couldn't say anxiety, the drug eliminated all of that—but there was a cognitive concern on my part to stay awake. Because it was a very drifty, very floaty, very dreamy type of thing, and I made a point not to go to sleep. Like I say, I think I did too much. Because, well, it was a very pleasant feeling. The experience as a whole was not altogether pleasant. It was a matter of the amount that I did.

I: How did you manage to stay unaddicted?

R: I've always felt that addiction was a result of the life style and not the substance itself. I've never lived a junkie life style, like I observed in my friend.

Although many of our subjects who had unpleasant initial reactions continued to use, many others did not continue even though they had not had a bad time. In spite of social support the next interviewee (one of the "significant others" group) gave up use.

I: Were you one of the first of your group to try heroin?

R: Well, there were quite a few of us that tried it at the same time.

I: All for the first time?

R: Yeah.

I: How many were there?

R: Oh, there must've been about five of us. Two of my cousins, and one woman and a man. Before this I had had other opportunities to try, but I passed it up. When I lived at home, I had no conception of what getting high was all about, really, and so I never had any desire to, you know, filch stuff from medicine cabinets or anything like that. And after this, I had no desire to use heroin again either.

Though the following user's declared moral motives sounded unconvincing to the research team, he stopped use after several positive experiences.

I: You had heard terrible things about it?

R: I heard it wasn't very enjoyable. It was like being very drunk, without having to drink, and all this stuff. So I tried it. Also, I knew that my high school was having a lot of trouble with downs, even some heroin, so I did want to try it because I was thinking of some time becoming a teacher. And I wanted to have experience with that drug if it was becoming popular. So I did try it, and it was all right. I didn't really find anything thrilling in it.

I: And you tried that on a few occasions?

R: Yeah. And I sort of liked it.

I: And no other times?

R: No, no. I don't have a source for a drug like that. Just the opportunity came up, and I tried it.

After the extremely negative experiences of the next user (a significant other) there was apparently no question of continuing.

R: I had been scared in the first place, but Alice kept telling me how good it was. She got it and I snorted it. For a little while I felt a sort of a glow; then I began to feel sick. I've never been so sick in my life. The nausea went on for hours, or it seemed like hours. Finally, I threw up two or three times. Then for a little while I felt better, and then I got sick again. It was horrible. I never would touch any of that stuff again. I told Alice if she even mentioned it to me again, we were all through.

PSYCHOLOGICAL AND SOCIAL EFFECTS OF THE DRUG. The following descriptions of the effects of opiate use show that some widely held views about these effects are misconceptions. Neither the actions nor the pleasures and difficulties of our using subjects were stereotypical. For example, there was little straight shooting up (intravenous injection) and little sudden nodding off (quickly falling asleep). In addition, their reactions were not so monolithic as laboratory experiments with the drug have led researchers to expect. Instead, both positive and negative responses were highly individualized and idiosyncratic, almost as much in the case of our compulsive subjects as among controlled users.

Subjects mentioned as the most pleasant effects the "rush" (glow or warmth), the sense of distance from their problems, and the tranquilizing powers of the drug. Pleasure that was experienced as bodily sensation often expanded into a feeling of psychological well-being. Many subjects linked the drug to special-occasion use: sex, eating, other specific activities, and socializing. The social aspects of drug use were regarded as very important—both the social group with whom use occurred, and the problems of association with non-using groups. The greatest danger faced by controlled users was the potentially disruptive result of their association with addicts, an association that was dictated by their need to obtain the drug but that threatened their own carefully balanced using style.

Although our interviewers obviously could not measure the degree of pleasure resulting from a subject's use, they were instructed to make a subjective judgment as to whether each user's responses were spontaneous and sincere or whether they sounded hollow. We knew that since our controlled subjects were not addicted, their opiate use would not bring them relief from any incipient withdrawal syndrome. Yet it was hard for the research team to distinguish between the kind of pleasure that comes from the relief of discomfort and that which is purely gratifying. Certainly we had expected more celebration of the famous "rush." The next subject was fulsome in his praise of this effect, but his response was not typical.

> R: The whole thing of getting off on dope is the rush. I mean, to me it is. That's the one thing about dope that I don't care what anybody says—you can get sick of any drug, I have of most of them, except for marihuana, and I do like a downer—but you never feel that rush like on dope and, I mean, that is the ultimate. That's the best. It is.

Later he described the sense of an immediate effect that propelled him from one state of consciousness "entirely" into another. His sense that use was relaxing was similar to that of the next respondent, whose calmer descriptions sounded more convincing to the interviewers.

> I: Is there anything in particular that pleases you about opiate use as compared with other drugs?
> R: Ah, yeah, you know, it's the rush you get, but it's very mellow. And it's a body thing. I can feel myself relaxing. And there's sort of, like, a euphoria sometimes. Especially with smoking. You just feel good, you feel calm. You feel warm, you feel relaxed, or I do. But it seems like other people do too.

The next excerpt resembles descriptions of the opiate high given by writers who have used the drug.

> I: Could you describe an opiate high for me?
> R: Well, I can try. You get warm. Your vision is definitely blurred. You're very, very lethargic, relaxed, almost to the point of falling asleep but not really asleep. It's like being in a dream and being awake at the same time. Your eyes will be closed and you can't keep your eyes open, but you're fully conscious. You can hear what's going on in the room; if there's music on, you can hear the music, but you really couldn't get up and walk around. Well, you could, but it would be more like bouncing around. It's more like lying back, half asleep, in a dream sleep, and it's very, very—mystical almost.

Almost all of our opiate users described their sensations much more in bodily terms than did our marihuana and psychedelic users.

> I: Could you try to tell me in your own words what the high feels like?
> R: Well, the first feeling I can say is, uh, heat, a welling up of warmth that

appears all over my body. My thighs and my stomach first. And it's a general relaxation. Warm feeling, associated with a calm, like a descending calm, like a fog settling in, over my whole body. I'd say that time seems to slow down, the thought processes seem to slow down, and get more rambling or associating, or dreamlike. Everything's being slurred, my gestures, my speech. Although with conscious effort this can be overcome, it seems to be a symptom. The rush is more pronounced some times than others. I don't know what that is due to. And by rush, I mean, you know, the immediate oncoming heat.

Most subjects attempting to convey their pleasure in the experience explained that the initial sense of physical relaxation gradually turned into a feeling of mental well-being.

R: I think there's a big physical factor involved in it. It's like a body stone kind of thing. But at the same time, the whole thing about the psychological thing that's involved in doing it—I think that carries over into the feeling afterwards. But psychologically, I feel good, I feel great, I don't know, I feel good [laugh].

What may be called the "distancing effect" was an almost universal reaction to an opiate high as distinct from a marihuana or psychedelic high.

I: Could you try to tell me in your own words what the high feels like?
R: It's like crawling into a psychic cloud. Everything is cushioned for you. Very, very little that's negative gets through to you. I don't know, I think it's very relaxed, very pleasurable. Very low anxiety level, very low desire level. I guess the high—uh, you feel full. You know, whatever kind of hole you might have in your being—I think people do, everyone feels lacks of one sort or another—you know, it fills in all those spots.
I: What happens when you come down? How do you feel?
R: You come down real slowly. Usually, if you get loaded any time during the day, you're still loaded when you go to sleep. You wake up in the morning, you're just your normal self. I don't, *I* don't feel any comedown from it.

The distancing effect seemed to be a sense that the user's "I," his perceiving self, saw what was going on outside, and apparently to a large extent inside, his psyche from a distant, sage vantage point. Many different descriptions of this phenomenon were given.

I: What in particular pleases you about heroin?
R: The feeling of nonexistence that I get.

> I: Have you ever had any unpleasant reactions?
> R: Oh, sure, I've gotten sick.
> I: Do you mind getting sick on it?
> R: It doesn't upset me.
> I: How does it affect your use?
> R: It doesn't discourage it any [laugh].

Another subject described it as follows:

> I: What do you enjoy about heroin?
> R: I like the feeling of getting totally numbed out, and not having to worry about anything, and having a place. I mean, I would feel like I had a safe place in the world, and before I didn't.

But not all aspects of this experience were pleasant. Several subjects found it somewhat disorienting.

> R: I got sick at first, and I thought, "This is supposed to be great?" And I didn't want to stay home and be like this all night long. And I just went out. And it was heavy winter and my coat was open and I was feeling great. And I went to a friend's house, smoked a little reefer, and just sat back and had, like vivid nods, vivid color nods. Just colors, like a rainbow in your head. It was sort of like an acid trip right in there. Or it was like hallucinating, like nods are. You close your eyes and they're all here. And it just turned me on, so much, to dope. "Forget it," I said, "I don't care if I get sick on this stuff. 'Cause it's so beautiful, beautiful."

It was clear to the interviewers that several subjects experienced this distancing effect as tranquilizing—that the drug was acting as an anti-anxiety medication.

> I: Could you try to describe in your own words what the high feels like?
> R: It feels, first of all, like there's a definite sensation of easing tension. Even if I'm not specifically feeling tense, there's a definite feeling of relaxation that kind of sweeps over you. And a loosening up and a kind of general un-uptightness that reflects itself in a lot of areas. In terms of the way I see the rest of my life, it makes everything seem beautiful. I feel a lot more optimistic. I'm able to handle all the things I have to handle. Everything seems like a nice challenge instead of a burden. I enjoy experiencing the things around me. I'm able to let the world back in a lot more, rather than when I'm in a normal state and just preoccupied with everything I have to do and problems and different things like that. When I'm high, I seem to be able to just forget about a lot of

things and deal with them one by one. And, it's a kind of letting-go feeling.

These subjective reactions of those who used the drug more or less "medicinally" (as a tranquilizer) but who also insisted on their enjoyment or euphoria made it very hard for us to be clear about the differences of opinion about heroin and euphoria as discussed by McAuliffe and Gordon (1975) (see chapter 2).

I: How important is using heroin to you?

R: Depends on the situation. Like, if things are going my way, that's the way I was takin' heroin. If things weren't goin' my way, if something happened to me—like, my mother every month or so she's going in the hospital, everything slams on me, plus exams at the school, plus dealing with whities, plus dealing with my social friends' flaky actions— then heroin's very important. But it feels good.

The extent to which most users did not want simply to nod off but wished to enjoy the high came as a surprise to us. Sometimes, but not always, this attitude was associated with a hyperactive personality.

I: What do you particularly like about heroin?

R: I'll tell you what I don't like. I don't like to use it to become unconscious. It doesn't heighten my senses, but I like to use it to the point where it relaxes me, to the point where my nervous system is not so overcompelling, where I'm not reacting so much to different circumstances. I'm very hyper anyway. It's almost like I'm speeding all the time. And it slows me down a little bit and I can think clearly.

I: You don't get off to nod?

R: No, definitely not. I think that anyone who does that is just wasting it or really just trying to put themselves out of the picture.

The use of heroin seemed to be idiosyncratic, related to the habits of the individual and his or her choice of special occasions for use. We were surprised how often the special-occasion use of heroin for sexual enhancement was mentioned.

I: What are your feelings about drugs and sex?

R: Umm, they can enhance the visceral experiences. I think sometimes they may alter emotional content somewhat. But the reason that I use dope with sex is primarily sensational, visceral.

For a sexually active person who was a controlled opiate user, the experience of sex tended to fuse with the opiate experience.

I: Do you ever use heroin with sex?

R: Sometimes. If you don't use too much, you can get more in touch with your body. But I don't use dope to have sex. It's usually more by accident. But I do get physical when I do dope. It's nice to have a lady to lean up against.

Several subjects, however, reported a sexual problem that was quite general among opiate users.

I: You say you often use heroin before sex?

R: Well, not as much as I used to. You see, when I was a kid and just starting to use, I thought it was great with sex. I felt all relaxed and I never had to worry about coming fast. Before that I had, I think you call it premature ejaculation. Then, later on, when Susie and I were together for a while, I began to find it very, very frustrating. You feel great, all sexed up, and for a while it's terrific, but then you want to get off and you can't. After a while it stops being fun and gets frustrating as hell. If Susie hasn't taken any—and she does it only about once to the three times that I do—she begins to get sore and wants to stop. It becomes a pain rather than a pleasure. You can't pee, you can't shit, and especially you can't come.

Sexual activity was not the only special-occasion use reported. The following account is typical of several subjects who, like marihuana users, found that the pleasure of eating was consistently enhanced and who were not bothered by nausea.

I: Did you do heroin when you were out in California?

R: I did it a few times out there. I had friends who were chippers and one friend who was a junkie, and we'd go and do it sometimes and go out and eat a big dinner and do some heroin. I didn't believe any of the bullshit about heroin. I still don't. It's an addictive drug. You've got to watch out, and when we went to eat, we'd shoot up and go eat a meal.

I: Sort of a social thing?

R: It was a social thing, yeah.

I: Was the high conducive to socializing?

R: Yeah. Well, it depends how much you do. If you do a bunch, you nod out, you know, but it's a weird drug too, because you can get the energy with it to do almost anything. You just put yourself in the right frame of mind. I guess the whole idea of being high on heroin is fighting the down effect. A lot of people do that with sopers, too. You're supposed to go to sleep on them, but you fight it and it's a nice high.

Obviously, most of our users ingested drugs to get high, a goal that would suggest rather spicy and even decadent activities. Yet one subject's special-occasion use could hardly have been more wholesome:

I: Are there any activities that your use of drugs makes more difficult or impossible?

R: No. Very much easier, if anything.

I: What activities do you particularly like doing when you're high?

R: Well, I like going out with my son to take in a movie or go to a sporting event, or something like that.

Another subject's use, which led to more mundane activities, illustrates how diverse the effect of the high state can be.

R: A lot of times I get high and wash a bunch of dishes and then wash the floor and stuff like that just because, you know, it's stuff that I've been meaning to do and should have done but I just didn't feel like doing.

I: But if you're high, it's easy?

R: I just [snaps fingers] breeze through it and that's that. "That wasn't bad!" And then I just go out and do whatever I wanted to do anyway.

It was also clear that the ability to function and to channel the high state increased with the user's drug experience.

I: Was there any special reason why you wouldn't do it during the week?

R: Well, during the week at night. When I was first doing it, I couldn't function too well after doing it. I could function, but I didn't do much but sit around. And talk, talk, talk. We'd talk a lot. But other than that, talking with people, I couldn't run around and do things. But now if I want to do it during the week, I—it's not that—I function. I function very well with it. As a matter of fact, I can sometimes, oftentimes, get more accomplished when I'm high [laugh] than when I'm not.

I: Oh?

R: Yeah. If I don't do too much. If I don't get too high, but just a little. I can run around and I get ambitious. I start running around and doing things. And getting involved in projects and stuff.

Not everyone, of course—and here is another example of the astonishing diversity of the drug effect—liked to be so active.

I: What do you usually do after you get high?

R: I like to lie back mostly when I'm high, you know. I'd rather not be doing anything too active because the more active you are, the more it interferes with experiencing the high. I mean, I would prefer just to lie on my back with my eyes closed, either listening to music or not, either with a friend or not. It's pleasant to get high with friends, though. And, just feel the high. I've done it with other activities, too, but I prefer to be as inactive as possible while high.

Those who reported the ability to do a circumscribed and meticulous task more efficiently when high made the interviewers wonder about the extent of the subjects' hyperactivity when they were not high, even if they did not report that condition.

R: With heroin, I can play the piano and feel very relaxed, and I can really get into it. The other day, I felt like playing the piano when I was real high. I just finished doing myself up and I felt great. I was real high, and I played one thing and I played another thing, and I was playing away. It sounded good to me, sounded really good, and I felt really relaxed, and I was expressing myself better.

The following excerpt from the response of a woman who was not hypersensitive showed well the extent of the variability of the drug's effect.

R: Actually, I've done a lot of good work when I'm high. I find that I can do a lot of work, say, on my writing, without tiring. I can concentrate on it more for long periods of time because I'll be enjoying it and won't have as much of a view to the end as to the doing. I can just keep going for a long time.

Perhaps more surprising than any other single finding were the consistent reports from controlled subjects that heroin and other opiates were used, very much like marihuana or alcohol, as part of an active social occasion.

R: And after we get off—you know all of a sudden everybody gets off— everybody feels real good and everybody's talkin', and everybody's gettin' to know each other, and it's good. It's a real good social drug, I think. All of a sudden your little social anxieties are gone. And people have told me, like my friends that don't use heroin—I've come home and said, "I've just shot some dope"—and they've told me, "You make more sense when you're stoned on a drug than any other time." And I believe them, I believe that's true. 'Cause I think, if you don't do too much, it's a real good social drug. You're real interested in everything.

Little has been written about the social aspects of opiate use. But interviews with several Iranians, whose country has a long history of ritualized use, were enlightening on this point. The Iranians pointed out somewhat condescendingly, because they felt that Westerners knew little or nothing about opiate use, that in Iran the drug was used quite generally in a social way. Indeed, they said, when a group of men shared an opium pipe after dinner, it made for a relaxed, talkative, and lively evening. Some of our subjects' experiences came close to this ancient tradition:

R: It's more a social thing—using occasionally. We would talk a lot while getting off. I've been in scenes where strung-out people would just, you know, all cop together, go into an apartment, all get loaded, and then split their separate ways. When you're using occasionally, even though there might be a lot of energy tied up with the ritual of getting loaded, a lot of anticipation, there isn't that same kind of desperation as when you're strung out. And there isn't that same isolation. If you're strung out in a city, after a while you become a lone wolf. And, you know, you see it in yourself; you see it in every other person that uses.

Another frequent finding that somewhat surprised us was the extent to which many controlled users echoed the sentiments expressed by the marihuana and psychedelic users about the influence of prohibitionary laws on what would otherwise have been pleasurable social use. Several users were knowledgeable enough to quote Thomas Szasz (1975) and to claim that more bad reactions occurred because of the functioning of the laws against drug use than because of the drug use itself.

R: I consider the laws concerning heroin use to be antiquated and ridiculous—I've read Thomas Szasz—because I know the kind of pattern that I've evolved in using it. I know I can use it without going out and doing harm to anybody else. I know that I can use without doing harm to myself. And the whole thing about—because you're using an illegal narcotic you're some sort of a criminal—or people say, "Heroin user?"—you know, that kind of thing. Just the whole connotation of people that use narcotics, you know, really turns me off. It's a real drag, and it's all because of the law.

Apparently using an opiate socially had a strong bonding effect. But the research team found that certain aspects of this bonding were different from those associated with marihuana and the psychedelics. For those two drugs it was the sharing of the experience, with all its strangeness, that seemed uppermost. With opiates, the sharing of fears concerning illegality seemed to be more crucial.

R: Illicit drug use is something that involves generally a great deal of trust. And if it's not there, there's a certain degree of paranoia that arises because after all, it's heroin. I guess it's a matter of trust. I have used with strangers, but the feeling is not the same.

The bonding that followed the drug experience could be extremely important and long lasting.

R: Actually, the best set of using circumstances I can think of is being with the old gang from back home. We began together, began experimenting together, have gone through other aspects of life together, and the feeling is definitely one of trust. In this as well as in other areas.

I: How long has it been since you've lived at home?

R: About six years now.

Those whose social relationships were based on opiate use were constantly concerned about the long-term effects of use on themselves and their friends and about the need for continuous checking and control. In their own eyes, of course, these chippers were breaking new ground.

R: Manuel and Nancy and I have been using dope together for years now. Because of our business and all, we're usually separated for half the year, when we come up north. But we keep in contact, and drug use is one of the things we keep on eye on each other about. I mean, like, how are you doin', how much have you been doin', and so forth. It's a subject of interest to all of us, and it interacts with our work, our individual art work, and our work when we're separate. Because we all use it to relax—while we're working sometimes, too—and we feel we've made some breakthroughs in the work as a result of being high. So, yeah, we keep in touch about it.

The drug effects were variable and sometimes difficult to deal with. Thus great importance was placed on having a social group that would be understanding about members' difficult moods or even their desire to absent themselves.

R: Well, it depends, but I think I can say I enjoy drugs more when I'm with other people. I know sometimes I get melancholy when I use heroin, and it's not always great to be melancholy with other people. And sometimes for that reason I do it alone. But it can be different, and if I do get melancholy, my friends seem to understand. Yeah, probably more enjoyable with other people.

It was also important for our controlled users to demonstrate to themselves primarily, and to others secondarily, that their heroin use had not interfered with their ability to keep up with many different social groups.

R: Even when I was in my heaviest drug period in California, I still kept my high-school contacts. I always keep my contacts up and I'll play the role, whatever it needs to be. I've never seemed to be so much out of control that I've had to cut off a complete group of people.

Yet in attempting to stay in contact with other social groups, users ran into the problem of having to conceal their heroin use. Quite in contrast to compulsives, most of our controlled subjects, like the next two, were morbidly concerned lest their use should become known to nonusing significant others.

> R: I had so much close contact with my mother and my other friends, whom I dug more than these other dudes. I dug the dudes because they dug heroin, but my other friends were more important to me. You see, I was living almost a triple life. I had to not only conceal from my mother, but also from the good guys, and then swing with the bad guys. Plus, you know, try to put out towards society—you know, looking good, not showing anybody that you do this. So I couldn't afford to do it every day.

> R: Most of my friends don't know. Or it's been mentioned a couple of times and then just dropped, and it's never been brought up again. So what they really know or what they think, I don't know, 'cause I don't go proddin' for it. Because they're sort of —some of them don't even smoke pot. The first time their initial reaction to it was just a shh, you know, it was just such a shock to them, sort of a thing, that their friendship means enough to me to want to keep it and not have that come between us.

For almost all of our subjects, the fear of nonusers' learning about their use proved to be well founded.

> R: The people who've never done it or people who used to do it—reformed junkie-types—are so against it that it's not even worth mentioning. I'd rather not cause a hassle. And when I have told people, they're always watching out to see if I'm doing it, and if I am, they'll give me a lecture. So it's not worth it to tell them.

Even friends who shared certain aspects of the drug experience might disapprove if a controlled user crossed the boundary from snorting to shooting up. This added to the "paranoia" our subjects felt about others' learning of their use.

> I: Have you had friends who don't use and know that you use and express disapproval?
> R: Yes.
> I: In strong terms?
> R: Yup.
> I: What sorts of things do they say?

R: Well, with one friend—one that's most adamant about it—there's a lot of concern involved. And lecturing. And usually by the time it gets to the lecture, it wears on me, you know. One time we snorted heroin before I started using it to any degree, and he didn't get off on it, and he told me about it. He said, "I spent ten bucks for it and I didn't get anything out of it." After the first time I shot it, I just went and told him, "Wow, I didn't have anywhere near the same experience you had—I thought it was great!" And he said, "Did you snort it?" and I said, "No." And that's when it started. And he started with this business about—he's my best friend—"I suppose I'm going to have to start watching my stereo equipment now." Just trying to lay it on like that. And then he started going into this lecture: "Once you start you can't stop; you do it once, and you're going to be hooked for life; stop while you can." And I just thought that the best way around this, I guess, is not to mention it.

It was clear from our interviews that nonusers could not believe that heroin could be used in a controlled way in a social gathering. As one subject put it:

R: I'd hear about it from her: "You're going to turn into a junkie; I don't want to live with a junkie." And I'd be getting all sorts of hassles all over the place. So a lot of times I just wouldn't say anything about it. I'd just get off, and I wouldn't say anything about it. And then, if she says to me, "Your eyes look like they're pinned; did you get off or something?" "Oh yeah, I got off." But unless she explicitly mentioned that, a lot of times I'd wear my glasses around the house to make it so that my eyes weren't—right out there. I kept it from her.

Users with significant others who were nonusers could run into an additional complication: criticism that was leveled not only at themselves but at their friends.

I: What does your wife think of your friends?
R: She doesn't like them at all.
I: Why?
R: Because she feels they're influencing me.
I: In other words, if they weren't around you at all and they didn't call you, you wouldn't even use on weekends. Is that it?
R: No, I'm not saying that. It's just that I'm a lot more apt to use when I'm out with my friends.

Despite the brave front they put on, our controlled heroin users knew that they were doing something extremely dangerous. Especially unpleasant, even frightening, was the association with addicts that usually was required in order to obtain the drug.

> R: One of the major problems with chipping is getting involved with the heroin subculture. One of the incredible problems arises when you only buy a gram or so. The people that you buy it from tend to call you back twice a day for two weeks, at least, and it's quite a hassle getting. First of all, you're always getting burned. You never get a really good deal. You're constantly getting harassed by these people on the phone. Every call is an invitation to join the addict subculture or the habitual using subculture, and there's nothing you can do about this. People you are buying from are in this subculture.

Association with junkies might not only lead to increased use and potential addiction but also to the risk of arrest.

> I: Is that where you score—on the street?
>
> R: Always on the street, practically.
>
> I: Is there some reason for that?
>
> R: Well, yeah, because the people are visible. I know one place where it's a house thing, but his dope is terrible. I wouldn't even go there as a last resort. I mean, if it came down to that I just wouldn't even get high. I wouldn't consider it. And that's within walking distance of my house.
>
> I: So that means you'd have to go to a scene set up for that.
>
> R: Yeah, which is why that thing happened the other night. They'd been hot in the area for, I don't know, a couple of months now. There've been police around and they've been shuffling from one corner to another, and this and that, and it's been, you know, touch and go. You've got to look in the mirror all the time you're down there. And as a matter of fact, I was there about, I think about ten minutes before they got busted.

The degree of association between our controlled subjects and opiate addicts varied. Some subjects had none because they bought through an intermediary; most of the others had contact only in the process of buying, but a few interacted with addicts in a variety of ways. All, however, were scared of becoming like the compulsive users they had seen.

> I: As you see it, when you were using it, did you identify yourself as an occasional user, a chipper, as—? What was your relation to your identity or image?
>
> R: As opposed to an addict or a nonuser?
>
> I: Yes.
>
> R: I considered myself just that, somebody who knew the junk world, who knew what went down in the street life, but yet who wasn't an integral part of the street life. I was separate from it. I had one foot in

it, and one foot in the life of the nonuser. When I worked in the organization and when I worked in the program, things like that kept that one foot out, kept me from jumping in the fire with both feet. And so I was in a unique position where I could observe. Once you're really tied up in it, it's really tough to observe. When you've got both feet in it and you're encircled in it, it's really tough. But I was fortunate enough to keep one foot outside of it, so that I could observe, and see what danger could fall upon me if the other foot were dragged in.

The next subject's fear of addiction acted like a sanction or rule to keep her use controlled.

I: And why did that period end?

R: I got to a state where I had no choice except to get pulled into the heroin scene for myself, which meant that I would have to do a lot of things, prostitute myself and stuff like that—a lot of heavy stealing. I couldn't see that it would lead to anything. I had higher horizons all the time.

This fear of crossing the line and becoming an addict or, more exactly, a junkie—because it was the life style as much as the actual physiological addiction that was terrifying—had to be dealt with. Subjects went to great lengths to deny their fear and to establish external controls. The next man, who couldn't bear the suspense, had to test himself once and for all to see if he could tolerate addiction without becoming a junkie. The experiment he carried out would be labeled counterphobic in ordinary psychiatric parlance.

R: They were all going through withdrawal when they came into the hospital.

I: Is that why they were there?

R: Yeah. Some of them much more seriously than others. And I got to learning about the nature of withdrawal, what it was that these guys were actually kicking, and what the nature of the habit was, whether it was a physiological process or whether it was psychological. A couple of them looked downright scary; they looked like they were going through hell. And a couple of them it didn't seem to phase, they just got chills and put up with it. But in the course of talking to them about their experiences, I became convinced that they were addicted to the rituals and the life style much more than to the substance. And so I wanted to experience that myself. Shortly after that time I bought a whole lot of heroin and did it daily for ten days.

I: Were you using it by yourself in that period?

R: Yes, although other people were aware that I was doing it. No one was sharing in my heroin. I had bought it for myself, for this experiment, as I thought of it at that time.

I: What was the object of the experiment?

R: To see what it would do to me. To see what quitting would be like.

I: What happened when you stopped?

R: I was nauseated. I had chills for about four or five hours. And I had a headache for two days. Other than that, it was an adventure.

Those occasional users who were in close contact with addicts invariably had experiences that indicated how real the horrors of addiction could be.

R: I got him into the clinic—if it wasn't for me, I don't think he would have gone. And he went to a halfway house, and I got really mad at him 'cause he wouldn't stay there. He split from there and he was facing jail. (This was a few years back.) And he said, "Well, damn it, I'm not going, they're crazy up there." So I went down, I went there [laugh]. This is Good News House and I went down there; I went there and I stayed there. He was sick; they sat him in a chair for about eighteen hours, looking at a wall. I knew what was going to happen   you start to get sick after you've been sitting there all night. He left after a day and a half. I stayed a little longer with him. I said, "I see what you mean" [laugh]. I think I did a lot of trying for him. The way I look at it, I tried to get him into a lot of different places.

I: Do you worry about his drug use now?

R: No, he's a big boy now. I worry more about myself. But he said he wished he could do what I do now. Just chip a little bit—I really think that's something.

Since almost half of our subjects had had a brush with addiction before they settled into a long-term controlled using pattern, they knew what they had to fear:

R: Yeah, he would shoot up more than I would.

I: More times?

R: No, not necessarily more often, but more—

I: More stuff each time? More junk each time?

R: Right. And I also had pains, so I was sure it was something we ate or something like that. But not like him, I wasn't hung up on anything. Also, I was taking care of him. It's common with women to be able to just pass over their own physical ailment to [laugh] take care of their men. I really became conscious of it, of what it meant to be strung out. And then I was very careful. And I tried to be careful with him. It was hard to control him. He went through that a few times, kicking, like that.

I: Did you ever have to go through that?

R: No. I mean, once in a while, I would get an upset stomach or some-thing, but that's the most I would get.

I: But you would continue to use even after that?

R: Yeah. But much less than I did before. It was not an everyday thing. I'd do like two days and then purposely abstain for a day.

The fear of being like a junkie, that is, accepting addiction and an addic-tive life-style, was very real to those who had had extensive contact with addicts.

R: I've seen plenty. The one time I woke up and thought I was sick scared the shit out of me. I told you about Penny—I used with her the first time. Six months later Penny was a whore and a cheap whore at that. She had been busted three times for boosting. I guess she couldn't even do that right. She just needed lots and lots of bread to keep that habit going. Doing it the way I do it, every other weekend or so, it doesn't cost me that much. I just don't want to see any more junkies. I just want to stay as far away from them as I can.

The fear of becoming an addict or a junkie or of being arrested was bad enough, but there were even worse concerns. Most of our subjects observed social sanctions that were really safety precautions to minimize the risks of an overdose and of infection. Yet they all had horror stories to tell.

R: I started shooting heroin for a while, but then I knew of some people who OD'd and died, and then I got pretty paranoid about sticking a needle in my arm. I was thinking that any time I stuck a needle in my arm, I was a potential OD and dying. And I felt anyway that cough syrup and Doridens produced about the same effects that heroin did. You know, the nod, the high, but you don't get the rush.

And once in a while the horror "story" became a reality for a controlled user.

R: It was really weird because I never had anything like that happen before, and then all of a sudden every vein in my whole arm just swelled up and turned red, and I could just see it climbing right up my arm, and I did it in this arm, and it was only from here to here. So I figured once it gets there, that's it, "see you later." And I thought, well, what should I do? And I thought, well, I'll just boost it. And I just kept boosting it, because it was to late at that point to do anything about it anyway, so I figured I might as well just enjoy it while it was there. And I said goodbye to John, I did. I said, "I think this is it." And the two of us were just really freaked out.

5

Research Findings: Drug-Use Rituals, Sanctions, and Control

STUDIES OF THE PHARMACOLOGY AND CHEMISTRY OF MARIHUANA, THE PSY-chedelics, and the opiates fill many volumes (see Grinspoon 1971, 1979; Kaplan 1970; and Goodman & Gilman 1975, for example). Fortunately, in order to understand the social-psychological relationship of each of these to personality (set) and to social setting, only a minimum of knowledge about their pharmacology is needed. Of greater importance is some knowledge of how these substances are used.

Marihuana

The common hemp plant, cannabis sativa, used for millennia to produce paper and rope, is the source of marihuana. The flowering tops, particularly from the female plant, produce an aromatic, sticky resin that contains the intoxicating properties. When the flowering tops themselves are gathered, the term marihuana is applied; when the resin alone is collected, the term hashish is applied. Interestingly enough, in contrast to most drugs, marihuana, in usual doses, cannot be classified pharmacologically as either a stimulant or a depressant. In heavier doses, it is more likely to act as a psychological depressant, even a sedative, but causes few of the physiologically depressing actions of such drugs as alcohol, barbiturates, benzodiazepines, and opiates, thus accounting for the low toxicity of cannabis. Although the action of marihuana is sometimes called psychedelic, the cannabis group is not chemically related to the psychedelics.

THC (delta-9-tetrahydrocannabinol) is considered the most active intoxicating ingredient, and the strength of any cannabis preparation is usually defined by its THC content. In fact, there are over 200 chemical constituents in the natural plant, some of which potentiate or inhibit the action of a particular

135

plant strain, giving different strains not only different strengths but also individual qualities of response. In contrast to many drugs, cannabis is not water-soluble but is soluble in fat, which explains the fact that it is retained in body fat for some days after use.

Marihuana use is not highly ritualized. It takes place in a wide variety of settings and circumstances, such as before going to a movie, during a party, while watching television, or during a walk in the woods. Users may sit alone at home, or they may join their friends. Controlled users do not usually get together specifically to take marihuana; they meet primarily to socialize, and if the drug is used, it is viewed as an adjunct to the occasion (Kaplan 1983; Trebach 1982; Weil & Rosen 1983).

The flexibility of marihuana rituals is partly explained by the pharmacology of the drug. Its effect, varying with the strength of the particular sample, is relatively mild and does not last long. My subjects, who were experienced users, found little difficulty in controlling the drug high, and usually they were able to function normally in that state if it became necessary to do so. This fact did not surprise me. As Becker (1963) had observed, because appreciation and control of the marihuana high are learned, the user eventually is able to function adequately while under its influence. Weil and I with Nelsen (1968) had expanded this finding by discovering that in a controlled setting experienced marihuana users were better able than naive users to control the high.

Flexibility in marihuana rituals can also be explained in terms of the drug's status. It is now widely accepted in our society that although marihuana is still a "bad" drug, it is "less bad" than heroin, LSD, or cocaine. This new attitude, coupled with the expanding use of marihuana, has created an environment in which rigid external controls in the form of rituals are no longer so necessary as they were in the 1960s. The more marked ritualization of the mid-1960s was described by research subjects who were twenty-five years old or over. They recalled with nostalgia and humor the dimly lit room, locked doors, music, candles, incense, people sitting in a circle on the floor, and one joint being passed ceremoniously around the circle. At the time of interview they regarded this earlier behavior as quaint and unnecessary. Nowadays, as the number of intermittent marihuana users in the United States has risen to some 31.9 million and the number who have tried the drug to 57 million (Miller & Associates 1983) marihuana use has lost much of its deviant character. Concurrently, social sanctions for controlled use have been strengthened and have become available throughout most of the using subculture.

Under these conditions considerable learning about controlled use can take place before actual use begins. Most American adolescents are well aware before choosing whether or not to use marihuana that the drug does not cause people to go crazy or fall apart. Our younger subjects (eighteen to twenty years old) had known of teachers in their high schools who used marihuana, and many of them had older siblings who used it. The same subjects had also acquired a knowledge of marihuana from friends, the underground press, popular music, or novels. Their first few experiences with the drug recapitulated many of the ritualistic elements of the early 1960s. These beginning sessions were rather formal affairs in which an experienced user introduced one or more newcomers to the drug, providing guidance, demonstrating how best to smoke the substance, and soothing the neophytes' fears. Very quickly, however, newcomers moved beyond these structured situations and began the process of adapting use to a variety of social settings. They had no difficulty in locating using friends with whom they also shared nondrug-centered interests.

The lack of highly specific rituals should not, therefore, be construed as evidence that controlled users are reckless in the way they use marihuana. Rather, the rituals that earlier served as rigid external controls have been replaced over the last decade by more general but still effective social sanctions. Through growing familiarity with every aspect of marihuana use, these sanctions, like those relating to alcohol use, have been internalized, and the rituals developed to support the sanctions no longer need to be followed so closely.

The research staff and I found it much more difficult to locate abusers than controlled users of marihuana. Our subjects described the drug as not particularly deleterious, easily controlled, and difficult though not impossible to abuse. Some expressed genuine disbelief when we asked if they had ever had any difficulty in maintaining controlled use. Still, they were not messianic about marihuana; they recognized its potential for abuse and offered guidelines for sensible use. As one subject said, "In spite of all the rationalizations about how good dope is, I don't see that I have to have a reason for getting high every time. Yet getting high consistently without a reason seems to be a reason to check things out with myself." Another subject commented that if one uses marihuana too much the quality of the high declines; when this happens, one should stop for a while and then adopt a pattern of less frequent use. Controlled users cited three reasons for not using too much marihuana at any one time: to avoid transient but unpleasant panic reactions or paranoia; to keep the high controllable so that other activities could be better enjoyed; and to avoid wasting the drug. Subjects generally subscribed to the ethic that they should not be high at work or at school. For example, Susan S., who worked as a housekeeper several days a week, explained that although she could clean when she was "stoned," she preferred to restrict her drug use to leisure time.

Although passing a joint around a group is no longer essential, it still serves on many occasions to assist the process of adjusting the intensity of the high. The time that elapses between inhalations permits the user to monitor his degree of intoxication. Several subjects stated that when using alone or with one or two other people, they stopped after several "tokes" to let the high catch up with them and then decided whether they wanted more. One subject commented that this was an especially sensible way to proceed when trying out a new batch of marihuana.

Many of the books and articles about marihuana that have been published in the past few years have warned the public, users, and potential users, about the dangers of the drug. Great stress has been put on the potential physical, social, and psychological harm that can follow use. Such writers as Peggy Mann (1978), Gabriel G. Nahas (1976), and Robert L. DuPont (1983) have increasingly returned to the position of the early 1960s, which barely differentiated use from misuse (Heller 1972; Kaplan 1970; *Marijuana and Health* 1982; *Report of the Liaison Task Panel* 1978).

Implicit in these warnings is the sense that the users themselves do not appreciate the difficulties that can arise from their drug use. Occasionally, of course, this is true, as the following two interview excerpts show:

I: And let's say that you're on one of your sprees, will you use marihuana too or will you not?

R: Oh, yeah. Give me anything and I'll take it.

I: I see, so it doesn't really matter. Have there been occasions . . .

R: If I'm loaded, if I'm doing both, I mean, you could give me anything . . . and like a dummy, I'd take it! You know?

There was every evidence that this young man's heedlessness about drug use was reflected in other areas of his life, and it was doubtful that any warning could have reached him.

Another subject exhibited the sporadic stopping and starting pattern that is also common among people who are having difficulty with alcohol:

I: Did you ever stop using it?

R: Yeah, but not for a very long period of time.

I: Why did you stop?

R: Well, sometimes it was inaccessible, and sometimes I just wanted to try and stop. No particular reason, just thought I'd prove to myself that I was not addicted to it or anything.

I: And for how long did your use stop?

R: I guess the most was one week.

I: And why did you go back?

R: Just because I felt like it.

Such an attitude, of course, reflected the user's lack of confidence in his ability to control drug use.

With these two exceptions our subjects were clearly aware of potential difficulties and were specific in their warnings about them:

R: There are some kids, adults too, that will just smoke to excess. And it can be an alternative life-style, practically. That isn't good, especially with kids in high school, when they might be doing things that are more constructive for themselves. They get involved in drugs, and all of a sudden it seems like the answer to all of their problems in the world. All their friends are smoking grass now, and I know in high schools there are a lot of problems with hard drugs. Hallucinogens, and downs, and things like that.

I: So you have genuine concerns about it?

R: Oh, yes, I think it definitely can be dangerous.

Similar sentiments were echoed in other interviews. Nevertheless, most of our subjects liked marihuana use so much that their recognition of its potential difficulties was balanced by more positive experiences with the drug.

Our interviews indicated that still greater confusion was likely to arise over the existence of effective sanctions. Frequently the sanctions that develop around illicit drug use are quirky and individualized, such as the following subject's sense that marihuana use was seasonal:

R: And also the springtime—I don't know—but people get high a lot. It's not that you smoke once a day or so—but you get high like several times a day—and you spend pretty much the [whole] springtime . . .

I: Has that been a repeated pattern most springs?

R: Yeah.

I: What about the summer?

R: The summer people, in terms of drugs, are the ones who use it in their travels. I do hardly any drugs in the summer when I travel.

This woman's preference for spring over summer made sense to her if not to others, and it had functioned as a rule of use for her for five years.

But more frequently the sanctions that controlled use were not entirely conscious or the subject was not accustomed to articulating them. He only vaguely knew he had them:

I: And did you have any particular adverse reactions to it?

R: No, not adverse reactions. Because I still smoke now, if the situation is right. But I won't go out and buy it myself. It's a good social drug, I guess. Very.

He also considered his rules for use to be logical:

R: I don't think you have to have a reason for getting high every time, but just getting high consistently without a reason for it seems to me to be a reason to sort of check things out with yourself.

Here the explanation ended. But to the research team this subject's insistence on using the drug socially or on having a particular reason or occasion for use constituted the most compelling of sanctions.

Such sanctions do not develop out of nothing. Marihuana users, unlike alcohol users, are not exposed to enough early education about use to develop an awareness of their limits and to test them (Maloff et al. 1982; Harding & Zinberg 1977).

R: I was smoking every day, which I did at one time. I did that before, for a long time, because there was just so much available to me at one time that I did it, and that was very bad [laugh]. In fact, I was talking to my roommate today, before I came up here, and he said there was a time last year when he felt he was just in a fog. That's all it is, a fog. And when I think of that, I have to agree. If you smoke grass every day, even if it's late at night, you can't do that, even if it's social. Because, I don't know, it numbs the brain.

This experience, which was not unusual, indicated how users develop respect for the drug and come to recognize the need for controlling sanctions.

Because few of our marihuana-using subjects had drug-related problems at work, their work-related rules were simple:

I: Do you have any rules, rules for yourself, about using drugs?
R: I guess the only rule is that I won't get stoned if I feel that I'm going to be confronting a potentially hostile situation—not hostile, but a situation in which drug use might not work out. I wouldn't get stoned to go to work. But I feel that I can take care of myself when I'm on drugs. I don't worry about that too much.
I: Would you have gotten stoned for this interview?
R: I could have easily gotten stoned; it wouldn't have bothered me. It depends on the situation. I wouldn't like to smoke in the middle of the day if I have things to do. Or I wouldn't smoke in the middle of a class. Things like that.

This was a general attitude. Most experienced users believed that they could get stoned and function pretty well, just as most experienced alcohol users think that, under special circumstances, they can have a lunch-time drink and return to work; but they realize that it is a strain and generally undesirable.

Many of our subjects were very specific in their caveats to new drug users:

I: If you were going to tell somebody who was going to try marihuana for the first time three important things to consider, what would they be?

R: Don't get carried away with it. Don't get into it as if it means anything other than it's just a drug, something to distort your brain; there's no deep meaning in drugs—that would be the second thing. And the third thing would be, be very careful about whom you initiate into drugs because you really have to realize that there are some people, especially young people—it can have a very devastating effect on them, if they get into it, if they think of it as something other than it isn't.

And some users were conscious of and extremely articulate about their own sanctions:

I: What does regular use look like?

R: Once or twice every two weeks or so. Maybe going sometimes a whole month without it, maybe taking two or three puffs, never smoking a whole joint, always sharing a joint with at least one other person.

I: Are there some times during the day or week when you're more inclined to use one drug or another?

R: Nope.

I: Mostly it's evenings?

R: Oh, yeah. I should say that I would be more inclined to drink in the evening related to dinner or socializing and use marihuana late in the evening.

I: Do you have any rules about using drugs? Things you check on before you use them?

R: Oh, yeah. With marihuana, I wouldn't use it unless I knew the person who was offering it to me.

I: You've had adverse reactions to marihuana?

R: Yes.

I: Would you use marihuana if you were in a bad mood?

R: [Laugh] No, but maybe in an uptight mood.

I: If you were to tell a new drug user three important things about using, what would they be?

R: To use moderately, to make sure what you're using—you know, to know what you're using—and not to use it as a crutch.

I: Are you more likely to use drugs in a particular place?

R: Yes, I'm more likely to use it in a home setting.

Such subjects had already learned why they needed sanctions. The question about what advise to give to a new user was valuable in that it often led them to articulate rules for safe use that they had not known they had.

Social rituals, which develop to support sanctions for marihuana use as they do for alcohol use, include choosing a special place, a particular time, and a particular activity. The following excerpt describes the beginning of a ritual:

> R: I was in one of these heavy roots-type bars, just sitting back and taking twenty minutes to drink a beer and listening to the Irish music. And then this old drunk started coming in and turning me on, you know, to drinks, and I sat down and started playing with this guy, playing chess with him. Because I was playing chess with him, he gave me a hit of hash, and that gave an opportunity for other people to take a hit and put it out and wait for a new move from there, so it was kind of a weird scene. But suddenly, I realized I had been in the bar for like five hours. All of a sudden, four games of chess and three weird conversations later it was one o'clock. And I had sort of a buzz. But I walked out, you know, walking straight; the only part I didn't like was sort of standing in a bar all night.

For years this man continued the ritual of playing chess when he was high.

Many of our subjects began marihuana use while listening to music. Some claimed that marihuana slowed down the time sense so that they could hear and experience music more explicitly and precisely, note by note, theme by theme.

> R: I've noticed some people have mellowed a hell of a lot more than I have [as a result of using marihuana]. The mellowing out that I'm into—I listen to Cat Stevens and that type of music, you know—is that I really feel what the music is trying to say, both in the words and the instruments themselves. It's a really strange experience listening to music when I'm stoned. It's like the music goes right through me, or like I can feel the music entering my heart or something. It's like eating a piece of chocolate cake: you know how you feel and you taste what that chocolate cake is, you experience it. Well, it's the same with music. You get really close to it, it enters you and you become very close to it. Not like, well, now he's doing that riff and now that's a piano and a violin playing. You just feel the sound and the emotion in yourself and it carries you away with it. Sometimes I actually cry or laugh with the emotion of the music. Most of all it's very relaxing. And I feel like I get to know personally the guy who's doing the music. With Cat Stevens, I've noticed the changes in his attitudes through his music. A lot of people who sing his songs, even, are the types that once went through some hard times—they are sort of establishment in their kooky little ways. I've noticed a lot of people like that.

The enhanced sensations that many subjects experienced by mixing marihuana use with eating and sex led them to associate use with these special occasions.

Most of our subjects maintained one ritual or another, but these might change as their tastes or their social circumstances changed.

In some instances rituals were used when sanctions appeared to be slipping.

> R: Yes, I was out there—well, as soon as I got out there I started getting high again [laugh]. This one relationship still was constrained, and I had to be pretty straight. At the time I was with her, my nervous system was such that when I got high, I still got a little bit uptight. When I first started getting high again, after having my central nervous system put together, it was beautiful. Everything was like when I first used to get stoned, so intense, no paranoia, and it was beautiful and exciting—the whole thing like that. And then I found myself in about two weeks really bitchy and irritable, and realized that I was smoking dope every day, and this was $10-an-ounce shit. Then I stopped getting high for a couple of weeks and I told her, "Don't smoke more than twice a day, more than once a day; if you catch me doing it more than twice a day, let me know." And about a month later she came up to me and said, "Hey, you're doing this," and I started rationalizing, and I caught myself, realized what I was doing, and had to watch myself much more carefully.

This man's reliance on his girlfriend as an external control can legitimately be described as a kind of ritual, but one born of necessity rather than used to buttress a sanction and increase the pleasure of use. It shows an awareness of the need for rules. But in the judgment of the research team, whenever a ritual is used to replace a sanction, the potential for loss of control is great.

Psychedelics

Psychedelics include a wide range of substances that vary in both potency and duration of effect: LSD, mescaline, peyote, psilocybin, MDA, DMT, and a few others. Originally this class of drugs was called psychotomimetics or hallucinogens, because their effects, it was thought, imitated those of a psychosis or hallucination. For some years before the drug revolution of 1962, psychiatric residents at some installations routinely took doses of these substances so that by experiencing the time-limited effects they might become more empathic with patients who were experiencing the real thing. Indeed, there are a number of articles in scientific journals attesting to the success of such experimentation (Kafka 1964; Kafka & Gaarder 1964; Mogar & Savage 1954; Savage 1952).

In time it became clear that the effects of these drugs were not psychotomimetic, and the term psychedelic, from the Greek 'mind manifesting,' came into general use. In nature there are hundreds of plants, barks, and vines with psychedelic properties that were discovered and used before the dawn of recorded history, often in religious rites. Chemically there are two broad classes of psychedelics: those based on an indole ring roughly related to the body's pineal hormone secretions, and those with a molecular structure closer to the adrenalin hormone and similar to amphetamines. Both groups have stimulant properties as well as the mind-manifesting intoxication. The best-known indole psychedelic, psilocybin, is contained in more than a dozen species of mushrooms (especially *Psilocybe cubensis*), but morning glory seeds contain a similar, though more toxic, substance. LSD (lysergic acid diethylamide), the drug many people believe to be responsible for the drug revolution and the most widely used of these substances, is a synthetic product developed in 1938 in the indole group which causes an intoxication lasting from ten to twelve hours. The buttons of the peyote cactus containing mescaline, long used in American Indian religious rites, are the best-known natural psychedelics in the adrenalin-amphetamine group. For inexperienced users, ingesting these cactus buds causes nausea and vomiting. Numerous synthetics, such as STP (2,5 dimethoxy-4-methylamphetamine) and MDA (methyldioxyamphetamine), have been developed with similar chemical structures.

The illicit status of these drugs creates a major problem for the average user in that he cannot be certain what is in the drug he buys. What he presumes to be mescaline may be LSD, or the mescaline may be adulterated with PCP, amphetamines, and other substances; therefore, he can only guess at the proper dosage. A few very knowledgeable users are in a better position. They have access to reputable sources, and some have their drugs tested by a chemist before use.

Unlike the marihuana high, the psychedelic high may last for six to eight hours, and it may differ substantially from one psychedelic to another (Zinberg 1974). It is an intensive though not uncontrollable experience, characterized by perceptual changes, sometimes of an illusory nature but distinguishable from genuine hallucinations. The risk of a bad trip, which is always present, is to some degree increased by the lack of quality control over the drug. For these and other reasons, within the drug subculture psychedelics are regarded as "real"—that is, dangerous—drugs. They neither have the widespread appeal of marihuana nor are they treated casually. Estimates of use are inexact, but it is frequently mentioned that between ten and twelve million people have tried psychedelics. Most of the rituals and social sanctions related to the psychedelics deal with making the specific drug experience as safe as possible for the user rather than with concerns about chemistry and frequency of use, as with the other drugs. Yet, as was the case with users of marihuana, we found it easier to locate users than abusers.

Psychedelic use is almost invariably a drug-centered group activity. Subjects talk about having others with them who can be relied upon to help them cope with a bad trip or with unforeseen events: "I have to do it with someone that I really know well, that I trust." Casual acquaintances are sometimes included in the group, but then the trip is commonly preceded by a discussion in which all the members try to get comfortable together, to determine who may need extra help or attention, and to establish ground rules. During this preliminary discussion, an experienced user may be assigned to act as a guide for an inexperienced or uneasy user. Group members may forbid anyone to wander away from the group without telling another member; otherwise someone might worry, and worrying is felt to be detrimental to a positive drug experience.

Subjects agree that planning the trip is an important matter, even when the participants have taken the drug together previously and feel quite close to one another. The need for structure varies, but pre-trip planning includes such issues as what foods or beverages to take along, what activities to engage in during the trip, whether thorazine or other drugs should be available in case of a bad trip, or whether talking people down is preferable to medicating them. This planning reaffirms the participants' sense of shared intentions and strengthens their ability to control the drug high.

Subjects are adamant about using psychedelics in a proper setting—"a good place." For many this means tripping in a relatively secluded spot in the country. In every case the space must be secure and comfortable. A city tripper said, "I'll take a walk outside, but it'll always be with the notion that I can come back to this sanctuary in the house, and so it's no threat." This subject and many others expressed some disdain for users who violated the principle that the drug experience should be confined to special settings. As one said, "I was living last year with a dude who's seventeen years old and is from the West Coast. He was telling me that when he was going to junior high school he would just drop acid in the morning and go to school, which completely weirded me out. He could just ride with any kind of horrible thing. Amazing!"

Another social sanction that subjects observe is the need to be internally prepared for psychedelic use. One subject described this as "making peace with the public reality: mentally putting your house, your affairs, in order; you know—what's the Zen thing—emptying out the teacup first." Others talk simply about needing to be in a "good mood" and needing "energy" to undertake the experience. Some subjects appear to ritualize this internal process by tidying up the space in which they are going to use the drug.

Beyond these conventions, which represent attempts to ensure a good trip and prevent a bad one, other rituals and social sanctions are directed toward inhibiting compulsive psychedelic use. Subjects repeatedly advocated using psychedelics no more than once every two weeks, and in practice their use was far less frequent than that. Less than once a month was the most typical using pattern, and over time, use consistently became even less frequent. Avoidance of compulsive use, however, is probably not so much the consequence of negative sanctions as it is the result of a combination of two other factors: the positive value that controlled users attach to the consciousness-altering properties of psychedelics, and the fact that tolerance to these consciousness-altering properties goes up very rapidly as use becomes more frequent. Our subjects who were interested in experiencing precisely these effects found that too frequent use of the drug was counterproductive.

Some psychedelic users who are not interested in the consciousness-changing qualities of the drugs may become compulsive users. For them, it is the speedy, stimulating effects that are appealing—effects that are enhanced by larger, more frequent doses of the drug. Assuming, of course, that these compulsive users are actually using psychedelics and not amphetamines that have been wrongly labeled (a mistake that could not be made by a serious user), I would conjecture that such users are associated with groups in the subculture that either put a negative value on consciousness change or do not recognize it as a primary drug effect.

By comparing the testimony of older and younger subjects, my research staff was able to identify some of the shifts that have occurred over the years in psychedelic-using rituals and social sanctions. The older subjects, who had begun use in the mid-1960s, often shared a sense that psychedelics should be used for "personal growth" rather than recreational purposes. They viewed tripping as an activity that was undertaken to accomplish a worthy goal—to learn more about oneself, to grow intellectually, or to transcend ordinary perceptual boundaries. By contrast, the younger subjects, who had been using psychedelics for only about five years, included among their reasons for use various goals that were plainly recreational. Younger subjects might trip for a rational purpose, but they seemed equally inclined to trip simply in order to enjoy the high state. Although I cannot yet account for these expanded goals, it is possible that they indicate a growing familiarity with the drugs and therefore less guilt feelings about their use. Perhaps when the older subjects began using psychedelics, they needed to assign some constructive purpose to tripping in order to justify their interest in this class of drugs, which was regarded as more dangerous and powerful then than it is now.

If the psychedelic-using population continues to grow, it is likely that recreational use will increase and, as with marihuana, will become less ritualized though not less controlled. It is unlikely, however, that psychedelic-using rituals will ever achieve the same degree of flexibility and diversity as marihuana-using rituals. Probably periods of greater interest in psychedelic use will come and go every few years and social sanctions will be more or less available, depending on the resiliency of social learning; but because of the high-impact, long-duration drug effect and the related tendency to keep psychedelic use infrequent, there are both less need and less social opportunity for the process of internalization of social sanctions to take place. Thus the dependence on rituals (on external controls) will continue to limit the flexibility of psychedelic use.

Even those of our subjects who were satisfied with their drug experience felt the same extreme concerns about using psychedelics that had been evident among early users. To counteract these fears they took care to follow various rules for safe use and the rituals supporting them.

The social sanctions and rituals that surround the use of psychedelics are stronger, better articulated, and more carefully followed than those associated with either marihuana or the opiates. The sanctions that developed in the 1960s had two purposes: to establish control over excessive use (which early users did not realize was not likely to occur) and to establish control over the immediate experience, which was more demanding than any other drug experience. Interest in developing and following sanctions and rituals for reasonable psychedelic use was considerably more important than whether the rules were sensible. Keeping a day free after a trip was eminently sensible, while eating bee pollen was a highly romantic ritual; yet both sanctions indicated respect for the drug and a decision to try to use it safely in order to avoid destructive consequences.

The user of psychedelics shared some of the marihuana user's concerns about possible health hazards, such as chromosome breaks or a defective conception, but his fear of damage along social and psychological dimensions was much greater than the marihuana user's. With marihuana, it was usually the beginner who was anxious about such things, whereas experienced smokers, though they knew of a few genuine misusers (abusers), generally felt they had enough control over the drug to avoid social and psychological harm. With the psychedelics, experienced users recognized that trouble would follow unless the sanctions were observed; and even if care was taken, there were still worries:

R: Once it would be beautiful sunshine, but then the next time it would be like, you know, hiding in the corner like a rat. Your throat is dry, you can barely speak 'cause you're poisoned 'cause you took a heavy dose and—I had a few of those.

Fifty percent of our subjects reported at least one adverse reaction to the drug—usually a bad trip; and 22% knew someone else who had had an adverse reaction. As one user put it,

R: This guy that I really knew well, a graduate student who published this political magazine—he was a physicist, a graduate student, more into studies than I was, but I was in mathematics—he used to take some really incredible stuff. And so in 1962, I guess, I guess it was '61 or '62, that winter, he went to Cambridge where they were doing the original Leary stuff, and he did a huge dose. I guess they didn't know in those days what was an appropriate dose, or something, and he went essentially psychotic.

Because of the power of psychedelic drugs to dislocate perceptions, it was recognized in the early 1960s that a beginning user might not know what was happening to him and therefore might need guidance.

R: It was important that the—whoever was the guide—should also have a light dose. And in two sessions I took psilocybin along with this person, and then in another session I was also operating as a kind of guide with two of my associates on the faculty of a theological school.
I: What did that entail, being a guide?
R: Well, I was just there as somebody who had had the experience. I was there to help them if they needed help.

The habit of having a guide was quickly translated into the social sanctions that someone tripping for the first time should always have an experienced user present.

R: In those days, everybody had a babysitter; you wouldn't do acid without a babysitter. Everybody had a babysitter then. That's the old days, man, the great days.
I: What had you heard about it before you tried it?
R: Nothing, really, except like what my friend told me and stuff.
I: What was that?
R: He hadn't done it either. But he just heard it from someone that heard it from someone that it was really fantastic. And you see all those lights and music. It's just fantastic, and you were just really planning for a trip. But now I just do it kind of whenever I want to. Then you planned all the environment, how you'd be. There was that big fear about freaking out.
I: Had your friends used it before?
R: A few of them had, yeah, but not regularly; it was like a special thing, you didn't wanna abuse it.

The guru or guide would soothe anxiety by telling the user: "It's OK. It is what is supposed to happen. Let it happen. Go with the flow." Some neophytes, anxious to use, found guides in odd places.

I: How old were you?

R: Sixteen.

I: Who showed you how to use it?

R: I read a book [laugh].

I: Which book?

R: *LSD* by Hoffman and somebody else.

I: And you really wanted to try it?

R: Uh huh.

I: Who turned you on to it?

R: A dealer that I met.

I: Where did you try it?

R: By myself, in my bedroom.

I: Did he tell you anything?

R: He said, "Have a good trip."

But even quite young, inexperienced people learned in a social way about this sanction without knowing how they had learned it, and they followed it carefully. Users also learned quickly how sensitive they could become to their own moods and surroundings in this alternate state of consciousness.

R: They told me to watch where I took it, that there were some places that one shouldn't take acid, like in resistance [to the draft during the Vietnam War] sanctuaries, or anything like that. Grass was cool, but acid's too strong. Watch where you get your acid because, like one experience I had wasn't real acid, and I had a really bad experience later with that. It was a headache. It was a physically bad experience. They told me to watch where I took it, watch where my head was at when I took it, and when I was taking it, I sort of already knew that.

An important factor limiting use was the difficulty most people had in arranging their highly organized lives to accommodate a drug "trip" that lasted a whole day and lingered on during the following day.

I: What is the next day like?

R: I like to have a day of recovery, usually I'm just tired. And not physiologically upset, but just, like, really tired out. I just don't want to have a lot of things to deal with. If I trip on Sunday and I have classes on Monday until three o'clock, I can't concentrate very well. I'm usually still tripping a little bit and I just can't attend to things very well. Sometimes the work in school is really important and I have to go to a meeting and really deal with something, and I can't really be—I have to be able to attend to it really well.

For most people, setting aside this much time required planning, and it was time that trippers either could not or did not wish to devote to mundane tasks (Bieberman 1967).

> R: I'd use marihuana any time I felt comfortable to do so. And alcohol any time I felt comfortable to do so. I don't feel compelled to use either, really. And LSD or some kind of hallucinogen, I would like to use more if I had the space to do it. I don't feel I have the space now. I have to work every day. I have to keep certain things together. That's an expansive kind of drug. Sometime, I'd like to be able to just sit down and expand.

From these discoveries about place and time another sanction emerged not only among beginners but also among experienced users: "Only use at a good time, in a good place, with good people." Originally this sanction was offered as advice from one friend to another, but soon users far removed from the initial advisor accepted it as an important and valid way to avoid trouble.

> R: I was, in some part of me, afraid of acid. I'd heard about bad trips and I never wanted to have one. So I tripped a few times, but I would never take a tab unless one of my friends had tried it first.
>
> I: Tried it first?
>
> R: Yes. They were real acid freaks; they were always tripping, but they knew that I didn't, and I trusted them to give me a tab that they found to be good or mild or whatever.
>
> I: Is there anything else you would do?
>
> R: I would never use it in the city, only in the country or in a park. I hate the city when I'm straight, too much noise, bad air, weird people. So I never wanted to intensify that experience. Also, when someone tripped, everyone else in the house would be informed beforehand, so they kept their behavior sort of, well, gentle and kind, I guess. No weird vibes, no head trips. And I would use on a weekend or when I didn't have to work so that I could come down and relax the next day because I always felt spaced out and tired. And I would trip on a pretty day with a friend. Never more than one person. Just one good friend I could relate to.

> R: I'm very much accustomed to getting into a situation that's as un-threatening as possible. Usually it's, you know, the room's kind of tidied up, I know exactly who's going to be around, everything is pretty much in order. I mean, I'll take a walk outside, but it'll always be with the notion that I can come back to this kind of sanctuary for myself in the house, so it's no threat.

I: How about the other people in the house?

R: If people in the house know that other people are tripping, I think that the effort that's made is to act as normal as possible. I think that's really necessary. I know that I feel really condescended to if people behave differently.

Psychedelic drug users illustrated more clearly than either marihuana or opiate users the interplay between sanctions and rituals.

R: OK. Now, I make sure set and setting are right. I have to do it in a really good environment, dig some of the people and the vibrations there, so I have to do it, maybe, with someone that I really know well, that I really trust, and there are some people like that. I have to do it where I have the freedom to, like, walk around outside, somewhere in the country, or something, and dig on trees or whatever, and I have to have my head in the right place, so that I'm not really angry or upset or anything like that.

These rules or sanctions were supported by individual quirky rituals involving seasons of the year, physical activity or lack of it, the state of the surroundings, and what to do when going up or coming down.

R: When you get ready for an LSD trip, there's a lot of preparation involved. It was in early, well, late springtime and, let's see, there were five us who dropped—we're still close friends. We took very small amounts of LSD, very small, because I'd never done it before, and everyone else had, but we wanted to. We thought if we all took the same amount, we would be on the same wavelength, and we sat down and listened to music the first part of the trip. And I did it. Nothing really happened to me for about two hours. I didn't know what to expect, and we started talking about all kinds of things—what we should expect, how to come down, and stuff. You know, it was just basically bullshit, giggling and stuff, a lot of nervousness. I was pretty nervous, and then it came on, and it was a very mild trip, as far as my trips have gone. I didn't get into any astral phenomena. I talked to my friends about what to do. It was getting late and we went out into some woods where there were no people around.

I: Were you out in Gloucester?

R: Yeah. At a friend's house. And we went into some woods and the trees looked more beautiful, and we watched the sunset. It was a really beautiful experience. I didn't really have anything religious; it was just really beautiful.

All of our subjects recognized the primary importance of social sanctions and rituals. All of them stated, in fact, that in order to contain comfortably the long-lasting effects of the drug, they followed several rules for use (mean number of rules = 3.2, S.D. = 1.665, range = 0–6). For the group as a whole these rules included: plans for use (61% of the sample), never use with strangers (44%), never use in a strange place (39%), never use alone (39%), do not let significant others know of use (22%), make special schedules for use (28%), clean the surroundings before use (11%), have rules about obtaining the drug (11%), keep a drug budget (11%), and various other specific rules (50%).

Opiates

Pharmacologically all narcotic drugs are depressants. Indeed, the term "narcotic" is rooted in the Greek word meaning 'stupor'. In legal terminology, the term narcotic has come to include many classes of drugs, but in fact, the term refers only to drugs derived from opium and synthetic variations of opium derivatives. It is important to remember that broad pharmacological classifications, such as depressants, tell us little about the individual actions of particular drugs, especially about their subjective effects. Thus the user experiences opiate derivatives far differently from other depressants such as alcohol or barbiturates, just as the subjective experience of the stimulant cocaine has little in common with the stimulation of psychedelics, although both are antistuporous.

The potency of opium as an analgesic and intoxicant when eaten or smoked goes back to prehistory and was known to ancient Greeks, Chinese, and Egyptians. If the pods of the opium poppy are cut just before they ripen, they ooze a milky-white substance which when dried turns brown and gummy, and that crude opium contains more than twenty-five ingredients. One ingredient, morphine (from Morpheus, the Greek god of sleep), was isolated in 1803. That event, followed by the invention of the hypodermic syringe in 1853, ushered in the era of modern analgesia and, of course, with it, modern addiction. Heroin is simply diacetyl morphine, a more potent product, developed in 1898. Codeine and Dilaudid are two other well-known opium derivatives. Demerol and methadone are the best-known synthetics, although a new generation of synthetics has become popular recently in such products as Percodan and Darvon.

More than any other illicit drug, the opiates have been the object of public condemnation. Popular convictions about the evils of opiates and particularly of heroin extend deep into the drug subculture itself. Many of the marihuana and psychedelic users we interviewed did not even recognize the possibility of controlled opiate use, even though they had identified and dispelled many of the larger culture's myths about their own drugs. (It is possible, of course, that standing with the larger culture against opiate use may help marihuana and psychedelic users to view their own drug use as comparatively "good.") Perhaps because of this general attitude of condemnation, we found it harder to locate controlled opiate users than abusers, just the reverse of the situation with the other two groups of drug-takers.

The controlled opiate users in our study—most of whom used heroin but some of whom used Dilaudid, codeine, and other pharmaceutical opiates, all on an occasional basis—were painfully aware that they were perceived as deviant. They tended to keep their use a closely guarded secret from everyone except one or two dealers and their opiate-using friends. During our study project, a woman who for several years had been a reasonably close friend of one of the researchers felt free for the first time to "confess" to him that she had been a controlled heroin user ever since she had known him.

The relationship of controlled opiate users to addicts, or compulsive opiate users, is as dangerous and difficult as it is necessary. One way in which controlled users can assert their normalcy is to spurn and condemn junkies, but often they must rely on junkies to obtain their drugs; and a few controlled users show impressive ingenuity in finding drug sources (Zinberg & Jacobson 1975). Addicts, for their part, do not understand and often feel threatened by the controlled user's "peculiar" relation to opiates. Hence, on the one hand, controlled users get poor-quality opiates at great cost from junkies, and on the other hand, they are repeatedly and seductively invited to become full-fledged members of the junkie subculture. The controlled user's constant dilemma is how to become friendly enough with an addict to establish a reliable contact for quality opiates, but not so friendly that his refusal to participate in the addict's subculture might offend the latter and lead him to cut off the supply.

Beset by danger on all sides, controlled users huddle together in small isolated groups that develop idiosyncratic, rigid rituals and social sanctions. These groups are fragile and drug-centered because it is difficult to find controlled users who would make compatible friends—the inverse of the situation with marihuana users.

Many of the rituals of controlled opiate users are hard to distinguish from those of compulsive users. In both groups, people squabble over who gets off first, belts are used as ties, eyedroppers are used instead of syringes, and booting is common. The main reason for this ritual-sharing is that in the absence of a highly visible, communicative population of controlled users with its own discrete rituals the addict subculture is the only readily available source of expertise about the drug. But there are also two other reasons for this phenomenon. First, although the life-style of the addict is repugnant to most controlled users, they sometimes find the addict's bold, outlaw stance attractive; hence, partaking of the addict's ritual may be an expression of wistful identification. Second, some controlled users (including several of our subjects) started out as addicts, and they retain and share with others their former compulsive drug-using rituals, of which booting is probably the best example.

Several controlled users have added new elements to the addict ritual. One subject, for example, shifted the emphasis away from "getting off" by tacking on middle-class amenities. He played the good host by serving wine and food to his user guests (without any of the nausea that is commonly accepted as accompanying opiate use), and all spent the evening together in conversation. Another user protected herself from a possible overdose by shooting a little of the drug, waiting to gauge its effect, and then shooting the remainder. By and large, however, controlled users' rituals are not clearly distinguishable from those of compulsive users, especially in the details of administering the drug.

By contrast, the social sanctions surrounding controlled use are distinctive. Most of the rules for opiate use to which controlled users adhere are summarized by the maxim, "Don't become dependent," because they realize that it would be relatively easy to become addicted. For example, our ex-addict subjects had firm rules about frequency of use. One such subject was a woman who had used heroin on an average of three or four times a month for more than four years. Occasionally, when her commitments to work and to her child permitted, she would go on a using spree that lasted about a week. Even on such a vacation, however, she would not use heroin more frequently than every other day. In general, subjects limited their opiate use far more than was necessary to avoid addiction. One subject had confined his use of heroin to weekends for the past five years. Another had limited her regular use over an eighteen-month period to twice a month, except on special occasions such as birthdays and New Year's. Then, troubled by her tolerance of some of the drug's effects, she deliberately cut back to only once a month. She ignored the possibility that instead of growing tolerance on her part, the problem might have been the variability in the potency of the drug she had used on the two occasions when it had happened. There was some question of whether she had really deveoped tolerance or whether she had simply bought some low-potency heroin.

These and other examples indicate that although many controlled users feel that heroin can be used moderately, they regard it as more rapidly addicting than is warranted by the pharmacology of the drug. This attitude, of course, is understandable in view of the prevailing myths about heroin's power as well as the exposure of controlled users to addicts who have succumbed to the drug.

Controlled subjects observed common sanctions against behaving like or becoming overly involved with junkies and compulsive users. One user might chastise another for manifesting irresponsible, junkie-like behavior or being unable to control the drug's effects. A user of codeine-based cough syrup and of

Doriden indicated that despite the somnolence induced by these drugs, people who used them were expected to act responsibly: "One cigarette burn and you're thrown out." Being cheated by dealers was a fact of life, but a controlled user who cheated his or her fellow users was punished by being called a junkie. Controlled users frowned upon spending too much money on heroin because it suggested the junkie's lack of control: "Just 'cause I had the money didn't necessarily mean I would cop. Of course, I wouldn't steal to get the money to cop; there's no need for it 'cause I don't have a habit."

Shooting up like a junkie was acceptable, but shooting up *with* junkies was not, because it symbolized a loss of control. A couple who had regular access to opiates through the wife's addicted sister and brother-in-law stopped relying on them for opiates because of the social pressure to use the drug with them. Instead the couple would borrow a car and drive several miles to a copping site in another city where they knew they could obtain heroin from street dealers.

This sort of behavior is not unique. It is indicative of the care with which controlled opiate users observe their social sanctions and, in sharp contrast to compulsive users, of their insistence on privacy. It is this insistence rather than their rarity that has raised so many questions about their existence (see appendix C).

The interview excerpts cited in chapter 4 on the effects of opiate use reveal more than the users' awareness of how the drug influenced their lives and psyches. These excerpts also indicate the existence of social sanctions and rituals that served to control use. For example, each response concerning special-occasion use shows the subject's recognition of a sanction that might be paraphrased as follows: "I do not take opiates at any old time, like an addict, but only or chiefly on special occasions." Even a user's constant fear of associating with junkies or of becoming addicted implies a sanction against uncontrolled use. In effect, our controlled subjects were able to construct a hierarchy of values—a list of activities that were important to them—and then to assign to opiate use a ranking somewhere within that hierarchy. Unlike compulsive users, they did not put opiates at the top of the list.

> I: In your mind, at what point does an occasional user become an addict?
> R: At that point when he decides he doesn't give a damn, you know.
> I: Could you ever be an addict?
> R: No.

Junkies invariably put opiate use at the top of their hierarchy, as the next subject, an ex-addict, pointed out.

> R: Well, I've used a lot every day in the past. At different times. I mean, I've been strung out at different times.

I: How do you use it now?

R: Well, chipping. I don't know what you mean by that, but chipping in my sense means that you have a little jones [habit]. But using it occasionally means something different to me.

I: What difference is there in your mind between someone who is an occasional user and someone who uses a lot? Is there any?

R: Well, of course there's a difference. When you're strung out, you can't work. I couldn't work. I ended up quitting my job 'cause getting really strung out, getting the dope is a full-time job. But when I was using occasionally, I lived like a normal life, I went to work every day. I decide when to use, who to use with, and what will go on when I use. I have lots of rules about all that, and now I follow them. I think that's quite a big difference from people who use a lot. Tomorrow maybe I'll go to work, or maybe I'll call in. I really haven't made up my mind. If I was strung out right now, I'd be in town tonight copping for a fix tomorrow morning. Or trying to make money. I think that's obvious. Being a junkie's a full-time job. And it's a hard one.

Compulsive users may also have certain sanctions and rituals; but theirs are not so well developed and reinforced or so consistently applied. Booting, mentioned earlier, is one example. Still more important, compulsive users are likely to adhere to and articulate rules that operate to support compulsivity rather than control it. One compulsive user, with great difficulty, would save some heroin so that he could begin each day by getting off.

All of our controlled users were obliged to abide by definite sanctions and rituals in order to keep their drug use under control. Usually they perceived and described their rules and ceremonies simply as safety precautions, that is, as the "correct" way of doing things.

R: I wouldn't do it daily. I didn't let myself do it daily for a period of time.

They did not want to become addicted, and they were keenly aware of that possibility.

R: I'd do it every day for four or five days and then I wouldn't do anything. I wouldn't do anything for about a week, try not to do anything for about a week. Because I was really wary about getting strung out.

I: Would you do it once a day then?

R: Yeah, once a day, sometimes twice a day, if I had enough money to do it. But sometimes I'd pick up like three bags at a time or something like that, and I'd do one and a half one time and then later on that day I'd do another half, or I'd do like two bags and then save the cotton and do the other bag. That sort of thing. But sometimes I didn't do it for a week or two weeks or something like that. Not at all.

I: In order to not get strung out?

R: Yeah. Because I just feel that—I knew that I was close and I could very easily. And there's a real psychological thing to it, you know. It's a real psychological trip. It really is.

Such subjects recognized external responsibilities and used them to keep themselves in line. They were not always aware, however, that the ability to do this differentiated them from addicts.

I: Were you ever an addict?

R: No.

I: If not, how did you avoid becoming an addict?

R: Well, I have responsibilities, you know, and I keep my use down. If I wasn't married and I didn't have my son or my business, then I think my chances of becoming an addict would be very strong.

I: Have you ever felt that you were getting a habit?

R: No.

Even if the following subject was fooling herself about the extent of her interest in opiate use, she was still stating the sanction that such use should not be at the top of her hierarchy.

I: How important is using drugs to you and your friends?

R: Well, it's one of those things that if it's appropriate and it works, it happens. If it's not, it doesn't. I don't really care that much. I doesn't make that much difference to me.

The controlled users' statements repeatedly indicated a rule that they would only go so far or do only so much to get the drug.

R: Some friends up there from Roxbury, the South End, that's how I made my connection.

I: I see. So it was kind of—it was chance, until you got a connection.

R: Yeah. If it was there I would have used it before, but I don't know, I'm not into the bag of chasing things down. If I had to hassle or something, forget it.

The decision as to what was too much opiate use was more conscious and specific with some users than with others.

R: So I just sort of said to myself, "OK, man, you're going to have to make a decision. You're at the point where obviously you're enjoying doing it, you know, but is it more than that? If it is more than that, are you going to continue like this, because if you are, you're going to have to go out and start hustling. You're going to have to find a new source of income because you're not going to make it this way. Or you're going to have to cut down." And when I thought of the change in life style that would be necessary, it just didn't appeal to me at all. I enjoy gettin' high, but I don't want to make it my life.

Money was often cited as a controlling factor:

R: I have one rule that I never, never break. I never spend more than $25 a week on dope.

But the research team was astonished to find how many people could get money for drugs if they moved drug use higher in their scale of values.

I: You said you had controls on yourself to make sure you don't get strung out. What are they?
R: Usually the cost of it is enough to control me because I start thinking about how much money I'm wasting. You know, I'll add up how much money I spend in the month. If it's more than $100 and at the time I'm broke, then I'll just stop for a while and say, "God, what am I doing?" [laugh].

Subjects frequently stated their sanctions as if they were purely expressions of their own personalities.

I: Could you be an addict?
R: No, I don't—because of the experience and everything else, I don't think I could be. I really don't. I couldn't—what is it—I couldn't throw myself into anything that much. Whether it were a good thing, a love affair, or a drug addiction. I don't think I could just put that much energy into any one thing.

But invariably such statements actually expressed sanctions against addiction.

I: What kind of user do you consider yourself?
R: I'm slowin' down a helluva lot. I think I'm becoming more mature. It's like smoking cigarettes. The two cigarettes I just smoked were the only two all day and I enjoyed them, you know, whereas if I had gotten up this morning and smoked up until now, I'd constantly be aware if I was smoking a cigarette, even if I was talkin' to you. I'd sort of feel it burning, you know, in my head and in my hand. And that shows me that my mind is getting older and is learning more, and I'm knowing myself better. I'm slowing down to learn more, to treat myself better. So I don't know—moderate use now is becoming more important. I never want to be a junkie.

And the familiar themes of staying away from junkies and from addiction could also be stated explicitly.

I: What advice would you give a new user?

R: I'd tell them not to hang out with, you know, superfly junkies, you know, pseudo-superfly junkies, and get into that whole scene. Like, don't let it be a jumping-off point for—I'm speaking in terms of, maybe, liberation. You know, so many people say opiates are—keep the people down in the ghetto. Keep the minds asphyxiated. And that's not true. In my case, it's not true. So don't let it become your master. There's some weird saying about that.

Some subjects gave their own special reasons for wanting to establish sanctions about frequency of use.

R: I was only doing it once every week or once every two weeks. The first time I went out and got high, my wife and I could function, but if I get high the second day, it really wipes me out, I'm really dragged out. If I get high on Friday and don't get high on Saturday, I'll remember what I did Friday, but if I get high on Friday and get high on Saturday, when I do come around and straighten out, I really don't know what I did on Friday. That was a major concern of mine, not knowing what I'd done.

In describing how they viewed use, our controlled subjects often sounded as if they were speaking about a more conventional experience, such as alcohol use, rather than about the esoteric experience of using heroin.

I: If you were to tell a new drug user three important things about using, what would they be?

R: I would say that the first thing, the cardinal rule about using drugs, about using anything in life, is to do it in moderation. That's the first thing. Do it in moderation. Now, there are certain nuances of using drugs that I can tell them. There are certain things, little things, that I could explain to them, but basically it's to use it in moderation. I'm not going to say, don't use it, or use it. I'm just going to say, if you're going to use it, use it in moderation. That way you'll never get burned. You're always one step ahead of your dope use.

The following excerpt emphasized that the drug was often used in social interaction:

R: I enjoyed the whole idea of being with people, you know. And getting the drug ready and shooting up.

A general principle or sanction underlying this behavior was the attempt by our subjects to choose using companions whom they knew well.

R: Well, there've been times when I've used heroin around other people that had been using heroin whom I didn't know, and I was sort of apprehensive about it. At first, I don't know, there's something that happens—there's something that's a little apprehensive in the first place about getting off. I prefer to either do it by myself usually, or with that girl.

I: Let's call her Mary.

R: Mary—with her, or with somebody else that I'm quite familiar with that does it. I won't do it with a friend of mine that doesn't have anything to do with it. You know, I'll either go off and do it some place else and then come back, or I won't do it.

Most of our controlled subjects did not use when those who were unsympathetic were around, but occasionally a subject did take that risk.

I: Do you feel more inclined to use drugs when you're alone or when you're with friends?

R: Well, it really doesn't matter much. If I feel like getting high in some manner or another, usually I'll do it independent of my surroundings, unless there are some really deeply personal feelings of the people that I happen to be with, which has happened a couple of times. And then I'll either go get high or I'll say, "OK, I'll see you in a few minutes; I'm just going to go to the bathroom." Something like that, but that doesn't usually happen. It's happened once or twice with a couple of friends of mine, like if I wanted to get high on heroin or something like that.

I: It sounds like it's more likely to happen with heroin.

R: Oh, heroin's the only one. But anything that I shoot, I don't do that in front of somebody else that doesn't do it because, you know, people have feelings about it. And they form opinions and a lot of the opinions I don't think are just. I just sort of feel like, "You like the way I am, so what you don't know won't hurt you." So that's the way it goes.

The research team doubted whether users who took such risks and violated what was an important sanction for others, had the ability to retain control. But the man just quoted apparently did have that ability because he had other sanctions that he observed carefully. The woman quoted next also broke a sanction that most controlled subjects observed—that is, not to use in a group containing both compulsive and controlled users. Her ability to rank her drug use much lower than her work on her hierarchy of values was in itself a controlling sanction.

I: Did you begin getting a habit during the time when you were working the afternoon shift?

R: I guess I came close to getting a habit, but I never really felt sick or anything like that. Like my friend, you know, he used to get up at 8:30 in the morning and get off, you know, while I was home sleeping. I wouldn't see him until about one o'clock in the afternoon and he'd already be high, and he'd say, "Come on, let's go over to my house and we'll do some dope." And I'd turn him down and say, "No, I'm going to go to work; I'll do it tonight," and I went to work. All during the day he might have got off four or five times, plus at night he used to do it a lot more than I did it, so he got a habit. Out of the six or seven people I hung around with, there were only three of them that really had a habit. The others sort of, they'd get off a lot, but they sort of controlled it in a way.

As might be expected, the commitment to earning a living was a crucial factor in limiting drug use.

I: What does your drug use look like?
R: What do you mean by that question?
I: Are you going to continue on weekends, or do it more than weekends? You've been doing it so many years, are you gonna stop doing it weekends, are you gonna do it every day?
R: I have a family to support and everything, so I have to be cool about the whole thing.
I: What do you mean about being cool? In which respect? What do you intend doing?
R: I'm gonna take it easy, don't overdo it. Control myself.

Many subjects had a primary commitment to work that went beyond earning a living. The next subject had not only made that commitment but had also learned to follow the essential rule propounded by Andrew T. Weil in 1972: "Less is more." By exercising care and specificity in the use of his drug, he was able to preserve his enjoyment of it.

R: So I really like working, you know, because if I wasn't working, I'd be drinking all day and smoking all day. And you know, when you do it like that, you don't even really want to. I enjoy it much more just doing it once a night, like having some beers and a few joints. I enjoyed it a lot more than if I had done it all day. Now I have ways to restrict myself. I talk to myself about when to and where to and whom to do it with. It's like having rules about when it's OK.

Controlled users generally valued the status gained from work far more than compulsive users.

R: I've done a lot of work. That's why it's very important that I remain in control, because I've done a lot of work in the union. I'm on the central committee and this would really destroy it. I'd have to take—maybe get thrown out altogether. Or I'd certainly lose my status and my position. I worked hard to get that. I don't think that there'd be any effect on my job, but I'd just as soon not let anyone know.

I: Is that part of the reason that you're interested in discontinuing use?

R: Yeah, very much so. It's the fear of someone else finding out in the union or at work. And I've worked with these people for seven years and been with the union for about eight years. And it's just too much for me to lose. It doesn't counteract the good feeling that I get from the heroin; it just doesn't balance it.

Controlled users also accepted the responsibility that went with work status.

R: Well, of course, nobody in the hospital is supposed to use narcotics. Nobody knew that I use. I never got a habit. I had too much work to do, and there was too much—I felt too much of a commitment to get strung out. But I have chipped for about five years.

The process of learning the technology or techniques of drug use is especially important in the case of the opiates because a mistake in quantity or in shooting up can have disastrous results. Thus beginning users gradually acquire technical sanctions and rituals, though sometimes with frustrating consequences:

I: When you got high, did you fix your own shot or did someone fix it for you and shoot you with it?

R: Most of the time we would fix everything together, and I would just get a smaller amount than they would. At first, someone would have to do it for me, until a while later I learned to do it myself. Because the times we would be around doing that, other guys would be so busy trying to get off themselves and I would be sitting around waiting on them to get through. When they got through, they'd be so high that I'd end up by myself waiting for them to come out of it before I could even get off.

The next response illustrates how fascination with the ritualized technique of use served as a sanction until the subject had greater faith in his own sense of control. It also shows that the same rituals do not have controlling power for junkies.

R: I've always had a fascination with the process of getting off. At my introduction to junkies, I thought maybe they were much more addicted to the ritual than to the substance, to the activity of sitting around, cooking the dope, and the act of injecting it. And when I first did that, it was a fascination with me. But I don't think of it so much any more. It's just merely the most efficient way to use the drug. And I think, you know, at one point there was a great deal of elaboration of tying off and pumpin' in, and all that. I was never really into it. I'm not now.

As the same subject pointed out, learning the techniques and the rules for safety that went with them was not like taking a formal college course.

I: Did whoever it was that showed you give you instructions and do's and don'ts?

R: No, I don't think so. I just think it's things that you pick up from standing on the corner listening to older dudes. Being around older dudes who knew more about it, you just pick up these kinds of things as you go along. Once you get into it, you're gonna pick up all these different things. Say, you run into a person who's dealing, and you've been down here all day trying to cop, and you say, "Well, I'm going to cook it. You all going to come on? Come on over?" You sit down. He says, "Yeah, man, you shouldn't do such-and-such a thing." You pick it up there, you pass it on. Pass it on, person to person.

Even in this casual way the information got transmitted.

R: Sometimes they tell you, don't use this spike here because this type of spike is too big. That's what they call a coke spike. But you shouldn't shoot heroin with that 'cause it puts a big hole in your arm, and all you do is flush blood back and forth. You'd be doing it all day long. Bleeding like a dog. Yeah, and don't get off on dirty needles, or on dirty water or with anything that's not clean or reasonably clean.

Another constant source of anxiety was the question of buying the drug and knowing something about its quality. That concern led many subjects to adopt a sanction requiring companionship when using opiates, and especially when using a fresh supply.

I: Do you have any rules about using drugs?

R: Oh, yeah, private rules. I'm always wary when I cop some heroin and I don't know what the strength is, what it's like. Usually, if you ask the person you buy it from, forget it; I mean, it's always "fantastic." So I'll always take too little. I'll always have to end up getting off again, a second time. If I'm snorting it's different, you can keep on snorting. One of my rules, which I find females have more than males, is never to get off shooting up alone.

Both that subject and the next woman subscribed to the rule of using a little at a time until they knew what the stuff was like. Only rarely did junkies subscribe to such a rule.

I: Are there any things you check on before you use a drug?

R: Well, I usually know who it's coming from, I make sure of that. I just won't buy it from anybody on the street. And I know the amount I'm doing, you know, so I don't do an overdose. If I have to break it up and do it in two or three hits, then that's how I'll do it rather than do it all at once.

Controlled users, again in contrast to compulsive users, did not just look for dope; they looked for a dealer in whom they had confidence.

R: I buy from this one guy who lives near work. I met him kind of by accident after I moved here. I really had no intention of using again.

I: Do you only buy from him?

R: Yes. I trust him in the sense that his stuff is always pretty good. I have no desire to make further connections with other people.

This caution meant that controlled subjects could use only under specific conditions, a restriction that would have been insupportable for an addict.

R: What I don't want is to get messed up by heroin, which for me in a strange city means that I don't really want to meet people who are into dealing drugs—just the way it's structured in this country right now—unless I can meet people who are friends of mine. I've always tried to score from people I can relate to.

Another issue that comes up in any discussion of opiate use is the difference that users claim exists between pharmaceuticals—that is, opiates such as Demerol, morphine, Dilaudid, codeine, or methadone that can be legitimately prescribed—and heroin, which cannot be prescribed in the United States and is reputed to produce a big bang. Until recently most pharmacologists, knowing that heroin breaks down to morphine in the body, denied any difference. But, according to C. B. Pert, G. Pasternak, and S. H. Snyder (1973), the most recent work shows that there is more than one kind of receptor site in the brain for opiates, indicating that the differences in effect claimed by users could have a physiological basis. Generally our subjects lauded the superiority of heroin and were suspicious of pharmaceuticals.

R: I never liked bottled pills too much 'cause there's always something involved that kind of scares me. If some person gives me a pill and I don't know what it is, I won't bother with it. I won't take it. No matter what they say it is. I wouldn't give it to anyone. I'd just either throw it away or try to find out what it is.

Nevertheless, a few subjects expressed a definite preference for pharmaceuticals, and they seemed to use that preference as a sanction. They could have used heroin, but this compulsive user regarded the pharmaceuticals as less dangerous.

I: When did you begin getting interested in heroin?

R: It was just this past summer, right around the beginning of the summer. We hit a car and we got a doctor's bag, and we got a big bottle of liquid morphine and a big bottle of liquid Demerol, a bunch of downs, and stuff, so we did that. We had that for a few weeks, about two, three weeks. And then, just when we ran out—you know, all along we'd been doing cars—we hit another doctor's bag and it had a lot more in it, and this we kept to ourselves and it lasted us about a month, a month and a half. And then after that, I was doing Dilaudids and stuff like that, and Demerol from doctors and such. And you know, all the junkies in town were getting scrips downtown—you could buy them pretty easily— and methadone. And then I was doing heroin at times with my friend, but I didn't really like that because usually it burned, you know. It wasn't worth all the money you put into it when you could get something pharmaceutical.

Some subjects saw the pharmaceuticals as safer because they felt they could be sure what was in them.

R: I prefer using pharmaceutical opiates. You always know the quality and the strength of the drug you're taking. With heroin it's something you can never know.

I: Which do you prefer?

R: I only take Demerols now. The price is about the same as heroin and you know what you're getting.

It is quite possible, of course, that users can be no more certain of what is in a bottle labeled "liquid Demerol" than of what is in a glassine bag that supposedly contains heroin. Certain pharmaceutical pills are clearly marked, but others are not, and counterfeiting has become sophisticated. It is probably true (but only probably) that sellers of pharmaceuticals are less likely to adulterate their product than sellers of heroin. Yet our controlled subjects seemed to have an overriding desire to seek out a safer way to use their prized intoxicant, and this led them to invent interesting and sometimes ingenious methods.

R: For a while I was strictly snortin' and it seemed to be pretty wasteful.

And so I went back to injecting it. But I got to feeling somewhat uptight about whatever impurities there might be in the substance. So what I do now is to dissolve it or drop it in my nose, in solution.

I: Why?

R: The nasal membranes, from what little I know about them, seem to be self-cleaning. There are a lot of capillaries there. Well, anyway, it ups the efficiency. There's very little waste with that method, and I'm not having to stick needles in my arm, which you know is somewhat of a trauma even still—the act of doing it.

This search for rules or sanctions sharply distinguished controlled users from compulsive users.

I: Can you recall being told any particular do's and don't's by whoever showed you how to shoot up?

R: Oh, yeah, I can remember when he told me, "When you tie up to hit yourself, when you get the hit, you loosen it [the tie]. Don't shoot up tied." And they'd always tell me never to shoot in the hand 'cause you'll blow it up. And always, when you cop, if you aren't sure about the person you're getting it from, taste it—make sure what it tastes like.

I: So you can get a sense of whether it's good stuff or bad stuff?

R: You can't sense whether it's good or bad dope. Not whether it's good or bad, just that it's dope or not.

I: So it's yes or no, rather than good or bad.

R: Yeah.

It cannot be overemphasized that the establishment of sanctions about the techniques of heroin use is not a mere question of manners but an important safety precaution.

I: Do you like droppers or syringes?

R: I like syringes; I'll never do another dropper again.

I: Why? What's wrong with a dropper?

R: I had a bad experience with one. I didn't like it. The points seem to be bigger in the droppers, and I don't like to leave a big hole in my arm. With syringes, those gauges are pretty small. And also I didn't like the disadvantage of disposal because I like to boil it, and it's not worth a bad case of anything.

Our subjects' responses also illustrated how rituals develop around sanctions. The rule that hepatitis can be avoided by taking care of the needles is strengthened by the choice of where to use the drug and who tries it first.

I: Do you have any special rules about using drugs?

R: Yeah, I don't like to let people use my needle. My boyfriend lets people use his, but he doesn't catch heaptitis. I'm petrified to get sick again. So I have this whole ritual when I do it, you know, including boiling the water. And I have my own needle, and no one can use it. We have other needles in the house. If someone wants to use a needle, there's a needle for them to use if they want to get off in the house.

I: Do you really get off at home?

R: Yeah, or down at my sister's apartment.

I: Is it usually just your boyfriend and you, or are there other people who join you?

R: Well, there have been times when there have been other people there, watching.

I: Who usually gets off first?

R: Well, if it's me and my boyfriend, he usually gets off first 'cause he doesn't go through all those rituals. He just does it. His body just has a tolerance to it.

Our next subject shifted from injected heroin to orally ingested cough syrup because he was afraid of needles. Nevertheless, he and his wife retained all of the rituals they had developed, including cleaning the house.

R: First of all, when I cop I don't take my Doridens too long before I drink my cough syrup, because the cough syrup is hard to get down. Your mouth becomes dry, you gag. Usually, my house doesn't get cleaned until after I get high.

I: Till after you get high?

R: Right. That's my way, anyway. My wife is the opposite. She'd rather tidy up before. She eats before she drinks her cough syrup. I don't eat. She has to eat. I don't or I do—doesn't make any difference. Usually I don't. I don't eat after I do my cough syrup because my taste buds are affected. After a while, after I get off anyway, the taste is ruined for just about everything, except maybe 7-Up or a Sprite (I have a constant supply at home, a couple of quarts), or orange juice. Another rule is, "Don't go over thirty miles an hour," 'cause I usually wind up being the driver on weekends.

Although the development of sanctions and rituals is usually unconscious—that is, the user believes he is only doing things the way he has to do them to be safe, or the way he likes to do them because that's the way he is—some users can articulate their rules very clearly.

I: Do you have any rules about using drugs? Any personal rules?

R: Most of the time I won't front money for anybody. And every time I have, I regret it. I did get ripped off recently, which really made me mad. Is that what you mean, that type of rule? Let's see, what else? As far as works go, I'm fairly picky about the works that I use.

I: Do you wash them, boil them?

R: Yeah, and I won't use the same works as somebody who's had hep. I don't use an old cotton usually.

I: Are there any things that you check on before you use a drug?

R: I taste it. A lot of good that does [laugh].

I: You test it for quinine or poison or whatever?

R: Yeah. Or coffee. I used to always want to get off first, and now I let other people get off first. Oh, one of my rules is that if I don't know the dope, I won't do a lot at once. Unless somebody else does it first.

By contrast, the next user was unaware that his sound reasoning about safety was indeed a rule.

R: I try not to smoke in bed. I've had some problems in the past with that. Nodded out with a cigarette, woke up with a big burned blanket or a small fire. I'm very super-conscious of that. Some people I used to chum around with used to come over to my house wrecked, and I used to give them a big pail for an ashtry, hanging around their arm, so they wouldn't burn my furniture.

I: I see. I think that's a very good idea.

R: It worked out well. You're allowed one burn and you're thrown out.

I: That was the house rule?

R: I wouldn't tolerate that shit. I gotta pay for it. I think that's about it on the rules. I've never really thought of that, do's and don't's, they just come natural, I guess. I've been doing them so long.

At times the ritualization of the experience began to carry the force of all the sanctions. For the next subject, using opiates at home was not necessarily safe, but it stood for the carrying out of other sanctions.

I: Where in fact do you usually get high? At home?

R: Most of the time at my house. The only time that I don't get high at my house is if I'm with some people that I don't know very well, or some people that I do know and for that reason don't want coming. And if they don't have a place to go for us to get off, then we either get off in the car or a restaurant, or anything like that. And even under those circumstances I'd rather go back to my house and do it. I'd rather just hold off and go back to my house. But under the circumstances if we have something planned, or you know, I'm gonna get looked at weird and they're gonna start wonderin' about me, I just do it the same as everybody else does. Get high, sit around, and listen to some music for a while. Then go out for a ride in a reasonably comfortable, smooth car. And just ride around, and maybe go to the movies. If I have an appetite, go get something to eat.

For the next subject, it was exactly the opposite: going to someone else's house had become ritualized, but it had the same effect of reinforcing the use of sanctions.

R: I go to someone else's house to get off. I'm afraid to use in my own house because it might somehow jeopardize my job. I used to shoot myself up, but I haven't done it in so long that I usually let someone else do it now, especially since I can't afford to have tracks on my arms. So I'd be, you know, going to someone's kitchen, getting a clean glass of water, getting the cooker, getting the matches, you know. Boiling the works, getting off, and hangin' out.

I: What do you do afterwards?

R: Usually play music and talk a lot. It's so pleasant. You just talk a whole lot, and, I guess, you fantasize a lot, you feel like your dreams can come true and you start to think about them and little things don't bother you so much. Usually we make sure the shades are drawn. That's about it. And the door's locked.

The next excerpt points up a number of rituals that many subjects followed to ensure comfortable drug use. Cleaning up in a general way supported the basic rule of cleaning the works. Many subjects reported insisting on a bowel movement before getting off, to minimize discomfort from the opiate-induced constipation. Also, the following subject reported the almost universal awareness that experience with the drug brought considerable control over the high state.

R: I usually make sure everything in the house is in order before I get off. So I can relax afterwards and not have to worry about anything, you know. Clean up a bit, make sure there are no loose ends, so I can relax afterwards. Clean up the bathroom, clean up the works, take a good shit. I used to take the telephone off the hook, but I don't now because I find I can control the high enough now to converse intelligently over the phone if I get a call. Get out my favorite records. Make sure the doors are locked.

The choice of a favorite time of day in which to get high, which varied greatly from subject to subject, commonly reinforced the method of getting high.

R: If I have someone here, I'd prefer to get high reasonably soon after I get up. I eat breakfast, sit around straight for a while, get a few things out of the way that I don't have to be troubled with later on. I'd just as soon get high during the daytime because that way I feel it longer. I'm not tired. You know, I'll get high anytime. But if I get high at nighttime, then I hate to go to sleep because I hate to waste the high 'cause it's so expensive. So I end up staying up most of the night or finally just falling asleep 'cause I'm tired.

Choosing a time to get high was not only a ritual. Those controlled subjects who used fairly regularly had to have strong and decisive rules about when to get high in order to prevent the drug from taking over their lives.

I: Is your weekend high confined to Friday, or is it Friday and Saturday, or—

R: Fridays and Saturdays. And Sundays I usually sleep it off. Every once in a while I'll do something on a Sunday too. If I plan on not going to work, I'll get it three days.

I: So that it's a planned thing. If you know you're not going to go in to work, if you have a holiday, or if you decide you're going to take a holiday, you feel free to get high on Sundays?

R: Yeah.

I: Otherwise, you—

R: Fridays and Saturdays, always.

The next excerpt illustrates not only that decisiveness was needed to keep use in bounds but also that this quality differentiated controlled from compulsive users. Although the subject was a relatively heavy user, he could leave the drug on a shelf for long periods of time.

I: Did you ever have any periods of heavy use or light use?

R: Well, from what they tell me, I have a very high tolerance, so on weekends I'll do quite a bit of it. And you know, other than on weekends I'll do it. Sometimes I'll do it from Friday night right through until Sunday night. Other times I'll just do it Friday night, but just about every weekend I'll do it now. That way a buy will last me for months.

The opulence reported by the next subject—evidenced in buying half an ounce of heroin and half an ounce of cocaine—seemed potentially dangerous. But as she pointed out, she kept use on a social basis so that the one buy lasted a year. Such behavior would have been utterly impossible for a compulsive user.

R: But one time when we did heroin it was very interesting. We had a huge round table and they put a set of works next to each plate. And we had like half an ounce of heroin and half an ounce of cocaine. There was a lot of dope around—we made a great big buy. And we went to dinner and it was an extremely social thing. It wasn't like an addict in the bathroom or in the hallway. It was a lot of fun, and we did it again and again that season.

6

Personality and Social Learning: The Theory of Controlled Drug Use

THE RELATIONSHIPS AMONG PERSONALITY (SET), SOCIAL STRUCTURE (SETting), and drug initially seem obvious. Everyone knows that psychic states vary greatly, that the environment affects them, and that drugs may make a tremendous impact on them. But these relationships, though easy to grasp in theory, are surprisingly difficult to accept as practical realities. Most of us are accustomed to thinking of drugs in a medical context, where they are used for the treatment of specific conditions. Thus we wrongly assume that the effect of a drug is constant—that it will have the same effect on different patients with the same condition, and moreover that its effects on the same patient will not vary over time. The physician is not eager to dispel this belief because he wishes to maximize the therapeutic effect of the drug he has prescribed.

In spite of this medical aura surrounding drugs, most drug experts have come to accept the importance of set and setting in influencing drug effects. Those who are not experts can perceive the significance of the drug-set-setting combination by examining their own or others' experiences with alcohol. The effects of alcohol vary from person to person and over time: there are happy drinkers, morose drinkers, belligerent drinkers, and flirtatious drinkers. Sometimes alcohol may be a relaxant (the martini after the hard day at the office) and sometimes it may act as a stimulant (the first drink at the party). Often it serves as a mood accelerator, deepening depression or heightening euphoria in accordance with preexisting conditions. At times it releases inhibitions, and at other times those who have already put aside their inhibitions will take a drink or two to provide themselves with a socially acceptable alibi. From the standpoint of pharmacology, alcohol suppresses the action of certain inhibiting centers in the brain and can have no result inconsistent with this action. Yet the range of actual effects in terms of both behavioral change and psychic state is extremely wide. It may be precisely this wide range of possibilities that makes alcohol such a popular drug. Admittedly, these eclectic effects serve my theoretical stance by emphasizing the importance of the interaction of drug, set, and setting.

The Psychological Viewpoint

The investigation of this complex three-way interaction is a comparatively recent phenomenon, even though the existence of psychic disturbances and varying psychic states was recognized long ago. Not until the end of the last century did a technique appear that made possible a systematic theoretical study of personality and personality disturbance: the technique of psychoanalysis developed by Sigmund Freud and his followers. Whatever one may believe about its therapeutic efficacy, this technique permits a thorough study of the individual, tracing the growth of personality structure from the earliest motives and relationships and showing the continuity between early development and later behavior. Freudian studies of individual lives have opened up vistas of perception that have not only influenced every aspect of psychology but have become embedded in the medicine, art, literature, sociology, and even politics of Western culture.

THE IMPACT OF FREUD. Most Westerners of the late twentieth century are aware—some would argue hyper-aware—of the intensity and influence of the inner, often unconscious preoccupations. A contemporary writer would not, like Ruskin, discuss in his diary his impotence and sexual dreams as if, like pneumonia, they had been visited upon him. Much more typical of this century was the amused public reaction to President Richard Nixon's parapraxes (slips of the tongue), as when he said in 1960, with his wife at his side, "I can't stand pat," or when he called his colleague and running mate, Henry Cabot Lodge, with whom he had been having disagreements, "my distinguished opponent." Such slips drew guffaws from the audience and made the front page of the *New York Times*. The twentieth century, indeed, can accurately be characterized as the century of individual psychology, the "I" years (Lasch 1979).

In the light of Freud's impact on Western thinking it is not surprising that the rapid increase of illicit drug use in the 1960s (the so-called drug revolution) evoked not just public condemnation but the question, "Why do they do it?" or "What makes them do it?" And it is understandable that in attempting to answer these questions professionals as well as the public turned first to the deep-seated and usually unconscious personal motivations. Before the drug revolution the theorists and clinicians who studied drug users and abusers had interpreted drug problems as stemming from extensive personality disturbances (the so-called addictive personality) (Zinberg 1975). At that time such users probably made up a far greater precentage of those who became addicted than they do today. The recent shift away from the all-importance of set to a recognition of the significance of both set and setting seems to be part of an ongoing social-historical process that had its beginning during the drug revolution itself. This process was set in motion in the 1960s, when people who were quite different from the earlier drug takers started to use illicit drugs. Weil and I with Nelsen became aware of it in 1968 when we were conducting our controlled experiments with marihuana users. The so-called chronic users in that study, those who had begun smoking marihuana before 1965, were more anxious, more antisocial, and more likely to be dysfunctional—therefore closer in spirit to the handful of musicians, "Bohemians," blacks, and browns who had used marihuana before the drug revolution—than were the naive subjects who were just beginning use in 1968. By the late 1960s, we found, marihuana use was being experienced as a much more normative choice than it had been before 1965. And by the early 1970s the change had become even more evident. The controlled marihuana users described in the present study (exemplified by Michael in chapter 2) could not possibly have been driven to drug use by deep-seated and self-destructive unconscious motives.

The situation with heroin is more complicated. Since the 1920s most heroin users have been low-skilled members of the working class, coming from poverty-stricken backgrounds and precarious family situations. Early studies of these users focused on the impact of adverse social conditions on early personality development, thus taking both setting and set into account. It is questionable whether these studies demonstrated that such social conditions were the underlying cause of drug problems; in any case, the immediate object of study was the bitter, deprived personalities that came from such homes. And material from these earlier studies is still being used to show a direct relationship between certain kinds of severe personality disturbances and drug use.

PERSONALITY THEORIES. The viewpoint that drug use can be explained primarily in terms of personality is based on one or another of the theories of early development elaborated by the followers of Freud. Although, in thinking about very early development, it is extremely difficult to distinguish between genetic predispositions and early postnatal influences, dynamic personality theorists postulate that for a variety of reasons some people, during the process of growing up, find it more difficult than others to deal with certain powerful, primitive impulses. The histories of a few of the compulsive opiate users we interviewed for the present study are typical of what has been called an "addictive personality." These individuals had often been in trouble in grade school because of various problems, some of which appeared to be school phobias.

They had begun to smoke cigarettes heavily before the age of twelve, and they had had consistent and vicious struggles with parents or other family members. Sometimes they had had early obesity problems or had been runaways. They had begun to have trouble with the police in their early teens, when they had also started using alcohol and any other intoxicating substances they could find. They had used these intoxicants to excess, which had led in turn to other troubles indicating lack of control, such as auto accidents, expulsion from school, loss of jobs, or getting into fights. Finally, they had concentrated on one drug, usually heroin but sometimes a barbiturate, and had used it often and compulsively. A few of the compulsive users we interviewed and assigned to a comparison group fitted this general description, as do some of the addicts I have seen in treatment settings.

Users with such histories have led many clinicians and theorists to conclude that drug use is related in an almost one-to-one fashion to the user's disordered personality. By delving into any subject's past, it has been easy for such investigators to obtain a more elaborate history indicating varying degrees of early trauma that might have led to such disorder. One obvious trauma would be the loss of one's mother (through early death, desertion, mental illness, or some form of addiction), or the loss of one's father, or the breakup of the family structure. Though lacking the more overt evidence of early trauma, including physical difficulties, a subject might reveal a deep sense of being unloved or rejected, usually by the mother but at times by various "significant others" (Mead 1934). Such powerful, unfulfilled longings for love, for acceptance as a worthwhile and lovable human being, and for a sense of basic trust in another or in one's self might lead to overwhelming feelings of desolation and rage, over which the individual had been unable to develop reliable internal controls.

Some personality theorists (Knight 1937; Rado 1958; Rosenfeld 1960; Wishnie 1971) have assumed that intoxicants can "help" people with these rending conflicts by providing the surcease from frustration that had not been provided by the absent or unloving mother. These theorists see the users' impulses to take in heroin, alcohol, or other drugs as a translation of those unfulfilled early longings or "needs," to use current parlance. Other theorists (Kaplan & Wieder 1974; Khantzian 1975; Khantzian, Mack & Schatzberg 1974; Krystal & Raskin 1970) have suggested that intoxicants, especially heroin, are used as anodynes to the rage resulting from excessive frustration: if internal controls over these feelings are poor or nonexistent, the drug will act as a tranquilizer. In that case the decision to use drugs is an attempt at self-medication—a misguided effort to adapt to the world and reduce the destructive consequences of one's poorly controlled feelings.

While the earliest psychoanalytic writers on the relation between personality and addiction drew a fairly straightforward picture of unrelieved impulse leading to intoxicant use, later writers have presented a far more complex thesis. In attempting to explain how unrelieved impulse may lead to disorganized and poorly functioning internal psychic structure, a weak self-image, and lack of self-esteem, they have emphasized the process of identification (or lack of it) with reasonable parental figures. Having observed, particularly in the case of alcoholics, that families with significant addicted members breed more addicts, they have theorized that unrelieved desires for acceptance and closeness can be expressed by attempting to be like the desired person, or "object." It is as if unconsciously choosing to be like the person will ensure *being* liked by that person.

This drama, which is usually played out entirely within the intrapsychic realm, is not recognized by the individual, and consequently the mere suggestion that he is drinking in order to feel close to an alcoholic father he now hates would be anathema to him. Yet most of the direct personality theorists attach great importance to the enormous guilt that arises in the individual, particularly the addict, because of the raw and uncontrolled quality of his impulses. Such theorists view the addict's sense of guilt as the cause of much of his self-destructiveness and difficulty with self-care.

Personality theorists use a variety of forms and terms. Today there is great interest in Heinz Kohut's concept that each person's narcissism develops in a more or less separate line from other aspects of his personality structure. Using Kohut's theory, intoxicant use can be described as a function of the "self-system." The sufferer from a narcissistic personality disorder uses an intoxicant in an attempt to avoid directly expressing his desire to merge with a longed-for, idealized self-object, and by this avoidance to keep from reactivating the possibility of a traumatic rejection. Instead, within the self-system, the sufferer is able to function at the high moment of intoxication as if he himself were the object he longs for and idealizes. But when intoxication has receded, that intoxicated aspect of the self has a different function in the self-system; it is more likely to represent the despised, unlovable self. Since this debased conceptualization of self touched off the search for a merger with an idealized self in the first place, it is logical, according to this theory, that the compulsive desire to reexperience intoxication should quickly recur.

There are many other more or less sophisticated variations on these psychoanalytically oriented themes, as well as a variety of behavioral-learning theories, which fall outside the scope of this study. Though their forms of expression differ, the purpose of all these theories is to explain intoxicant problems as principally a function of personality—to trace, as was stated recently, the "developmental stages" as well as those "factors [that were useful] in countering the rage and depression that had to be defended against through drugs and alcohol" (Zaleznik & Schwaber 1976). And although little writing has appeared that specifically utilizes personality theory to explain controlled use,

personality theorists would doubtless explain the *lack* of addiction under the
same rubric. For instance, they would see Michael's capacity to control his use
of marihuana (chapter 2) as having been engendered by a coherent early development and good early relationships with significant others, a condition that
would lead to a personality structure well defended against the impulses of
desolation and rage and well equipped with internal controls to deal with those
impulses if they should get out of hand.

SET-SETTING INTERACTION. As shown in a recent compendium entitled
Theories on Drug Abuse (Lettieri, Sayers & Pearson 1980), the complexity of
drug use by any individual within a given social milieu is appreciated by more
theorists today than it was a few years ago. This move away from thinking almost
exclusively in personality terms jibes with my own position that both individual
personality structure and social setting must be included in any coherent explanation of the way in which the social learning process makes controlled intoxicant use possible. But how can the interaction of set and setting be explained in
psychoanalytic terms? Traditionally, Freudian theorists have been concerned
not with the effect of the social setting on the individual but with the impact of
the basic, inborn "instinctual drives" and the individual's need to gain control
over them in order to achieve a manageable social existence. Freudians have
continued to think in terms of these primitive, biologically given drives operating out of a core substratum of the personality that was formed during early
development, with emphasis on the management of the aggressive drive (self-
preservation) and the sexual drive (preservation of the race). They have assumed that, because these drives are universal givens transmitted through a
family environment and because the personality structures that are developed
to control them are relatively immutable, the consideration of social structure
has a low priority. They have, of course, seen and explicated in great detail the
significance of the child's early years and early relationships, but they have
failed to emphasize the continuing significance of the broader physical and
social environment.

Yet two of the constructs of psychoanalytic theory—relative ego autonomy
(REA) and average expectable environment (AEE)—which have been much
used in other contexts, can be very helpful in explaining how social learning
produces limited changes in ego structure and functioning. REA, a concept first
put forward by Heinz Hartmann (1939), signifies the capacity of the ego to
balance and synthesize the inputs from the instincts with those that arise from
the press of the environment (Gill & Klein 1964; Rapaport 1958; Zinberg 1975),
while AEE refers to the kind of physical and social environment in which REA
can be delineated and maintained by the individual (Gill & Klein 1964;
Rapaport 1959, 1960).

These two constructs have had an enormous impact on post-Freudian psychoanalytic theory. And although Freud's followers have never parted with the notion of instincts, their interest in the functions of the ego and its capacity to adapt to change in the environment has increased. Edward Bibring (1954), for example, includes the adaptive capacity in his list of six ego functions: perceptual, discharge, executive, mastery of anxiety, sensorial, and adaptive. In addition, other theorists (Rapaport 1958; Zetzel 1949; Zinberg 1975) dealing with the metapsychological level have included the ability to adapt among the following five capacities of the mind: the adaptive, the dynamic, the economic (mental energies, not quantified), the developmental (a genetic developmental sequence), and the structural (the coherent mental structures, or the id, ego, and superego). These five capacities of the mind, including the capacity to adapt to the social environment, are seen as biological givens that are based in the individual and are potentially mutable.

Because no single biological structure—that is, no individual human being—can be considered infinitely adaptive, the individual's capacity to adapt is assumed to function only within a reasonable range of experience. This range is determined after birth by the inputs of the physical and social environment. Of course, individuals with different biological endowments deal with their environmental opportunities differently; they develop different personality structures and adaptive capacities (REA), which function within the range permitted by their particular environment (AEE). For instance, a child growing up in the jungle will have different skills and capacities from a child growing up in the city; while the jungle child is learning about edible wild plants, the city child will be learning not to touch hot stoves. This comparative example is obviously only qualitative; the differences it specifies are not scientifically demonstrable or quantitatively measurable. Like the concepts of AEE and REA, which it is intended to illustrate, it merely suggests the types of differences and limitations that arise for human individuals of different inheritances living in different physical and social environments.

Relative Ego Autonomy

Psychoanalytic theorists who are particularly concerned with ego psychology, most notably David Rapaport, recognize that changes throughout life in not only the physical situation but also the social situation, including social setting and social attitudes, threaten ego autonomy and continually force the ego to reach a new balance or homeostasis.

RAPAPORT'S THEORY.   Rapaport began his work on ego autonomy by distinguishing the effects of the environment on living and nonliving matter.

Nonliving matter, he wrote, cannot escape the total impact of the environment, and the results of the interaction are invariant and statistically predictable (Rapaport 1958). This is not true of living matter, however, in spite of the claims of some psychoanalytic theorists that inner forces are strong enough to nullify the effect of the environment and thus make human behavior predictable.

Rapaport developed his argument by referring to the opposing positions of Berkeley and Descartes. In the Berkeleian view, man is totally independent of the environment and totally dependent on inner forces and drives. He need have little concern for the external world since it is "created" by inherent forces. The cartoon psychiatrist who is shown asking someone who has been hit by a car, "How did you cause this to happen to you?" is taking an exaggerated clinical view of this position. Descartes, on the contrary, saw man as a clean slate upon which experience writes. Man is totally dependent upon and thus in harmony with the outside world, and totally independent of, or autonomous from, internal desires. In essence, Cartesians, like some behaviorists, view such drives and the unconscious that supposedly contains them as nonexistent.

In explaining the factors that enable the ego to maintain its relative autonomy, Rapaport accepted neither the Berkeleian nor the Cartesian view of man. He reasoned that in order to understand how the ego, whose functions determine and delineate a sense of self, remains relatively autonomous and copes with the demands of the external environment as well as the instinctual drives, one must consider both of these elements and their interactions. On the one hand, the primitive drives provide the ego with the energy to prevent man from becoming a stimulus-response slave. As examples Rapaport referred to the man who did not march in step to an enthralling military band because he was deep in thought, and to Orwell's protagonist in *1984* (1949), who was saved, at least temporarily, from the press of his overwhelming environment by falling in love. On the other hand, the ready availability of a constant stream of stimuli from the environment permits the ego to mediate and moderate these drives by sustaining the primary ego apparatuses—motor capacity, thinking, memory, the perceptual and discharge thresholds, and the capacity for logical communication. Here Rapaport referred to the story of the great king who had been told by his wise men and phrenologist that Moses was cruel, vain, and greedy. Upon finding Moses gentle, wise, and compassionate, the king planned to put his seers to death. Moses demurred, saying, "They saw truly what I am. What they could not see was what I have made of it."

We constantly forget, wrote Rapaport, that what we permit ourselves to perceive of as external reality is an ego function. The soldier, the artist, the dendrologist, and the botanist see the same tree, but each perceives it differently. Moreover, the threshold at which each one discharges his response varies in accordance with his age, personality, ethnicity, social circumstance, and other factors that the ego collates. External reality also nurtures the secondary ego apparatuses, such as competence, cognitive organizations, values, ideals, and a mature conscience, and allows these characteristics to become successfully estranged from the original drive functions. Of all the gross misconceptions about psychoanalytic theory, one of the most egregious is the notion that the sadistic factors that led a little boy, for instance, to tear off a fly's wings propelled him later into a surgical career. In that reductionistic explanation many positive qualities are ignored—his manual dexterity, intellectual capacity, diligence, and regard for the health of others—which had been recognized, nurtured, and rewarded by many significant others, eventually including his patients, and which enabled him to choose a medical career, to complete it successfully, and to use the surgical knife without guilt.

Thus the relationship between the ego's relative autonomy from the id and its relative autonomy from the environment is one of interdependence. To put it another way, the autonomy that Rapaport postulated is always relative, always dependent upon the balance between the inner drives and the outer environment. When these two forces are nearly equally balanced, the ego remains relatively autonomous from both. But if the balance is upset—if the drives take precedence over the stimulus nutriment flowing in from the environment, or if external stimuli overpower the natural instincts—the ego's ability to function is endangered.

When the drives are at peak tension, as in puberty, the ego's autonomy from the id is in jeopardy. Although adolescents try to combat their tendency to subjectivity, seclusiveness, and rebellion by the external reality-related converse of these qualities—intellectualization, efforts at total companionship, and distance from primary objects—it is an unequal and often painful struggle, one that may be played out in part by experimenting with intoxicants. The ego's autonomy from the id can also be disrupted when the balancing input from external reality is minimized. The stimulus-deprivation experiments (Bexton, Heron & Scott 1954; Heron, Bexton & Hebb 1953; Heron, Doone & Scott 1956; Lilly 1956) confirm that when individuals are deprived of the normal, varied stream of external stimuli they become autistic and suffer from magical fantasies, disordered thought sequences, disturbed reality testing, primitive defenses, and poor memory. When the subjects of those experiments were in a state of reduced ego autonomy from the id, they were subjected to such an insistent stream of bizarre instructions, including the order to believe in witchcraft, that their lifelong convictions were shaken. So shaken was their hold on external reality that two weeks after the experiment, when asked about witchcraft, subjects continued to display uncharacteristic doubts about the invalidity of magic. This instructional part of the experiment demonstrated the interaction between the two guarantors of ego autonomy. It showed that when stimuli from the environment were minimized, resulting in a loss of ego autonomy to the id, the ego became an easy prey to the press of the external environment.

REA may also be impaired by conditions that supply frightening forms of stimulus nutriment. In the concentration camps, where external factors maximized the individual's sense of danger and aroused fears and neediness, the primitive drives, instead of acting as guarantors of autonomy from the environment, prompted many to surrender to it. During the stimulus-deprivation experiments, too, the replacement of varied stimuli by streams of official instructions gave those instructions power and engendered belief in their authenticity. It is not surprising that Rapaport used George Orwell's *1984* as a text, for this work describes in clinical detail how the deliberate upsetting of the balance between drives and environmental stimuli can reduce REA and turn individuals into stimulus-response slaves. If human beings are to maintain their sense of identity, their values, ideologies, and orderly thought structures, they need to receive constant environmental support for their existing verbal and memory structures.

Rapaport did not limit his discussion to the ego. He showed that the superego is even more dependent on consistent stimulus nutriment. The so-called convention syndrome—the situation in which respectable men and women who are removed from their usual routines and social relationships behave in an impulsive and uncontrolled manner—illustrates how heavily the rulings of conscience depend on social structure. When the usual constraints are left behind and the individual faces a new, short-term environment, the balance between id and environment is upset and the superego becomes subservient to the id. Thus the sailor in a strange port either must limit his exposure to the new environment or must find acceptable interests to balance his sense of alienation and depression, which might otherwise lead to some form of debauchery.

THE HEROIN ADDICT. An understanding of REA with its dependence upon the balancing inputs of id and environment sheds a good deal of light on the mental state and behavior of the heroin addict. Obviously the addict has lost or been cut off from many sources of stimulus nutriment. He is alienated from his family and friends, or if such relationships still exist they center on acrimonious pleadings that he give up drugs. Moreover, his inputs from the larger society, which regards him as a deviant, give him an entirely negative view of himself. His only other environmental input consists of the limited litany of his drug-using group: "Have you copped? When? Where? Was it good? What do I need to cop? What if I can't? Who got busted? Will I get busted?" The addict, in short, resides in a relatively stimulus-deprived environment. His dependence on whatever is left of the environment is further heightened by his need to continue coherent relationships with the few remaining external objects. He suffers constantly from doubts about his ability to maintain such relationships, and he readily accepts society's condemnation. This holding to what remains of the external environment maximizes the ego's autonomy from the id, but it does so at the cost of impairing the ego's autonomy from the environment by minimizing the input of those affective and ideational signals that usually regulate judgment and decision.

Thus the addict is caught on the horns of an environmental dilemma. His dependence on environmental support is increased by his need to cop, but his access to that support is curtailed by the deviant label society has pinned on him. At the same time, the addict's drive structures, derived from his primitive instincts, are kept at peak tension by his desire for gratification from the drug, as well as by his deep fear of the result of being unable to get it, the withdrawal syndrome. He is at the mercy of primitive impulses and of an overwhelming sense of neediness that invades or, rather, blocks out the capacity to perceive and integrate "objective" reality. Filled with doubts, he gullibly responds to those in the external environment who offer schemes that promise magical succor, and he continues to seek the drug that will provide relief.

When REA is upset, the ego tends to seek a new homeostasis. In the case of the drug addict, the new balance is likely to be relatively inflexible and to have a slow rate of change. This balance is established under very unfavorable conditions. At the same time that the input from both the id and the environment is insufficient or distorted, the drive structures are making variable but insistent demands for drug gratification, and the ego is struggling, as the clinical evidence from our subjects has shown, to retain whatever level of ego functioning is still left to it.

This internal struggle is the principal reason for the rigidity therapists have found in their work with addicts, both in and out of methadone clinics. The addict's new homeostasis of ego functioning cannot easily absorb fresh stimulus nutriment, not even an input so neutral and sustaining as that of a reasonable therapeutic relationship. In fact, the therapeutic relationship is particularly difficult for the addict to tolerate because it is *intended* to be at variance with the addict's usual relationships and to make his reliance on selective perception, quick repression, projection, and denial more difficult. All of these intrapsychic defenses are used by the addict to avoid coming in contact with perceptions, affects, and ideas at variance with his acceptance of himself as an addict and with the internal state he has derived from that acceptance. This is in distinct contrast to the psychological state of controlled users. Yet, as long as addicts continue to be classified as deviants, they will find it extremely hard to see themselves in any other light. And as long as their relationships with the external world continue to supply only restricted stimulus nutriment, they will probably continue to block most affective environmental inputs that are not oriented toward drug gratification and their accepted view of themselves.

The psychological state (set) of the addict, which resembles that of the subjects of the stimulus-deprivation experiments, is reminiscent of the regressive state described in the discussion of REA. In this state—the result of the ego's inability to maintain its relative autonomy from either the id or the external environment—the barriers between the ego processes and the id processes become fluid. Images, ideas, and fantasies based on primary-process thinking (according to Freud, thinking from the instinctual depths of the mind) rise to consciousness; and interest in magic, belief in animism, generalized unfounded suspiciousness, and acceptance of extremely childish rhetoric become regressively active in ego functioning. As the individual is forced to rely more and more on primitive defenses, his sense of voluntariness and his inner control over his actions tend to disappear.

The addict often seems to be vaguely aware of his own primitive responses, but he cannot bring them into consciousness long enough to question them: not only does his ego struggle to retain its existing capacity to function, no matter how unsatisfactorily, but his primitive feelings usually seem so real that he is unable to transform them into secondary-process thinking. His primary-process responses are not unlike those of the LSD user of the 1960s, particularly the user whose trip experience had little in common with his previous social and psychological experiences. By the 1970s, however, the changing social setting—the appearance of well-defined social groups that were knowledgeable about tripping—enabled the user to respond in a secondary-process way (Zinberg 1974).

Rapaport's writings on REA, which make it clear that the impact of the social setting on ego development is an ongoing process, tend to support my view that continued personality development and social setting are interdependent. Just as REA rests on a relatively stable but continually shifting balance between internal forces (which change at different life stages) and an external environment (which is constantly in the process of change), so the relationship between personality and social setting involves a relatively stable but continually shifting balance. Changes in that balance often result in changed social attitudes toward particular patterns of behavior. Thus behavior patterns that were once perceived as deviant and as the source of disruptive emotional conflicts may gradually become socially acceptable and even normative.

Average Expectable Environment

Rapaport's explication of Hartmann's concept of REA depended upon and included the equally important construct of AEE: the idea that a consistent, regular relationship between the individual and his social environment guarantees him a coherent series of mental functions free from domination by primitive impulses. This construct makes it possible for psychoanalytic theory to take account of the role of social change—the changing attitudes and behaviors of the social setting—in the development of that subtle complex of self-awareness that is variously called a mature ego, an identity, the self, a sense of self-actualization.

SOCIAL CHANGE AND PERSONALITY DEVELOPMENT. Although much of the writing of psychoanalytic theorists seems to imply that the early social environment alone constitutes the AEE, it is apparent that changes in the environment continue to affect ego development throughout life, and further that the kind of environment experienced by the infant may change from one generation to the next, if not from one decade to the next. Take, for example, the subject of breast feeding. One decade, breast feeding is out of fashion; the next, it is in fashion. And whether it is out or in makes a marked difference to the child in his earliest relationship with his environment.

Up to now the study of the influence of social change on personality development has not demanded full attention because the investigation of the way in which individuals master their early primitive drives and longings has in itself been sufficiently preoccupying. And the view that environmental change does *not* contribute to the process of essential personality development contains some seeds of truth. Personality has only a few basic building blocks, which include only a few fundamental affects (feelings); and the essential structure, whether based on genetic predispositions, early experience, or early introjections (internalizations of significant others)—and it is impossible to differentiate these—is laid down very early. Therefore, social change has a greater impact on what happens *after* the basic structure of personality has been established than on the original formation of that structure. The building blocks are in place; the cornerstone cannot be moved. But considerable rearrangement of the secondary structure is possible, on both a short-term (consciousness change) basis and a long-term (personality modification) basis. Each person, as a result of his genetic predispositions, early development, and social circumstances, has available a limited range of ego functions that can become relatively autonomous. But the social setting determines exactly which of these perceptions, discharges, and capacities are most likely to achieve REA. The active process of social learning will affect different personality structures differently, but there will always be a balance between the inner drives and the outer environment.

It is also true that the opportunities offered by the environment for the expression of individual psychological states in certain forms of behavior may change in ways that affect the emerging personality fundamentally and irre-vocably. For example, social attitudes toward sex changed so rapidly in the United States after the Second World War that a period of even a decade or two made an appreciable difference in individual sexual behavior. For the sake of illustration, consider the hypothetical cases of three sexually inhibited twenty-year-old women, the first living in the 1950s, the second in the 1970s, and the third in the 1960s. (The contrasts presented in this illustration are sharpened by not following chronological order.)

The woman of the 1950s experienced psychological conflicts about sex but remained aloof from sexual experience until custom forced her into a predict-able marriage and a sharply defined sexual role. The similarly inhibited twenty-year-old of the 1970s behaved very differently, entering into a variety of sexual experiences before marriage, because as an adolescent she had internalized a more permissive set of social mores that permitted some relaxation of her superego. In spite of underlying inhibitions and doubts, she was pushed by peer pressure, technological "advances," and the changing value system into a more direct expression of sexuality. Finally, the twenty-year-old woman of the 1960s behaved differently from both her counterparts. During her adolescence she had experienced far greater anxiety about pregnancy than the girl of the 1970s: the Pill had not yet been accepted, and she had not received much information about sexual activity and homosexuality from the media. She there-fore felt threatened by the new social attitudes, and although she experimented with premarital sex, she experienced psychological conflicts akin to those of the woman of the 1950s.

The different forms of sexual behavior manifested by these three women can best be explained in environmental terms. Viewed psychologically, all three were conflicted about sexuality, but each woman's behavior reflected the mores of her time. The social inputs of each decade delineated the AEE and brought about the ego development that enabled each woman to adapt to the new situation.

TECHNOLOGICAL AND SOCIAL-PSYCHOLOGICAL CHANGE. Social-psy-chological change is often touched off by technological change—for the women of the 1960s and 1970s by the development of the Pill. Technological change occurs obviously and relatively rapidly and is therefore quickly transmitted through the process of social learning. By contrast, social-psychological change takes place slowly and is more subtle, but it is no less critical to personality development. Two of the best examples of technological change and its social-psychological consequences come from the area of drug use.

The development of drug technology has had two major effects on drug use in America. First, technological advances, which have resulted in a proliferation of new, powerful drugs and the rediscovery of older ones, have vastly increased the number and availability of psychotropic substances. Some of these are concentrates, produced by extracting the active ingredients from natural drugs: heroin, for example, was derived long ago from opium. Others are synthetics, such as LSD, which are powerful substances but have no previous history of use. Several observers, notably Andrew T. Weil (1972) and James V. DeLong (1974), have stressed the importance of this first effect of new drug technology.

But the second effect is much more significant. Although it is not generally recognized, the fact is that the rise of interest in the consciousness-changing illicit drugs was preceded by a rise of interest in the consciousness-changing *licit* drugs. Until the 1950s, medical practitioners had few psychoactive substances, and those they did have, such as the barbiturates and the amphetamines, had only very general depressant or stimulant effects. Before the late 1950s, literally tons of phenobarbital were prescribed each year in the hope that this drug would reduce the edge of anxiety for some individuals. Then, quite suddenly, the phenothiazines, the tricyclics, the monoaminooxidase inhibitors, the benzodiazepines, and other new drugs appeared. Each of these new classes of antipsychotic, antidepressant, or antianxiety medications spawned numerous variants and combinations intended to achieve specific psychoactive changes for many types of people. It would not be going too far to say that the entire community mental-health movement and the press for deinstitutionalization of the enormous state hospital systems could not exist were it not for the phenothiazines.

Is it any surprise, then, that in a society made aware of the existence of many substances that might change consciousness for the better, some individuals have begun to take a new look at all sorts of drugs, both licit and illicit? Recently I appeared on a panel with a prominent psychopharmacologist who was describing the successful treatment of a complex case of mixed paranoia, depression, and anxiety. The doctor explained that by carefully titrating a mixture of a phenothiazine, a tricyclic, and a benzodiazepine, he had been able to help the patient significantly. In reply I said that I had just returned from Washington where I had heard young men in important political positions describing their daily lives: long hours of hard, intense work followed by a round of official cocktail parties. They said they enjoyed the tension-relaxing drinks; and the parties, attended by Congressmen, Congressional aides, political appointees, and other Washington-based power brokers, gave them an opportunity to do business. Later in the evening, in order to cut through the alcohol effect and get back to work, they found a little sniff of white powder just the ticket. Then, when they finally reached home exhausted, they relaxed by puffing on a thin cigarette filled with brown material, called a joint. "Was this careful titration of *illicit* drugs," I asked the panel members, "very different, except in the degree of emotional difficulty, from the medication regimen described by the psychopharmacologist?"

THE IMPACT OF SOCIAL LEARNING. For individuals with certain kinds of personality structure, such as those who are apprehensive about controls or those who are morally opposed to anything illicit, the presence in the AEE of licit consciousness-changing drugs has not weighed heavily enough to change the perception of drug-using behavior. For others with a different personality structure this social input has made a difference. It is clear, for example, that in the case of those who chose to use or not to use marihuana after its use became widespread, the nonusers were no longer necessarily the good guys, although plenty of decent, reliable, interesting, and adventurous youngsters decided that marihuana was not for them. And, conversely, those who chose to use were no longer necessarily the bad guys, although plenty of pleasure-seeking, anxiety-avoiding, passive youngsters decided to use.

The impact of social learning is not confined to behavior. It also affects internal perception and the capacity to activate internal controls. Our recent interviews with marihuana users revealed that naive subjects no longer need to try marihuana several times before they experience a high—a phenomenon characteristic of the 1960s, observed by Weil, Zinberg & Nelsen (1968) and others (Becker 1953; Goode 1972; Kaplan 1970). Nowadays, as a result of accumulated knowledge about the effects of marihuana use, even first-time users are prepared to experience the high and therefore many have done so.

The recent history of LSD use also exemplifies the impact of social learning. Howard S. Becker's prediction (1967), made at the beginning of the drug revolution, to the effect that after the intoxication induced by psychedelics had become more familiar and the users knew what to expect, their fears would be minimized and their reactions would be less severe and less frequent, proved to be correct (see chapter 1). Becker did not underestimate the extent of the changed consciousness state produced by LSD; he knew the drug to be many, many times more powerful than marihuana. But he was also aware of the power of the social learning process to socialize users to the experience. Verification of Becker's point was offered by my phenomenological study of the "high state" (Zinberg 1974). I discovered something that had not been so obvious to Becker and others: that when an individual experienced the psychoactive effects of LSD, he would select explanatory constructs out of the range of cognitive and emotional percepts available to him, and his responses would follow the available explanations of his situation. In effect, the boundaries of his AEE, which were determined in part by the social learning process, also determined the drug response to a great extent.

It may be that society is facing not only the powerful impacts of widespread drug use on individual behavior and internal capacity but also a striking change in the influence of social learning itself. Technological change, or more precisely the growth of knowledge, is one of the most important elements affecting the AEE. And philosophers of science point out that the rate of growth of knowledge has increased exponentially, as judged by rates of publication, patents, and other measurements. Before 1945, it took over 100 years for the sum of knowledge to double; then, amazingly, it doubled between 1945 and 1960 and again between 1960 and 1970. What is more, as of the early 1980s, the totality of human knowledge is expected to double every twelve years.

This rapid change means, for one thing, that parents have a different AEE from their children. Parents born in the 1920s or 1930s often find computers and their accessories strange and forbidding. They must restrain themselves from fulfilling a wish to "bend, spindle, or mutilate." By contrast, people born in the 1960s or later regard the computer, whether pocket, desk-top, or any other model, as just one more familiar article that they have learned about and used in school.

The splendid works of Thomas Hardy describe a society in which most learning took place vertically from one generation to the next. In Hardy's Wessex, children learned from their parents about work, relationships, and customs, and they followed the family pattern. Leaving one's village was a major step. When Jude left home to live in far-off Oxfordshire, he broke away from the family pattern, and his life broke up in consequence (Hardy 1895). In such a society, social learning hardly went on outside the family or the close social group.

Today much learning and perhaps most social learning is horizontal, that is, intragenerational. The peer group is mainly responsible for spreading information about work, relationships, and customs. Certainly most information about drug use, including particularly sanctions and rituals, is being transferred through peer groups, although the specific informational content may vary enormously from one group to another. It seems likely that this growing familiarity will permit future generations to make distinctions among drugs and forms of use that are not being made today by either parents or policymakers. It is also possible that social learning relating to drug use will in the future be transmitted within the family, as is the case with alcohol use now, and that the role of the peer group will be less important. A change in that direction seems to be taking place already in relation to certain illicit drugs, in particular marihuana.

The first generation of illicit drug users is always regarded as deviant. They have strong personal motives for seeking out such a drug as marihuana, and they use it with great anxiety. Gradually, as the deviant activity catches on (as marihuana use did in the mid-1960s), knowledge increases, misconceptions are corrected, and the users become more confident and tend to stop thinking of themselves as deviants.

The second generation of users tries the illicit drug not primarily because it wants to rebel against the straight society (the larger social setting) but out of curiosity or because they are interested in its effects. When the second generation supports the arguments of the first generation and opposes the cultural stereotypes about marihuana use and users, it is more likely to be heard: there are more of them; they are more diverse in background; and their motives, which seem less personal and less antagonistic to the reigning culture, are more acceptable to society.

By this time even the straight society has moved away from its formerly rigid position toward marihuana and has become mainly confused. Such confusion encourages others in the larger social setting who are not primarily motivated by either drug hunger or social rebellion to experiment with the drug. Their reports have an even greater effect on the larger society; and in addition, the new diversity of the using population makes it possible to develop various using styles that work better and cause less trouble.

NEGATIVE EFFECTS OF NEW TECHNOLOGY. Although advances in drug technology have enormously increased the availability and use of both licit and illicit substances, they have at the same time inhibited the development of rituals and sanctions like those that accompany the social use of many natural drugs. Before the American Indians use peyote, they all take part in the ritual of preparing the drug. This ritual puts them into the right frame of mind for use, gives them a knowledge of the drug, and emphasizes the quality of use, thus providing social learning and social control of the drug. But when, as in our culture, drug preparation is transferred to the technical expert or manufacturer, the natural social method of control is lost. The first-time user can be suddenly confronted with a substance that he does not understand and for which rituals, sanctions, and other social controls have not been developed or disseminated.

In addition to providing society with new, more powerful drugs that lack built-in social controls, technology has supplied the means of publicizing the worst effects of these new drugs. In the 1960s, at the beginning of the drug revolution, the reading and viewing public suddenly learned from widely disseminated media reports, principally on television, about the disastrous results of a psychedelic trip. The discovery of this new experience, experimentation by a few individuals who had a variety of reactions, and further experimentation by others were all kaleidoscoped into a few searing media presentations. These presentations gave the impression, accepted by most of the public, that such disastrous effects were the normal response to psychedelic drug use. Those whose personal experiences or observations had shown them otherwise were forced into a sharply opposing position, as has often happened in the field of illicit drugs. Neither of these responses allowed room either for reasonable social learning about the range of responses to the drug and how best to cope with them or for the development of social sanctions and rituals that might prevent many of the dysfunctional reactions.

Drug Use, Personality, and Society

Most proponents of Freudian instinct theory do not deny that technological change brings about social change, but they do question the view that social change contributes to continued personality development. They say instead that the two dominant drives, sex and aggression, are aroused in all individuals and that society works out ways for those impulses to achieve a degree of discharge under acceptable circumstances. For example, when an individual uses alcohol to remove his inhibitions, society accepts his flirtatiousness and his argumentativeness within limits that are subtly but differently defined by various ethnic groups and social classes. But why do such Freudian theorists not apply the same reasoning to the individual who uses marihuana in a *controlled* way in order to focus attention on a particular event or to reduce the boundary between himself and his sensations? Both the alcohol user and the marihuana user feel caught between sensations that pull in various directions, and they find reassurance in the capacity to focus for a time on a socially acceptable discharge or a derivative discharge of a primitive impulse. In both cases, the ego's usual relative autonomy from the id is maintained by its traditional guarantor of such stability, the external environment, which determines the acceptability of each form of discharge.

Unlike those, including Andrew Weil, who believe that the search for intoxication and consciousness change is instinctual, I see these interests as an integral function of the ego, part of its capacity to develop and change thresholds for discharge and to limit perceptual capacities. The ego has the potential to achieve discharge of primitive affects and fantasies in various ways, including that of consciousness change. Thus in this and many other societies the use of intoxicants is closely linked with impulse discharge. The group ceremonies and other elaborate social mechanisms developed by primitive societies not only define these discharges as acceptable but also control them, often claiming religious exemption for them. Those South American Indian societies that have used psychedelic drugs on special occasions have managed to control their use in this fashion. It is interesting to note, however, that such societies have not been able to cope with a new, technologically advanced intoxicant—distilled alcohol.

No society can hold back technological and social change. New substances, along with ideas about their use, are continually being introduced, and it takes time for society to find out which of them affect personality development and personal relationships. Not only the drug and the personal needs of the user but also the subtleties of history and social circumstances must be taken into account. No one has understood this more clearly than Griffith Edwards, director of the intoxicant research center at the Maudsley Hospital in England. He once remarked, in pointing out the fallacy of trying to separate the specific incident of drug taking from its social matrix, "One could not hope to understand the English country gentleman's fox-hunting simply by exploring his attitude toward the fox" (Edwards 1974).

The view that intoxicant use depends only on the drug or on a disturbed personality may seem attractive to those who accept the moral condemnation that society has visited upon illicit drug use. But for experts to use psychoanalytic theory to further such a view would be to belittle their own clinical and theoretical aims as well as the capacity of that powerful theory to incorporate social structural variables and the social learning process.

7

Reflections on Social Policy and Drug Research

INDIVIDUALS WHO EITHER DO NOT USE INTOXICANTS (WHETHER ALCOHOL OR illicit drugs) or who use them only infrequently in order to keep up with their friends often fail to recognize that others may benefit from regular, controlled use because it brings them relaxation and a sense of freedom from inhibition. This lack of understanding does not necessarily mean disapproval. At a cocktail party someone who has an extra drink or two may be treated with amused tolerance and, especially in middle-class circles, may be looked after and even seen home safely. In other social groups permission may be granted to "turn on" with marihuana, take a sniff of white powder, or tell of an experience with a psychedelic. Nevertheless, the general lack of understanding of those who use intoxicants, particularly the illicit variety, has led to public disapproval and moral outrage and to a desire to prohibit drug use rather than find out how to bring it under control. This prohibitionary attitude presents a major problem for contemporary America in at least two ways.

First, the prohibition mentality directly opposes the interests of most users, who place intoxicants near the top of their hierarchy of values. According to interviews conducted with people who were not specially selected because of their drug use, intoxicants (and food) rank next to the two activities that Freud claimed were the most important in life: "to work and to love." It is undoubtedly true that our commitment to work and thus to self-esteem and our relationships with others are our overriding daily concerns; much of our energy is spent in balancing, developing, and at times deprecating them. Religion used to be considered the third most important interest; but now the interest in intoxicants and food has begun to claim that position. This concern for ingesting, however, differs from interest in work and love in that most people disapprove of it and hesitate to admit it to others or even to themselves. Because society and therefore government reflect this personal ambivalence, they have refused to invest the time and thought that are needed to formulate coherent personal and institutional policies about such substances.

The second aspect of the cultural problem results from the recent very rapid growth of the use of intoxicants other than alcohol and the timing and pace of their acceptance (or rejection) by society. Since about 1962, America has been in the throes of a drug revolution in which millions of people (in the case of marihuana, 57 million; psychedelics, 16.5 million; and cocaine, 22 million) (Miller & Associates 1983) have tried substances that previously had been used only by a very small minority who were easily dismissed as deviant. By the early 1970s the enormous growth in the use of psychedelics, marihuana, and especially heroin had led to the creation, in the White House itself, of a Special Action Office for Drug Abuse Prevention (SAODAP), and to the appointment of the National Committee on Marihuana and Drug Abuse (the Shafer Commission). The Shafer Commission, made up of distinguished and acknowledgedly conservative (anti-drug) professionals from various fields, issued two reports— *Marihuana, A Signal of Misunderstanding* (National Commission on Marihuana and Drug Abuse 1973) and *Drug Use in America: Problem in Perspective* (National Commission on Marihuana and Drug Abuse 1972)—which considered the terrible difficulties that could arise from the new and extensive use of illicit substances. Nevertheless, their main message was a plea that society come to grips with phenomena that were not going to go away in the foreseeable future. These reports (whose antihysteria message is central to this book) were also noteworthy because they paid only slight attention to the use of cocaine. When they were written, no one could have predicted that interest in cocaine would expand as it has in the last few years.

Yet in the last twenty years use has not been confined to the four drugs mentioned. Significant interest has also been shown in amphetamines, PCP, and a variety of "downers" such as Valium and Quaaludes. But the four waves of psychedelic, marihuana, heroin, and cocaine use have been the most prominent, and they have given rise to the speculation that our culture, in an unconscious and inchoate way, is engaging in a vast experiment. A sustained effort is being made by at least parts of the culture to "find out" about various intoxicants and to see whether they can be used in a controlled and reasonable manner, despite the public wish that the use of such substances will go away.

Critique of Current Social Policy

Because this vast social experiment is going on, the question of what our society is willing to pay for the regularization of the use of any intoxicant must be raised and answered. It is certainly clear that our present prohibitionist policy, which requires society to regard all illicit drug users as criminals, deviants, or even "miscreants," and which encourages physicians to diagnose all such users as mentally disturbed, is being maintained at a heavy cost. Nor has it been successful, if success is measured by the number of smugglers and traffickers arrested, the number of individuals who have been persuaded not to try illicit drugs, the number of users who have been prevented from becoming compulsive, and the number of compulsive users who have been induced to take treatment. Moreover, debates over drug policy continue to ignore two related factors that make the issue of permanent prohibition largely academic. First, although drug use, like pregnancy, could be avoided by abstinence, mankind has not yet opted for total continence in the case of either drugs or sex. And second, the attempt to prohibit the use of drugs in this country has not been any more effective than the attempt to outlaw alcohol use in the 1920s.

The framers of current social policy, who hope to reduce the number of users by restricting drug supplies and punishing any use, argue that if there are fewer users there will automatically be fewer cases of dysfunctional use (Moore 1982). For example, if there are 10,000 users and 10% of them get into trouble, there will be 1,000 cases of misuse; but if the number of users is reduced to 2,000, there will only be 200 cases of misuse. This argument implies a straight-line arithmetical relationship between use and misuse, which does not exist. If the same type of argument were applied to alcohol use, it might lead to the highly debatable decision to raise the price of alcohol in order to discourage use! A rise in price would discourage some use, which supposedly would result automatically in fewer misusers. This, of course, ignores the strong probability that only the less committed moderate users who propound the social sanctions would be the ones discouraged. Interfering with existing alcohol consumption patterns with the aim of promoting reduced overall consumption rather than promoting moderate controlled using patterns is different from the use of formal legal controls with intoxicants where there has been little opportunity for informal social controls to develop, as with heroin, for example. However, by following the same mathematical argument and adding the assumption that all users are misusers, advocates of current social policy conclude that *total* prevention of use is crucial because of the large number of users. What is needed, they say, is not a reassessment of policy but more of the same policy—that is, better law enforcement and stricter penalties for trafficking and consumption.

But what have been the results of our present drug policy? Unsophisticated anti-drug legislation has led to a loss of respect for the law and the persistent flouting of it, to increased corruption among enforcement and other public officials, and to a virtual consensus among informed persons that although they may support these laws in principle, they will go to great lengths to circumvent them if a close friend or relative is involved. The labeling of individuals as criminal who would otherwise not be so considered has been more widespread under the drug laws than under the Volstead Act. The huge majority of those affected are young, the penalties are more severe and therefore more life-changing, and often the offender is forced to choose either to be branded as a criminal or to submit to "treatment." This choice, which ties the therapeutic process to criminal justice, has bastardized and denigrated a significant aspect of the mental health system and has had a profound effect on the way the individual drug-taker functions in society and views himself. These legal and social conditions have actually affected mental health more severely than has the controlled use of drugs themselves, and in some instances just as destructively as compulsive use. Finally, it is likely that current social policy is discouraging primarily those who use drugs only moderately, while heavy users, to whom the substance is more vital, are flouting the law in order to make their "buys." Thus, since it is the moderate, occasional users who develop controlling sanctions and rituals, the policy whose goal it is to minimize the number of dysfunctional users may actually be leading to a relative increase in the number of such users.

In 1972 the Shafer Commission recommended a change in our drug policy in the direction of dealing with each intoxicant individually and realistically. The Liaison Task Panel on Psychoactive Drug Use/Misuse of the President's Commission on Mental Health made a similar recommendation in 1978. In addition, the government's *White Paper on Drug Abuse* (1975) and the Strategy Council on Drug Abuse's *Federal Strategy for Drug Abuse and Traffic Prevention* (1977), both of which were aimed at the elimination of drug abuse, called for more distinctions between types of use, acknowledging that the elimination of "drug abuse" from our society was an unrealistic goal (1975) and that drugs were "dangerous to different degrees" (1977). But the Shafer Commission to a certain extent, and the President's Commission on Mental Health to a much greater extent, went further. These two commissions, which were well funded and had large staffs, concluded not only that it was important to make distinctions among different types of drugs and different types of use but also that the failure to make such distinctions had resulted in an extremely costly social policy, just as the Volstead Act had.

After the publication of the Shafer Commission's report in 1972, about a dozen states decriminalized marihuana use; that is, while continuing to impose criminal penalties for selling the drug, they reduced the first-offense penalties for possession of small amounts for private use to a fine similar to that for illegal parking, without labeling the individual a criminal. Few authorities, including the Shafer Commission, believed that this policy, which punished the seller more than the buyer, would resolve the marihuana issue. Decriminalization was intended as an interim solution: it would buy time to see whether the use of this particular drug could be integrated by society—that is, whether serious health and social consequences could be avoided.

The Shafer Commission also gave the traditional conservative response to the drug dilemma. Its members sought to delay major decisions by calling for more research. They assumed, or hoped, that researchers would come up with new facts that would provide clear, complete answers to difficult issues of social policy—that new data would magically eliminate the necessity for difficult intellectual or moral choices. Research might even show that the nonmedical use of drugs was severely damaging to health!

The experiment of decriminalization itself did provide critical data. Studies done in several states, notably Oregon (*Marihuana Survey—State of Oregon* 1977), California (*Impact Study of S.B.* 95 1976), and Maine (*An Evaluation of the Decriminalization of Marihuana in Maine* 1978; *Maine: A Time/Cost Analysis of the Decriminalization of Marihuana in Maine* 1979), indicated that the use of marihuana had not increased at a significantly greater rate since decriminalization and that some law-enforcement resources had been freed to deal with more serious criminal activities. But in spite of this evidence, drug policy did not change in such a way as to encourage the establishment of formal social controls; that is, it did not encourage the passing of new laws and institutional regulations. Instead, it tended to move in the opposite direction.

Several papers appeared claiming that marihuana presented greater health hazards than had been previously supposed. The validity of these studies, apart from those showing that the drug may cause lung damage as severe as that caused by tobacco and that it is probably bad for heart patients, is at best debatable (*Marijuana and Health* 1982). But even more damaging to those who hoped to move away from the policy of total prohibition was the appearance of survey research indicating that the age of first use of marihuana had dropped substantially and that heavy use among the younger groups had increased substantially. These findings led to the formation of parents' organizations that worked to "save" their children by campaigning for "education and prevention" (anti-marihuana indoctrination and prevention of all use) and by advocating stricter penalties and more stringent law enforcement. These groups were very effective in bringing direct pressure to bear on political officials to put their wishes into action.

Interaction of Formal and Informal Controls

One of the implications of my research on the controlled use of intoxicants is that in the absence of reasonable *formal* social controls, the age of first use will tend to drop. This is because *informal* social controls—sanctions and rituals—

are less effective when there are no acceptable formal social controls to support them. (As it happened, in 1979, 1980, and 1981 the earlier drop in the age of first marihuana use was reversed; whether this resulted from increased anti-marihuana activity or whether even under unfavorable circumstances some informal social controls were beginning to function is a question for later evaluation.)

The relationship between formal and informal controls is astonishingly complex. There are two kinds of formal controls: those enacted by law and those provided by controlling institutions. A high school, for instance, can forbid the consumption of alcohol at a senior prom and punish those who disobey—even if some students, according to state law, are old enough to drink. Similarly, such an institution can expel a marihuana user even though the state has de-criminalized use. An example of the interaction between an informal control and a formal control is the case of the boy who is nineteen and legally entitled to drink, who happily gives a beer to his eighteen-year-old brother but will not give one to his thirteen-year-old brother.

The absence of any clear formal standard for marihuana use, such as an age limit, has led youngsters to think that they can lower the actual age of first use without arousing concern or opposition. These youngsters know that even though society has outlawed marihuana, the effect is not the same as if the drug were socially unavailable. Very different degrees of deviance and of punish-ment are involved. At the same time, official disapproval of marihuana use, for example, by those under eighteen may be more effective than all-out prohibi-tion in setting discriminating standards. The high-school rule that forbids the consumption of alcohol at a senior prom does not forbid students to drink on all social occasions. The rule does indicate, however, that it is neither safe nor appropriate for them to drink if they cannot control their use. In the same way, the social sanction "Know your limit" does not condemn drinking but does condemn drunkenness.

The interaction of formal and informal social controls is most crucial in the case of young adolescents. In the first place it has been traditional in our society for this age group not to be allowed to use any intoxicants, licit or illicit. Second, when they do experiment with illicit drugs (and such use always goes on underground), it is particularly difficult to set standards for use, either formal or informal (parental). Many parents have said that they can deal more easily with their children's tobacco smoking than with their marihuana smoking. As one parent put it, "We can at least talk about cigarettes. I can bribe, wheedle, cajole, or threaten. But with illicit drugs there is a code of silence. I'm afraid that this attitude may move over to alcohol, which we used to be able to talk about." As has been noted in earlier chapters, parents today are in a very difficult position in relation to illicit drug use. In regard to the licit drug, alcohol, they have a much easier task, for the formal social controls associated with it (such as a legal age limit), insofar as they promote safety, often match the parents' aims, and thus many families can inculcate and strengthen their own informal sanctions and rituals about its use.

In the case of illicit substances, institutional controls can at least offer some help. A secondary school, by enforcing such formal controls as the banning of illegal alcohol and drug use while at the same time offering a reasonable educational program about these substances, can strengthen the parents' hands. Then youngsters eager to experiment cannot claim, "It must be OK any time, any place, because even the school doesn't make a fuss." Such attempts at institutional regulation give the parents the opportunity to think through with their children such questions as what intoxicants to use, where, when, how, and with whom—questions that are critical to the development of both formal and informal controls.

Drug Research and Social Policy

Because current social policy is aimed at decreasing the use of illicit substances (*Report of the Liaison Task Panel* 1978), the question arises whether research efforts must adhere to this policy in order to be considered ethical. If research is to be judged in ethical terms, and to a large extent it is, what effect does this have on the selection of research projects to be funded, how the research is done, and how the findings are treated by the public, as represented by both professionals and the media?

Almost everyone doing drug research would agree that it is extremely difficult to have one's work in this field perceived as objective and relatively value-neutral. Not only do popular presentations of any information about drugs insist on a "balance" that includes specific "anti-drug" material, but often scientific programs have been obliged to follow a similar procedure. In this kind of climate almost any work or any worker is quickly classified as being either "for" or "against" use, and halfway positions are not acknowledged. A diehard advocate of the National Organization for the Reform of Marihuana Laws (NORML), for example, will dispute any evidence that marihuana use can be disruptive. At a recent scientific meeting, when it was suggested that marihuana users should not drive when intoxicated, several floor discussants were quick to point out that some experienced users claim they can drive better when intoxicated. Conversely, a later statement that no deaths had been attributed to marihuana use during the past fifteen years, although over fifty-seven million people had used the drug in that period, was greeted by a retort from the floor that marihuana is not water-soluble and therefore is retained in the body. This reply was obviously not intended to counter the original statement but merely to show that no one could get away with saying something good about marihuana.

It is easy to ridicule these extreme positions, but the ethical issues themselves are serious; and the results of publicizing and exploiting drug effects in order to make use glamorous, in the Timothy Leary fashion, have given rise to grave concern. There is little doubt that the explosion of LSD use in the sixties was touched off by the wide publicity given such use. Although this explosion did not result primarily from the presentation of drug research, the drug hysteria very quickly affected research, as was evidenced by the declaration of one previously objective inquirer that he was setting out to prove the drug's potential for harm (Cohen, Marinello & Bach 1967; Cohen, Kirschhorn & Frosch 1967). Since the appearance of this kind of attitude—and it has surfaced in many places, including even the premises of the National Institute on Drug Abuse (1977, 1980; Johnston, Bachman & O'Malley 1982)—every researcher has had to consider whether his work is more concerned with discouraging use than with looking for the facts.

Truth in its basic sense is not the issue. Probably no one in the field, no matter how misguided he or she may be thought to be, has set out purposely to falsify the facts. But within a certain framework of values—the outlook that any illicit drug is so bad that efforts to prove it so are legitimate and serve the greater good—the search for truth tends to become deductive rather than inductive. And since all scientific inquiry must begin with an operating hypothesis, the issue of the aims of research is not a black and white matter. It raises the subtle question whether the culture's current policy of attempting to reduce illicit drug use should be allowed to outweigh objectivity. Researchers who treasure objectivity and neutrality and who accurately present their data, whatever these are, may end up carrying on work that contravenes dearly held cultural beliefs. These beliefs are felt to be sacrosanct because they supposedly help to prevent something bad from taking place, namely, an increase in illicit drug use.

As mentioned in the preface, in 1968, when Andrew T. Weil and I with Nelsen began to conduct the first controlled experiments in administering marihuana to naive subjects in order to study the effects of acute intoxication (Weil, Zinberg & Nelsen 1968), we were heavily criticized. Our critics thought that if marihuana should prove to be as dangerous to health as many people believed it was, we would be running the risk of addicting or otherwise damaging innocent volunteer subjects. But we were also told by many (most amazingly, including a senior partner in the law firm representing Harvard Medical School) that if marihuana should *not* turn out to be so deadly, our findings could be morally damaging because they would remove the barrier of fear that deterred drug use. It is, of course, impossible to say whether these experiments and

others that produced similar findings were significant in increasing the popularity of drug use. Even in 1968, when the experiment took place, it was clear
that marihuana was not the devil drug of "Reefer Madness." During that initial
period of criticism (and ever since then) Weil and I believed that supplying
credible and responsible information about the drug was essential, whether
that information supported our biases or not.

In this field, those who either withhold or distort information in order to
support the current social policy run the risk that potential users will detect this
falsification and then will tend to disbelieve all other reports of the potential
harmfulness of use (Kaplan 1970; Zinberg & Robertson 1972). Conversely,
those presenting the information that not all drug use is misuse, thus contravening formal social policy, run the equally grave risk that their work will be
interpreted and publicized as condoning use.

It is a frightening dilemma for a researcher, particularly for one who cannot
believe that the truth will set one free in some mystical, philosophical way. Of
course, neither can one believe that hiding facts, hiding the truth, will make
everything come out all right. And when the research concerns powerful intoxicating substances, abstract principles about truth and objectivity are not all
that is involved: human lives are at stake.

It was relatively easy to face up to the criticism of our marihuana research.
The growing popularity of the drug was evident, no fatalities from its use had
been reported, and there was a need for more precise information about its
effects in order to differentiate myth from fact. For example, at that time police
officers and doctors believed that marihuana dilated the pupils, and this misconception had to be cleared up because it was affecting both arrests and
medical treatment. But when it came to studying drugs like heroin, whose
physical properties, unlike those of marihuana, can cause disastrous effects if
control is not maintained, the ethical problem grew more serious. Moreover,
the effort to inform the professional community and also the public (by way of
the media, to which anything in the drug area is good copy) that heroin use is
not inevitably addicting and destructive involved the risk of removing that
barrier of fear that might have deterred someone from using. This has been and
continues to be a tormenting possibility. However important knowledge may
be, research cannot be countenanced if subjects are not protected from the
harm that may be caused by it, either directly or by withholding information—
as, for example, in the case of the unfortunate U.S. Public Health Service
research on syphilis, which withheld a treatment long after it had been proved
effective (Hershey & Miller 1976).

Nevertheless, even my preliminary investigations of heroin and other
opiate use confirmed what had been found in every other investigation of drug
use: that the reality was far more complex than the simple pharmacological

presentation given in medical schools. Certainly, heroin is a powerfully addicting drug with great potential for harm, but some users managed to take it in a controlled way, and even those who did get into trouble displayed patterns of response very different from those of the stereotypical junkie. In addition, other investigators, such as Leon Hunt and Peter Bourne, were beginning to report similar phenomena (Abt Associates 1975; Bourne, Hunt & Vogt 1975; Hunt & Chambers 1976). Once it became clear that these phenomena were extensive and significant, it was also clear that any attempt to remove such behavior patterns from the scientific purview because they were morally reprehensible or socially disapproved would reduce the credibility of all scientific enterprise. Further, it was possible that these heroin users, in the process of controlling their use, had developed a system of control that could be an extremely valuable basis for designing new approaches to the treatment of addiction (Zinberg, Harding & Winkeller 1981; Zinberg, Harding & Apsler 1978; Zinberg et al. 1978; Zinberg & Harding 1982).

That such research has a potentially positive application and is not for information alone does not, however, figure in the principle of what makes work scientifically acceptable. Basic research needs no defense here. But the way in which the work is received and treated, particularly by the media, can raise grave problems. Though researchers may be as accurate and careful in their statements as possible, they cannot control what others say or do with the information. Yet in the present climate of emotionalism about drug research, they would be naive indeed if they did not realize that certain findings are susceptible to distortion by the press. Unfortunately, several researchers have called press conferences before publication in order to herald their findings (*New York Times* 4 February 1974 and 9 April 1974), and they have not been unwilling to venture into far-reaching speculations that go well beyond the published data.

It is not enough to avoid carelessness in one's work and the reporting of it. Researchers must also do their best to avoid causing those who would not otherwise use drugs to do so. One way to shift attention away from the preoccupation with illicit use is to emphasize the potentially positive application of the work. Even here, however, the researcher who discusses his work as a therapeutic aid can run into another brand of sensationalism and misrepresentation.

The difficulty of defining and maintaining objectivity and the ethical problems associated with carrying out certain research and imparting its results are not confined to research on illicit drugs. Few investigators today, when individuals are faced with an overwhelming number of choices, are able to preserve the image of the disinterested scientist actuated solely by dedication to the purity of science. A searching article by a prominent jurist, David L. Bazelon, published in *Science* in 1979, comments on matters that are pertinent to this discussion even though it does not mention illicit drug use specifically:

> In reaction to the public's often emotional response to risk, scientists are tempted to disguise controversial value decisions in the cloak of scientific objectivity, obscuring those decisions from political accountability.
>
> At its most extreme, I have heard scientists say that they would consider not disclosing risks which in their view are insignificant, but which might alarm the public if taken out of context. This problem is not mere speculation. Consider the recently released tapes of the NRC's deliberation over the accident at Three Mile Island. They illustrate dramatically how concern for minimizing public reaction can overwhelm scientific candor.
>
> This attitude is doubly dangerous. First, it arrogates to the scientists the final say over which risks are important enough to merit public discussion. More important, it leads to the suppression of information that may be critical to developing new knowledge about risks or even to developing ways of avoiding those risks.

Who is willing today to assume the responsibility for limiting our scientific knowledge? The consequences of such limitation are awesome. The social risk of opening up areas of research on heroin use can hardly be equated with the frightening consequences of failing to disclose problems associated with nuclear reactions, but the principles are similar. It is understandable that government agencies, already overwhelmed by the number of factors that must be considered before reaching a decision, and buttressed by the righteous sense that what they are doing is for the public good, would want to protect society from the confusion that might be engendered if still more controversial information were made public. In principle, a bureaucracy wants to get all the information possible, but once it has settled on a course or a value position, it believes that new information raising further doubts may lead to greater risks and therefore should be kept quiet. As our cultural belief in the disinterested scientists wanes and our disillusion with the omnipotent court decision as a righter of wrongs grows, bureaucratic paternalism becomes the obvious alternative. But unfortunately, when the governmental acceptance of responsibility for a decision shifts to the assumption that the belief that supports a decision (illicit drug use is bad) is more important than the decision itself, there is bound to be difficulty in achieving a flexible social policy. This is exactly what has happened to the policy on illicit drugs.

Bazelon (1979) makes another point that upholds my position as well as that of John Kaplan (1970, 1983) and other researchers (McAuliffe & Gordon 1975; Herman & Kozlowski 1982; Waldorf & Biernacki 1982). Regulations that attempt to limit risks have their own social cost. This does not mean that we should not have regulations. But there must be a keen assessment of the risk cost of the regulations themselves. This is especially true in the area of drug use, where much of the damage being done today results from the illicit status assigned to marihuana and heroin and not from their pharmacology.

Policy Proposals

Many experts who have offered critiques of our current drug policy have made the radical proposal that all illicit drug use should be either decriminalized or legalized. A case in point is Thomas Szasz's laissez-faire approach (Szasz 1975). However, as John Kaplan (1982) and Mark H. Moore (1982) have pointed out in recent articles, such an approach would increase the number of drug users and consequently, at the very least, the absolute number of drug casualties. Because of this risk a more cautious approach to change is needed, and one that offers a responsible and workable alternative to the present policy of prohibition.

The leading recommendation to come from my years of research on controlled drug use is that every possible effort should be made—legally, medically, and socially—to distinguish between the two basic types of psychoactive drug consumption: that which is experimental, recreational, and circumstantial, and therefore has minimal social costs; and that which is dysfunctional, intensified, and compulsive, and therefore has high social costs (*Report of the Liaison Task Panel* 1978). The first type I have labeled "use" and the second type "misuse" or "abuse."

In order to distinguish use from misuse, greater attention will have to be paid to *how* drugs are used (the conditions of use) than to the prevention of use. Researchers must study both the conditions under which dysfunctional use occurs and how these can be modified and the conditions that maintain control for the nonabusers and how these can be promulgated. The goal of prevention should not be entirely abandoned, but emphasis should be shifted from the prevention of all use to the prevention of dysfunctional use. When this new focus is adopted, policymakers may decide not to treat all intoxicating substances as if they were alike. Careful studies of the use of various kinds of drugs and of the varying conditions of use may reveal the need to create a different policy strategy for each type of drug.

To study the conditions of use for each drug will require consideration of the following topics: dosage, method of administration, pattern of use (including frequency), and social setting, as well as the pharmacology of the drug itself. Consider, for example, the question of frequency of use. It is only at the extremes that frequency is not necessarily related to the harmfulness of a drug, as described in chapter 2. A policy aimed solely (or mainly) at reducing frequency would not only mask the significant differences between the drugs themselves but would deny the importance of the social setting, including when, where, and with whom the drug is used. These social factors, which may vary across cultural and ethnic lines, combine with frequency and quantity of use to determine the quality of use. A policy aimed at encouraging a shift from those drugs that are generally considered to be the most harmful to those that on all counts are the least harmful (even though some may at present be illicit) would result in a considerable reduction in social cost.

Further study of those conditions and patterns of drug consumption that enable users to establish and maintain control will underscore what my research has already suggested—that significant informal social controls over illicit drug use are now in the process of development. Drug policy should encourage the development and dissemination of these controlling rituals and social sanctions among those who are already using drugs, while at the same time continuing to discourage the general use of illicit drugs. The aim of this strategy would be to alleviate the worst effects of the current social setting on drug-takers without greatly increasing access to drugs.

Informal social controls cannot be provided to users ready-made, nor can formal policy create them. They appear naturally in the course of social interaction among drug-takers, and they change gradually in response to changing cultural and subcultural conditions. This is the primary reason why any abrupt shift in present policy would be inappropriate. The sudden legalization of marihuana, for instance, would leave in limbo those who have not yet had the time to internalize informal social controls. There are, however, several steps that can be taken now to demystify drug use and thus to encourage the development of appropriate rituals and sanctions. These steps include disseminating information (education), improving treatment programs, encouraging medical research, correcting negative attitudes toward drug users, and undertaking legal reform. The first two of these steps, education and treatment, will be discussed in some detail.

Education and Prevention

Many policymakers have assumed that behavior can be shaped by providing individuals with "information" on the consequences of behavioral decisions. The emphasis, however, has always been placed on the prevention or avoidance of behaviors presumed to have a negative impact on the individual or society. Such information has frequently been laden with ethical and moral judgments so that the "proper" decision for the individual has been preordained.

Drug abuse education and prevention efforts in the United States have burgeoned since 1968, coinciding with the rapid increase in the use of illicit psychoactive substances, starting with marihuana and LSD. Between 1968 and 1973, for example, the National Institute of Mental Health produced and distributed more than twenty-two million pamphlets on drug abuse and supplemented this effort with a continuing mass-media public-service campaign. During that same period departments of mental health in the individual states initiated drug education programs, and many of the 17,000 school districts in the United States followed with their own drug education efforts. The Advertising Council, a national body representing the advertising industry, estimated that the value of time and space donated by the private sector for the dissemination of drug information approached $937 million in 1971. In addition, numerous drug education programs were conducted by churches, civic groups, businesses, national voluntary organizations, and the military services. It was, as President Nixon had proclaimed, an all-out war on drugs, with education and prevention efforts centering on the elimination of illicit psychoactive drug use.

Both the private and the public agencies that promoted drug education added their own values to their educational materials, often distorting the information and discrediting its sources. In 1973, when the National Coordinating Council on Drug Education reviewed 220 drug education films for accuracy and appeal (*Drug Abuse Films* 1973), it found that 33% of the films were so inaccurate or distorted as to be totally unacceptable, 50% were not suited for general audiences unless a skilled instructor was present, and only 16% were scientifically and conceptually acceptable. Another government publication, *Federal Strategy* (1977), noted that even the best factual information often helped to stimulate curiosity about drugs, and that curiosity was becoming a major cause of experimentation. According to the Shafer Commission, these massive efforts, focused exclusively on promoting abstinence, may have actually increased psychoactive drug use.

In 1973 the Shafer Commission drew two conclusions about drug education and prevention programs: most information in the field was scientifically inaccurate; and most education programs were operating in total disregard of basic communication theory. The commission recommended a moratorium on all drug programs in the schools until existing programs had been evaluated and a coherent approach with realistic objectives had been developed. A federal moratorium on drug abuse prevention materials was ordered in the same year.

New federal guidelines were issued in 1974, emphasizing the notion that it was possible to develop "discriminating" materials that could reinforce or encourage drug-free behavior. Presumably, these materials would delete all references to the positive reasons given by individuals for using drugs, would avoid differentiating between the relative benefits and harms of a variety of drugs and patterns of use, and would emphasize the values of a drug-free existence. This sounded strangely like the approach abandoned in 1973, except that the new thrust would be labeled "discriminating and sophisticated."

A discussion of recent national education and prevention strategy is contained in an interagency report, *Recommendations for Future Federal Activities in Drug Abuse Prevention* (Cabinet Committee 1977), prepared in 1977 with the National Institute on Drug Abuse as the lead agency and presented as a "major refinement" in federal prevention-policy development. The federal strategists suggested three ways to reduce what they called drug casualties: limit the variety of drugs used, reinforce the drug-free experience, and reduce the frequency of use. The focus on prevention activities, they believed, should be on the drug use that had the highest social cost, as well as on the general drug-taking experience; the main efforts should be directed toward moderating the effects of taking drugs. The strategists, accepting adolescent experimentation with psychoactive drugs as part of the normal maturing process, did not view such experimentation as particularly distressing. The overall objectives of the federal government, they said, should be to reduce the number of new users (incidence), to delay incidence, and to reduce frequent or daily use. Their report suggested the following specific targets (*Report of the Liaison Task Panel* 1978):

> to reduce the percentage of frequent users of three gateway drugs (tobacco, alcohol, and marijuana) by 15% among 8- to 20-year-olds;
>
> to reduce the destructive behavior associated with alcohol and other drug abuse by 20% among 14- to 20-year-olds as evidenced by a reduction in overdose deaths, emergency room visits, DWI [driving while intoxicated] arrests, and other alcohol/drug-related accidents;
>
> to promote and reinforce restraining attitudes toward the use of psychoactive substances, especially use of the gateway drugs, by maintaining current levels of awareness regarding the addictive nature of heroin and alcohol, and by raising the awareness level of the addictive nature of tobacco by 50%.

That drug education and prevention programs should be broadened to include alcohol and tobacco (the first two psychoactive substances used by most youngsters) has also been indicated by my research. To ignore them would destroy the credibility of such programs because, although these drugs are legal, they are certainly drugs, are certainly intoxicants, and are certainly psychoactive—and yet alcohol may be useful. Moreover, the reasons why society is able to exercise some control over alcohol use but is not able to exercise control over tobacco use should be made an important focus of educational efforts.

My research findings also suggest that attention should be given to the various patterns of use that may be followed for different types of drugs, and to the consequences of these differing use patterns. Then more sophisticated educational efforts can be made to reduce destructive drug-related effects, such as overdose deaths, accidents, and arrests for driving while intoxicated; and these efforts can be conjoined with those aimed at reducing alcohol-related effects. For such campaigns to be credible and successful they must recognize that there is an enormous difference between drug use patterns that have potentially dangerous consequences and those more common, controlled patterns of use that are not destructive per se. Drug-using behavior that impinges upon public safety must be strongly discouraged, but this presumes public acceptance of the notion that not all psychoactive drug use is destructive.

In those health and mental health areas that are unrelated to drug use it is common for prevention efforts to be aimed at positive outcomes as well as at the avoidance of deleterious consequences. For example, although our society does not condone teenage sexual activity, it has decided that those who are unwilling to follow its precepts should be given the basic information needed to avoid disease and unwanted pregnancy. Drug education and prevention efforts should do no less. They should provide information on how to avoid the effects of destructive drug combinations (for example, barbiturates and alcohol), the unpleasant consequences of using drugs of unknown purity, the hazards of using drugs with a high dependence liability, the dangers of certain modes of administration, and the unexpected effects of various dose levels and various settings. These potential hazards are a particular threat to youthful experimenters, who unwittingly expose themselves to a wide range of untoward drug reactions. Does society really wish to continue tolerating education and prevention strategies that suppress information which could help hundreds of thousands of youngsters stay out of trouble? The posture that "they deserve what they get" is no longer tenable, and it is no longer officially espoused. Yet the fear still remains that if our education and prevention efforts do not condemn intoxicating substances, then potential users may interpret the lack of condemnation as tacitly condoning drug use. This dilemma has inhibited effective teaching in the drug area.

These recommendations for a change in the purpose and content of drug education programs apply equally well to some of the "new" prevention efforts that claim to represent a major departure from traditional approaches. One of the most prominent of these programs advocates the theory of a drug-free existence by promoting interest in such "natural highs" as yoga, meditation, and other nonchemical experiences. But many parents would rather have their children receive information on the responsible use of marihuana than be encouraged to seek "higher" states of consciousness. These parents may be skeptical about drug use, but they are also uneasy when traditional education promotes nonchemical highs.

A further problem with the so-called natural high is that it may not be regarded by adolescents as equivalent or superior to a drug-induced high. And even when the two are experienced as similar, many adolescents may seek to expand their repertoire of ways to get high rather than abandon drugs. Several years ago, when an exclusive preparatory school was considering the pros and cons of building an expensive swimming pool, it was persuaded that swimming would provide a recreational alternative to drug use. After the decision to build was announced, the administration was shocked to hear several students expressing joy at the prospect of swimming while stoned! It is not surprising that if adolescents find they cannot get high on swimming or in some other "natural" way, they may turn to drugs to achieve that well-advertised state.

Another relatively new drug education strategy has turned away from the earlier emphasis on the direct transmission of information through drug courses by offering the same information in courses on family development, nutrition, hygiene, safety, or interpersonal relationships. Although this diffuse educational approach relies upon different techniques, the message is the same. The older line that psychoactive drug use is destructive has simply been carried over into "values clarification." This new approach also overlooks distinctions between drug use and misuse, and it does not offer information on how to minimize or avoid drug-related difficulties.

If the "facts" about the consequences of drug use fail to convince the potential consumer of the impending peril, should these so-called facts be doctored to fit the policy, or should the policy be changed to fit the real facts? Prevention strategies talk about the need to develop more "persuasive" lines of communication and more "discriminating" materials. But doesn't this mean not just presenting the facts in a more attractive package but also altering them or suppressing helpful information? Wouldn't it be better to recognize explicitly the benefits some individuals get from some psychoactive drugs, licit or illicit? Or are we to continue to accept the notion that illegal drugs are ipso facto harmful, quite apart from the way in which they are used? Understandably, the legality-illegality quandary is especially difficult for drug educators to handle.

Several obstacles must be overcome before drug education and prevention can proceed from realistic premises. The foremost obstacle is the lack of knowledge on the part of those who are the most involved in educational efforts, particularly the physicians. Medical students are trained to view all nonprescribed drug use as misuse or abuse. A survey of medical school courses has shown that they deal only with the pathology of extreme drug consumption, including alcoholism, and neglect the possibility of controlled use and moderation. Hence physicians are often unable to answer patients' inquiries concerning different patterns or frequencies of use. Unless physicians are taught to differentiate between the various drugs and their effects, their patients' questions will remain unanswered. Medical education should be broadened to include comprehensive information on the effects of psychoactive drugs, the various patterns of use (including alcohol use), and the factors that promote control, as well as the signs and symptoms of dysfunctional use. Physicians would then be in a position to predict positive outcomes, counsel the avoidance of deleterious consequences, and give early diagnoses of drug-related dysfunctional behaviors. Physicians and other health professionals must be taught to recognize the subtle, individual, drug-related behavioral changes that foreshadow serious dysfunctions. They must also learn to identify the consequences of the differing patterns of use, ranging from the experimental to the compulsive, and to understand that not every nonmedical use of drugs is necessarily dangerous.

It is important that the use of psychoactive drugs for mind and mood alteration be considered in a social, scientific, and literary context. Educators should be familiar with the historical importance of the opium wars, the traditional ritualistic use of various psychoactive drugs, and the literary allusions to drugs by such great writers as Homer, Ovid, Baudelaire, de Quincey, and Coleridge. Then students will learn that man has always had psychoactive drugs at his disposal, that attitudes toward them have been constantly shifting, and that such drugs have been used for a variety of purposes. As the emotionalism surrounding drug use recedes, it will be possible to build such an approach into the educational process.

Treatment Systems

Because the focus of my research was on controlled use and controlled users, relatively little attention has been paid in this study to dysfunctional users and their obvious need for treatment and regulation. My long-term contacts with such users have revealed that today the drug treatment system is caught in a confusing dilemma about what it is supposed to be treating. The formal institutional structures of the system are not only unwilling to explore the distinction between the use and misuse of psychoactive drugs but do not know whether they are treating drug abuse or crime. Who, in fact, is to identify and pass judgment on the adverse consequences of drug use—the patient, the physician or counselor, or the agencies affiliated with the criminal justice system? The law labels any use of illegal psychoactive substances misuse (or abuse), while the medical establishment calls only nonmedical use misuse. Thus, by legal definition, any psychoactive drug use is seen as demanding legal intervention, while by medical definition any nonmedical use necessitates medical treatment.

All treatment programs, including so-called methadone maintenance, are abstinence-oriented, differing only as to the time period permitted to achieve that goal. This has not always been the case. The pioneer Dole-Nyswander projects on methadone maintenance (Dole & Nyswander 1965, 1966, 1967; Dole, Nyswander & Warner 1968) were designed as genuine maintenance programs. Although the patients' addiction to opiates (especially heroin) was initially replaced by addiction to methadone, the project workers expected that eventually the compulsive use of methadone would change to controlled use and that this improved situation would become the basis for social and psychological rehabilitation. Thus the use of a substitute drug was not the dominant factor. Methadone had several advantages: it could be taken orally, was long-lasting, seemed not to interfere with the individual's capacity to function, and, above all, was legal. But the basic aim of the program was to establish a clinical situation (controlled use of a substitute) in which patients freed from heroin addiction would be able to think through their problems and gain confidence in their capacity to manage their inner state and function reasonably well in society.

From the start, maintenance programs were highly controversial because of their retreat from abstinence and the introduction of a synthetic opiate. Since it was necessary to present some justification for their use, and since crime and drugs were being linked as the nation's number one domestic problem, it seemed reasonable to measure "treatment success" in terms of a reduction in arrest rates and criminal activity. Justifying treatment in this way made the use of a synthetic drug to treat heroin addiction more acceptable to those who saw abstinence as the only acceptable solution.

As a matter of fact, the initial evaluative studies showed that patients on methadone maintenance did improve considerably according to most social indicators. These studies, coupled with political pressure to do something about crime, led to a tremendous expansion of this treatment system. Methadone maintenance, which had been conceived originally as a medical treatment for voluntary patients, was presented to the public as a means of stopping drug abuse and crime by getting deviants off the streets.

Today the term methadone "maintenance" is a misnomer. Methadone treatment clinics have changed radically in that they have become openly abstinence-oriented. By federal regulation they are required to have physicians and nurses to dispense the medication. Some also offer a variety of ancillary services, such as vocational rehabilitation and individual and group counseling.

The other broad class of treatment programs, the various nonprofessional therapeutic communities, have always had goals that are wholly compatible with those of the larger society. They have aimed to eliminate drug use and have assumed that once abstinence was achieved, the client would become a model citizen. The early communities dealt with a few carefully selected, voluntary, heroin-dependent clients; but when enrollments burgeoned in the late 1960s under the pressure of the "drug epidemic," these communities began to test the client's motivation to rid himself of heroin use by putting obstacles in the way of his enrollment, in much the same way that a fraternity ritual screens candidates. It was assumed that if the individual could overcome these obstacles, his desire to become drug-free was genuine.

Therapeutic communities stress self-help, as does Alcoholics Anonymous; and in order to reinforce drug-free behavior they encourage intense interaction within the group and enforce firm rules of conduct by punishing infractions. The community setting promotes reform of the individual, not only by helping him to overcome drug dependency but by giving him a positive image of himself. Nevertheless, becoming socialized in the hothouse atmosphere of a therapeutic community does not guarantee success in the larger society. Initially, during the period of rapid growth of such heroin treatment programs, many successful "graduates" were able to remain in the field, working as counselors or administrators. Later on, when the employment opportunity disappeared and "graduates" had to return to the broader community for employment, they found it increasingly difficult to survive. One early community, Synanon, at one time tried to respond to this problem by developing self-contained communities where individuals lived and worked, abandoning reentry to society. Follow-up studies confirm that the self-help techniques of therapeutic communities can be beneficial, but retention rates are far lower than those of methadone programs.

The confusion about the goal of drug treatment programs—whether it is to cure drug dependency or to reduce criminal activity—worsened in the 1970s because of the increasing use of the nonopiate psychoactive drugs (cocaine, Quaaludes, Valium). These were assumed to have the same effects and consequences as the opiates—dependence liability, amotivation, and crime—and therefore the solutions were seen as the same: either to send users to jail or to remand them to treatment. The spread of such drug use among youth, added to the continuing heroin "epidemic," led to the rapid expansion of what the Shafer Commission termed a "drug abuse industrial complex." The budget for treatment services funded by NIDA grew from $18 million in 1966 to $350 million in 1977, shrinking to $155.4 million for fiscal 1981, with a total of 3,449 drug treatment centers and a static treatment capacity of 208,000 slots, of which federal funding provided approximately 102,000. But unfortunately the commitment to treat all psychoactive drug users ignored the essential differences among the various types of drugs and their using patterns.

The treatment services required for opiate dependents differ from those needed for users of other drugs. Services are also needed for those clients with emotional difficulities that are unrelated to drug use. With the trend toward polydrug use, there is a greater need than ever to integrate and coordinate drug treatment services with the broader health and mental health delivery systems to meet a variety of diverse client problems. According to data from the National Institute on Drug Abuse (Miller & Associates 1983), for the year 1981, 15.1% of all clients entering drug treatment programs reported *no* use of their drug during the month prior to admission; 5.9% had used it less than once a week; and an additional 5.1% had used it only once a week. Among those clients who did not take opiates, 19.1% used marihuana, 8.5% alcohol, 7.7% amphetamines (nonprescribed), and 5.8% cocaine; the use of inhalants (1.1%), barbiturates (nonprescribed) (2.9%), hallucinogens (4%), and other sedatives and hypnotics (3.1%) ranked lowest (Miller & Associates 1983). All of these nonopiate users required treatment that was drug-free.

Similar treatment problems exist with regard to the legally prescribed amphetamines, barbiturates, and minor tranquilizers. Users of these drugs, which have a high dependence liability, may require hospitalization for detoxification. Because they tend to be far more emotionally disturbed than opiate users (Benvenuto & Bourne 1975; Khantzian 1978; Smith 1975b; Vaillant 1978), their needs are only superficially addressed by the typical drug treatment program; and yet they do not readily fit into any of the other conventional areas of mental health treatment. It is likely that they could be more effectively served in a community mental health setting if space and expertise were available. Then drug treatment slots and funds could be exclusively devoted to providing services for clients who are suffering from the dysfunctional effects of chronic and long-term use of the opiates.

Opiate users in treatment centers usually live in areas characterized by glaring poverty, unemployment, and discrimination, where the use of drugs may seem to be the only alternative to despair. As of 1981 (Miller & Associates 1983), about 64% of these patients were black or Hispanic, although these two ethnic groups together made up only 18.1% of the national population (11.7% black and 6.4% Hispanic) (U.S. Bureau of the Census, 1980a, 1980b). Nearly 74% of these groups in treatment were black males, nearly 50% had had less than a high-school education, and 60% were twenty-six years old or over. Slightly less than half had been arrested within the past twenty-four months; about half of those with an arrest record had had one or more arrests.

The minority groups have often viewed drug treatment as a noxious form of social control, particularly if it substitutes one chemical dependency for another. This concern becomes even stronger when long-term maintenance programs are proposed. But recently many minority group leaders have begun to be less preoccupied with the evil magic of drug use per se and more concerned with the quality of treatment programs and the need for staffing patterns that are diverse enough to fit a range of cultural differences. The increased emphasis that minority leaders are placing on the *quality* of treatment services may be an important factor in improving these services.

Although treatment programs that are targeted at interrupting illicit drug use are important, treatment can be considered successful only if it prevents clients from returning to destructive drug use and gives them the emotional stability and technical skills needed to function adequately in society. The records show that this is not taking place. In 1981 65% of opiate users under treatment were unemployed at admission and at discharge; only 3.5% completed a skill-development program during treatment, while an additional 11.5% were in an educational or skill-development program at the time of discharge. Two-thirds of the clients entering treatment had been in treatment previously, and nearly two-thirds were discharged from the program for noncompliance, were incarcerated, or dropped out before completing treatment. Obviously, the rehabilitation needs of these drug treatment clients simply were not met.

In 1977 V. P. Dole and H. Joseph surveyed a stratified random sample of 85,000 current and former methadone-treatment clients in New York City. The results, which were consistent with reports from comparable studies, indicated that treatment "success" (defined as abatement of illicit opiate use accompanied by good functioning) was most likely for those patients who remained in treatment for the longest time, but that the overall level of success was low. The follow-up data on those who left the treatment program showed that although there was a dramatic reduction in their illicit opiate use during treatment, the majority relapsed after leaving treatment. This was also true of those who reentered treatment for a second or even a third time. In general, then, maintenance treatment is effective while the medication is being taken, but it usually does not cure the underlying problem, whatever that may be.

Obviously, those who have a long history of intractable heroin use should remain in treatment, whether drug-free or chemotherapeutic. Their earlier immersion in a deviant subculture has given them an identity, a community, and a way of life that have isolated them from the mainstream culture. Retention in treatment is essential in order to establish the kind of therapeutic relationship these people need to begin the long, slow process of working through their personal, social, and economic problems.

The indications of a need for long-term treatment are less clear for those with a favorable cluster of attributes—for example, for responsible young people who have a job, a stable home situation, and no history of alcoholism. For such a group, which is somewhat similar to the sample of controlled users described in this book, the expectation of a good outcome after detoxification is significantly higher than it is for all patients as a whole.

It is not easy to define "quality care" in terms that satisfy everyone who is concerned with the health, mental health, and drug treatment services. The difficulty of reaching a consensus on what constitutes such care in a health or mental health setting is multiplied in a drug treatment setting by the common practice of using abstinence as the criterion for success. If the less demanding criterion of controlled use were substituted, these programs would be able to achieve a much higher degree of success. This conclusion, at least, is suggested by the fact that almost 50% of the controlled opiate users in my research project were former addicts. It is clear that many individuals who have long histories of getting high and who do not want to give up an experience they find pleasurable may still be shown how to control their use. Unfortunately, such a criterion is unrealistic today and will continue to be so as long as the present policy of prohibition remains in force. Any program adopting it could be justly accused of condoning an illegal act—the use of illicit drugs.

Nevertheless, once it is clear that the purpose of drug treatment is to alleviate drug abuse, particularly dysfunctional aspects of opiate dependency, then the false hopes that have been raised regarding the elimination of all drug use and the reduction of criminality will be replaced by more reasonable criteria for success—such as reduced use, increased employment, and more adaptive social relationships.

The narrow and unreasonable assumption underlying the goal of abstinence—namely, that any drug use is misuse or abuse—not only has given society a drug policy with an unrealizable goal but has often prevented those in authority from recognizing dysfunctional use and dealing with it constructively. This is particularly true in the case of young adolescents. Recently a group of parents expressed concern about the frightening extent of drug and alcohol use in a regional public high school. A survey was made and the stories were found to be exaggerated: intoxicant use in that school turned out to be somewhat below the national average. When in-depth interviews were held with teachers, parents, administrators, and students, only a very few students were found to be in real trouble, and there was high consensus in regard to their indentity. Then it became clear that the exaggerated reports of use had so preoccupied parents and administrators that constructive efforts had not been made to get those who were in serious trouble into treatment. Overconcern about use by the many had stood in the way of active attention to the misuse and serious difficulty of the few.

Future Research

It is my hope that this research will stimulate other investigators to undertake long-term, longitudinal studies of psychoactive drug-using behavior as a socially evolving process which develops controls that affect a majority of the using population. Since such studies will require careful selection and special training of researchers, modest budget increases for research may be required; but the focus of the research rather than the total dollar amount should be the primary concern.

To date, five large and important areas of longitudinal research have been either neglected or treated only superficially: (1) the sequence of drugs used and the development of different drug-using patterns; (2) the individual, group, and cultural factors influencing low-risk and high-risk outcomes among equivalent drug users; (3) the changing attitudes of both users and nonusers toward psychoactive drug use; (4) the impact of the media on drug use and drug choice; and (5) the process of socialization as it applies to patterns of drug use. Three other topics need to be investigated by prospective studies: how drugs influence individual health and behavior, what use is being made of drug research, and how its findings influence public policy decisions.

Because of the expense of identifying illicit opiate users, who make up less than 1% of the U.S. population (see appendix C), it might be wise to adopt the suggestion made by Lee N. Robins in 1980. She proposed that when survey researchers identify an opiate user, they should ask if he or she "would be willing to be followed [up] at another time," thus permitting the creation of a pool of randomly selected subjects for intensive longitudinal study. This subject population would be more representative of the normal population than either the groups of subjects commonly used now, who are drawn from institutional settings, or the group analyzed in this book, which was a collected rather than a random or representative sample.

Besides the expense of conducting research on use of illicit drugs, there is the definitional problem. It is often very difficult for one researcher to know exactly what another researcher means by his terminology (see chapter 3). To minimize this problem, investigators could include detailed case studies to illustrate the category of use or user under discussion. To a certain extent, my study has employed that method, as have other investigators such as Bruce D. Johnson and P. J. Goldstein (1979). They interviewed their subjects daily for at least twenty-eight days at intervals of a few months. Their preliminary data include valuable details about the patterning, stability, and consequences of use (for example, the amount of money spent on drugs), which make it easier for other investigators to understand the meaning of their categories. Many of their subjects, incidentally, resemble my sample of controlled users.

Comprehensive and detailed case studies, tedious as they are to compile, would also supply the natural history of use called for by L. G. Hunt and others (Hunt 1977; Zinberg & Harding 1982). Today misconceptions abound about the patterns of use of all the illicit drugs, most particularly the opiates. At the least, what is needed is some knowledge about the change or transition from one stage of opiate use to another. For example, the latest data (Johnson & Goldstein 1979) show that, contrary to the popular view that heroin addicts inject themselves at least once a day throughout their using career, only 10% to 20% of the entire using careers of most addicts is spent using.

These kinds of data have powerful implications for treatment programs. Unfortunately, not many program evaluators attempt to identify the using styles of clients prior to and following treatment. It should be possible, however, to identify those in treatment who have the potential for controlled use. If a number of variables pointing to that potential (such as the ability to keep drugs on hand for some time without using them) could be isolated, questions relating to those variables could be incorporated into the screening procedures employed by drug treatment programs. Similarly, the characteristics of addicts who have been unable to achieve control over their opiate use could be identified and compared with the characteristics of ex-addicts (like those in our sample) who have managed to change their addictive pattern to one of controlled use.

When the proportion and characteristics of addicts who seem to have a reasonable chance to become controlled users have been determined and some understanding of the factors that facilitate the transition to controlled use has been gained, the stage will be set for a small, experimental program in which a few carefully selected addicts can be helped to establish control, and their capacity to maintain controlled use can be evaluated. Such an experiment is feasible; it could be done with some dispatch; and it would provide an enormous amount of useful information about heroin use and the treatment of those who are addicted to it. In the current climate of opinion about drugs, the major obstacle to launching such an experiment would be the reluctance of government agencies to support research on a treatment program condoning the continued, recreational use of heroin or some other opiate.

Probably the most convincing demonstration that control breeds control comes from the longitudinal studies of George E. Vaillant (1983). Through a variety of circumstances he had access to data on two groups of subjects from quite different economic backgrounds, collected over forty years ago, and he has continued long-term follow-up on these groups. On measures such as capacity to relate to others, to maintain close friendships and family ties, and to continue in good physical and mental health, the abstinent or near-abstinent score as poorly as the serious problem drinkers or the alcoholics. Statistically, moderate drinkers score significantly higher on each item. Vaillant says, only partially in jest, that his "findings have caused me to increase my drinking."

This approach to research—the development of long-term samples for study, the publication of detailed case histories, and the analysis of controlling and noncontrolling variables—would go a long way toward answering questions raised concerning the changing historical patterns of use. Some questions about the past are, of course, unanswerable. How can we find out, for example, whether occasional opiate use and the influence of the social setting on users' behavior have a long history or are relatively recent phenomena? Nevertheless, such an approach could still reveal important information about changing use patterns—what drugs are being used, how they are being used, and how that use is being socially integrated. Certainly, if our understanding of drug use is to improve, we must obtain more information about the social context of use, including a knowledge of how group customs and norms operate to shape different styles of use, how these customs (controls) arise, and how new users acquire them. Further research can discover ways to strengthen these informal social controls (sanctions and rituals) that encourage abstinence, promote safer use, and discourage misuse.

A final caveat. Throughout the duration of my project my subjects continued to make one point clear: at certain times, if not during the whole of their using careers, they experienced benefits from their intoxicant use and from different patterns of use. Thus, despite the reigning cultural morality, future studies of intoxicant use should take into account not only the liabilities but also the benefits of drug use itself and also of the differing patterns of use.

Initial Interview Schedule

Background Information

How old are you?
Where are you currently living?
  With whom do you live?
  What do they do?
  How long have you lived there?
  Do you like it there?
Where did you do most of your growing up?
  What ages were you?
Who was included in your living situation when you were growing up?
  Was your family closely knit?
Were you in the military? What was your discharge status?
  How did you feel about it?
What is your present marital status?
  Have you ever been married or engaged before?
  If married, what does your spouse do?
How do you feel about Sundays?
  What do you do?
  Did you always like Sundays?
Do you keep the house neat?
How interested are you in your clothes, hair, general physical appearance?
Do you like to tell stories or do you prefer to listen?
Are you ambitious?
  Were you always?

Parents/Family

What do your parents do? How long have they done those things?

Have there been any major changes over time in what they do?
How do your parents get along with each other?
Do you get along better with one than with the other?
Which?
In what ways?
How many brothers and sisters do you have?
Where do you fit in?
Are you closer with some than with others?
In what ways?
How was discipline handled in your house?
Was there violence in your family?
How would you assess your parents' relationship to you?
What is your parents' marital status?
Do your brothers and sisters get along with your parents the way you do?
Better?
Worse?
Has your drug use had any influence on your brothers and sisters?
Has anyone in your family, either immediate or extended, been an alcoholic or drug-dependent person?
Who?
On what?
Currently, or for how long?

Work

Do you work?
At what?
Salary? (approximate)
Do you like it?
Do you do well at it?
What sorts of things give you trouble?
What sorts of things are easy for you?
How do you get along with the people at work?
How do you get along with your boss or supervisor?

Schooling

What is the highest number of school years you have completed?
What degrees, diplomas, or certificates do you have?
How did you do in school?
What did you particularly like about it?
What sorts of things gave you trouble?

[If In School Now:]
    What extracurricular activities do you engage in?
    How do you get along with the people at school?
    How do you get along with your teachers, coach, etc.?

Legal

Have you ever been in trouble with the law, school, or work (drug-related or not)?
    Over what?
    What happened? (time)
    If not, have you ever had any serious brushes?

Activities

What are your politics?
    Did you vote in the last election?
Do you belong to any clubs, unions, or organizations?
In a week, about how much television do you watch?
How do you spend your leisure time?
    (Examples: movies, sporting events, concerts, museums)
Do you spend time by yourself?
    What do you do?
What are your goals for the future?
    Are they the same as your parents' goals for you?

Friends

How many different circles of friends do you have?
    Would you please characterize each group (kind of group—work, school, neighborhood, etc.; number in each group; sex; age; religion; length of time you've known them)?
Is there some place where you're inclined to hang out?
    Where?
    Why?
Were there any major changes in your groups of friends as you were growing up?
    How old were you when the changes happened?
    What were the changes?
    Were any of these changes associated with drug use?
Do your different friends or groups of friends know one another?
Do all your friends use drugs?

Do some friends or groups of friends have patterns of heavier use than others?

Are some friends or groups of friends drug-abstinent?

Do you have one best friend or group of best friends?

How long have they been your best friend(s)?

With which circle of friends is your best friend connected?

Does your drug use vary from one friend or group of friends to another, or is it pretty consistent no matter whom you're with?

Are some friends more than others associated in your mind with drug use?

Which ones?

Why?

Do you feel more inclined to use drugs when you're alone or when you're around friends?

How important is using drugs to you and your friends?

Do you usually feel on the inside or the outside of your groups of friends?

Do you see some friends more than others?

Which ones?

Have you used drug(s) when you've been around strangers?

Was that the same or different from when you're around friends?

What became of the friends you started using drug(s) with?

Do you still know them?

Do you still use drug(s) together?

Relationship(s) to Other Subject(s)

(Use this sequence when the subject is socially connected to another subject. Repeat all questions for each subject to whom he or she is connected.)

I understand you know ——, who also came in for an interview.

Is there anyone else you know whom we have interviewed?

What is your relationship to ——?

How long have you known ——?

How do you get along?

How often have you met with —— over the last two years?

How often do you speak to each other by telephone or write?

When do you get together with ——?

Special occasions?

Dinner?

Alone or with others?

Have there been any major changes in your relationship to —— over time?

When?

What caused the change?

Which drugs, including legal drugs like alcohol and tobacco, does —— use now?

About how often does —— use each of these?

Have there been any changes in the drugs —— uses or the way he/she
  uses them over the last two years?
    When?
    What changed?
    How would you explain the change?
Do you and —— ever use drugs together?
    Which ones?
    How often?
    When?
Do you and —— use drugs in the same way?
    The same dose?
    Under the same circumstances?
Do you ever share drugs with each other?
Does one of you ever supply drugs to the other, either for profit or at cost?
Has using drugs together affected your relationship in any way?
Do you think —— is reasonable about his/her drug use?
    Does use interfere with his/her life?
    Does use benefit him/her?
How would you compare your drug use to ——'s?
Is there some part of your drug use —— doesn't know about?
    Why not?
Do you think drugs are more or less important to you than to ——?
Have you ever been worried or concerned about ——'s drug use?
    In what way(s)?
Has —— ever got into *any* trouble with the law or at work or school with
  drugs?
    Were you involved in any way?
Has —— ever had any adverse reactions to a drug?
    When?
Has —— ever received treatment for drug use?
    When?
Has ——'s drug use ever been out of control?
Do you think —— will continue to use drugs?

Boyfriend/Girlfriend, Husband/Wife

Do you have a boyfriend/girlfriend, husband/wife?
    How long have you been seeing him/her/them?
    What does your spouse think of your friends?
How many serious relationships have you had in the past?
    How long did they last? (and/or)
    Are you inclined to have a lot of quick relationships?
Do you and your mate have a sexual relationship?
Is the sexual relationship satisfactory or are there problems?

How about the relationship in general?
>Like it?
>Troublesome?
>Something you worry about?
>Always a hassle?

Do you and/or your mate use drugs when you have sex?
>Always or occasionally?
>What are your feelings about drugs and sex?

Compared to your friends of the same sex, did you have sexual relations with a mate earlier, later, or about the same time?
>About how old were you?

Have you ever had homosexual relations?
>As a regular pattern?
>To the exclusion or in addition to heterosexual relations?
>What are your feelings about homosexual relations?

Drug History—Alcohol And Tobacco

What substance did you use first?

What earliest memory or association do you have about drinking, that is, not you yourself drinking but:
>Seeing someone drunk in your family?
>Seeing someone drunk on TV or the movies, etc.?
>How did you feel about them?

What memories do you have about the first time you drank?
>Who were the people you drank with?
>Where were you?
>How old were you?
>How old were your friends?

Did you actively search it out or did you come across it?

How long did it take for you to use alcohol regularly?
>What did regular use look like?

Where did you usually drink?
>With whom?
>How long did this period last?

Were you a heavy drinker, moderate drinker, light drinker?

Was your use ever out of control?

Was your use always consistent or was it in fits and starts?
>Have you ever stopped using it? Why? For how long?
>Did you go back? Why or why not?

What is your alcohol use like now?

Do/did your parents use alcohol themselves?
>What kinds of drinkers are/were they?
>Did you ever see your parents drunk or hear of their being out of control?

Were you ever worried that they might be alcoholics?

Do/did your parents take prescription drugs such as tranquilizers, barbiturates, amphetamines, etc.?

What did you think about that?

Did your parents ever talk with you about alcohol or tobacco?

What did they say?

Were you using at the time?

How long did it take before you started using?

Can you remember any time your parents stopped using alcohol or tobacco?

Why?

For how long?

Did they continue use at any time?

Was there any point when you were formally given a drink with your parents?

Offered a cigarette?

When you were little, did they ever share their drink with you or let you take a puff?

When did your parents become aware (find out) that you were using alcohol?

What were the circumstances?

What was their reaction?

Have you ever been publicly intoxicated?

Have you ever been sick on alcohol? Nausea, vomiting? Passed out?

Compared to your friends, did you get sick more or less often?

Did you ever go into a bar and get served even though you were underage?

Drug History—First Illicit Drug Use

(Use this sequence for first illicit drug used only.)

After alcohol and tobacco, what was the next drug you tried?

How old were you?

Who showed you how to use it?

What specifics can you recall about the first try?

What was your reaction to the high?

When you first started using, did you tend to use alone or with other people?

Who were the people you used with?

Where did you usually use it?

Did you actively search it out or did you just come across it?

Had you thought about trying it before you actually did so?

Were you curious? Afraid? Excited?

Had you ever sworn to keep away from it?

As you think back, when did you first become aware of —— (drug)?

When did you first hear about it?

What did you hear about it?
What did you feel about it?
When did you next try —— (drug)?
    With whom?
    Why?
    What were the circumstances?
How long after the first try did it take to become a regular user?
    What did regular use look like for you?
When was the first time you tried it by yourself?
    How did you feel about the experience?
When did you first buy —— (drug)?
    How did you feel about that?
Would you please describe your use of —— (drug) from the time you began to the present?
    Did you ever have any period of heavy or light use?
    Was your use ever out of control?
    Have you ever stopped using it?
    Why?
    For how long?
If you have phased out use of a drug, please describe that process.
    How did you feel about it?
Did your parents ever talk to you about —— (drug)?
    What did they say?
    Were you using at the time?
    How long after you started using did they talk to you?
    What do you think made them decide to talk to you?
How long did it take before your parents found out you used it?
    How did they find out?
    What was their reaction?
Did you ever have any adverse or unpleasant experience with it?
    Please explain?
    How did that affect your use?
What in particular pleases you about —— (drug)?
Who knows about your use of —— (drug)?

Drug History—Other Drugs

(Use this sequence for chronological use of other illicit drugs NOT including opiates.)
    What was the next drug you tried?
    How old were you?
    What specifics (circumstances) can you recall about the first try?
    What was your reaction to the high?
    When you first started using, did you tend to use alone or with other people?

Who were the people you used with?
Please describe your use of —— over time to the present.
    Did you ever have any periods of heavy or light use?
    (For heavy use) How did you feel when you stopped or reduced use?
    Was your use ever out of control?
    Have you ever stopped using ——?
Did you ever have any adverse or unpleasant experience with it?
    Please explain.
    How did that affect your use?
Who knows about you use of ——?

For Opiates Specifically

How old were you when you started using?
Who showed you how to use it?
What specifics can you recall about the first try?
When you first started using, who were the people you started using with, if any?
    Where did you usually use it?
Did you actively search it out?
Did you just come across it?
When do you first recall knowing about it?
Prior to using —— (opiate), what was your information or your opinion about it?
Had you thought about trying it before you actually did so?
    Were you curious? Afraid? Looking forward to it?
    Had you ever sworn to keep away from it?
Did your parents ever talk to you about —— (opiate)?
    What did they say?
    Were you using at the time?
    How long after you started, before they talked to you about it?
    Why did they decide to talk to you about it?
How long did it take before your parents found out you used it?
    How did they find out?
    What was their reaction?
When did you next try it?
    With whom?
    What were the circumstances?
How long after the first try did you become a regular user?
What did regular use look like for you?
When did you first buy it?
    How did you feel about buying it?
Please describe your use over time to the present.
    Did you have any periods of heavy or light use?

Have you stopped using it? Why? For how long?

When was the first time you used —— (opiate) by yourself?

What did you feel about it?

Have you ever had a habit? (How many and for how long?)

When did you first realize you had a habit?

How did you kick?

How long were you clean (not physically addicted)?

Could you be an addict?

If not, how do you avoid becoming an addict?

Have you ever felt that you were getting a habit?

What did you do?

What does the term "dabbler" mean to you?

What does the term "chipper" mean to you?

Describe what happens when other chippers or compulsive users move into your neighborhood.

Who knows about your opiate use?

Only other occasional users?

What in particular pleases you about opiate use?

Do you usually use opiates by yourself or with others?

Have you ever had an adverse or unpleasant experience with —— (opiate of choice)?

What was it?

How did it affect your use?

Now, I'd like you to describe an average using situation for me, in as much detail as you can. I'll help by asking some questions.

To begin, tell me how you go about getting the drug.

Procurement

Whom do you buy from? Addict or fellow dabbler?

How long have you known this person?

How is the quality over time?

Who buys? Does he/she always buy for the group?

How much do you pay for how much?

How long does this last?

Does the buyer get a "present" of an extra taste?

Getting Ready

Where do you usually get off? Whose place? Which room?

What's the lighting like?

Is there usually music? What kind?

Do you use glasses, syringes, and ties?

Who provides these? Who cleans up? Does everyone share, or does
    each person have his own works?
Do you use droppers or syringes?
What do you do with doors, windows, telephone?
Do you have a favorite part of your works—bottlecaps, ties?
How much time elapses between the idea of getting high and actually
    doing so?
Do you usually use indoors or outdoors?
Do you have other drugs around (for added high or just in case)?
How about juices (beverages)?
Who cleans up the house afterwards?

Getting Off

Who gets off first?
Does everyone self-inject or do people get one another off?
Can you get yourself off?
Is there anyone in the group who can't get himself or herself off?
How many times do you get off?
Do you boot? For how long?
What kinds of things do you talk about while getting off?
    (Example: The quality of the drug)
Do people usually throw up?
Is there a group somatic complaint, for example, headache?
What do you usually do when high?
    Listen to music? Watch TV?
What kinds of things do you talk about when high?
    For example, group reminiscing about the dope in the good old days
        or talk about who has good dope.
Do you get off at a special time of night/day, week, season?
How long do people stay around:
    When high?
    After they've come down?
I know it's hard to describe, but try and tell me in your own words what the
    high feels like.
    What do you like most about it?
    Does the drug have different effects at different times or in different
        situations?
    In other words, is the high a constant thing that you can count on, or
        does it vary with the particular batch or circumstances?
What happens when you come down?
    What do you do when you're coming down?
    What does the next day feel like?
    Is it just like any other day, or does it feel different in some ways?

Are you a little wasted, burned out, or tired?

Do you find yourself easier or more difficult to please?

Do you get over the experience quickly or do some effects last a day or two?

Does this help you control your use, or does it tempt you?

Drugs in General

Were there one or more periods of time when you tried a variety of drugs:
> For the first time?
> When was this?
> How long did it last?
> What drugs did you try?
> Which drugs did you use regularly in this period?
> When did the period end?
> Why did it end?
>> (Left geographic area?
>> One or more friends moved away?
>> Went back to work or to school?
>> Arrested?
>> Developed new friendships and interests?
>> Other?)

Do you find you usually have one drug as a mainstay (use more often), or do you switch around?

Do you enjoy drug(s) more when you're alone or when you're with others?

Are there some drugs you use with some people and other drugs you use with other people?

Do you usually plan when you'll use a drug or is it more by chance?

Are there some times during the day, week, month, or season when you're more inclined to use one drug than the other?
> (For example, Psychedelics in good weather?
>> Psychedelics in the spring?
>> Heroin on the weekends?
>> Marihuana before dinner?
>> Daytime versus nighttime?)

> Why?

Which of the drugs that you either have used in the past or currently use do you prefer?
> Why?

Do you mix drugs or do you prefer to keep them separate?

Do you have any rules about using drugs?
> Are there any things that you check on before you use a drug?

Do you know anyone who has got into legal difficulties with his/her use of drug(s)?
> What happened?

Have you ever got into legal difficulties with your use of drug(s)?
    What happened?
Has anyone you know ever overdosed or died from drug use?
    How many?
Have you ever overdosed or had an adverse drug reaction?
Will you use a drug in a strange place?
Is acquiring drug(s) easy or difficult for you?
How much do you pay for what amount?
Can you keep drugs around without using them up quickly?
What activities do you particularly enjoy when you're high?
Are you more likely to use drugs in a particular place, or will any place do?
If you were to tell a new —— (drug of choice) user three important things
    about using, what would they be?
        Where did you get this information?
Have you ever turned anybody on for the first time?
    How did it come about?
Are there drugs you have refused to try?
    Which ones?
    Why?
Are there any drugs you'd really like to try?
    Which ones?
    How is it that you haven't tried them yet?
Have you ever dealt drug(s)?
    Which ones?
    To make money or to cover costs?
Were you ever in a drug-education program or did you ever hear a special
    drug presentation?
        What was talked about?
        Who ran the program?
        Did you think the teacher knew what he or she was talking about?
        What was your response?
        Did your drug use change in any way?
Have you ever done any reading about drug(s)?
    (Books?
    Magazines?
    Pamphlets?
    Newspapers?)
    What was your reaction?
    Did what you read influence your drug use?
        In what way?
        For how long?
Have you ever seen movies or television programs in which there have
    been references to drugs?
        What was the nature of these references?
        What was your reaction to them?

When someone tells you something about drugs, what causes you to believe or disbelieve him or her?

From what source have you obtained your most reliable information about drugs?

Your most unreliable information?

Do you feel closer to the drug world or to the nondrug world?

How do you feel about the drug culture now compared to when you first started out?

Where do you think it's going?

What do you think about the laws relating to drug(s)?

Too harsh or too easy?

Should drug(s) be legalized or decriminalized?

If drug(s) were legalized, do you think your use would change?

Have changes in your pattern of consumption been caused by:

A geographic move?

A change in friends?

Going to or leaving work or school?

Breaking up with or meeting a girlfriend/boyfriend, husband/wife?

A change in health?

A change in interests?

Have you ever spoken to a doctor or a nurse or to a counselor about your drug use or about drugs in general?

When did this happen? (Why?)

What were the circumstances? (In a hospital? In a drug treatment center? In the course of a regular checkup?)

How did the drugs come up?

How did he or she react to your drug use?

What did he or she say about drugs?

Was he or she helpful to you? Would you talk with him or her or someone like that person again?

Do you plan to keep on using drugs?

How do you feel about your current pattern of use?

Are you satisfied?

Do you think you are using too much?

Do you think you'd like to use more?

Reinterview Schedule

Background Information

How old are you?
Where are you currently living?
   Is it the same place as the last time we talked?
   With the same or different people?
   If there have been changes in your living situation, please explain
      them.
Has there been any change in your marital status?
   If so, when and what?
   If you have been recently married or divorced, what does/did your
      spouse do?
Do you have children? Ages?

Family

Have there been any deaths, births, or marriages of note in your family?
   When did they occur?
Have there been any family disagreements or reconciliations that have
   affected you?
   When and what?
Please describe your current relations with your parents, brothers, and
   sisters.
   Do you get along better with some than with others?

Work

Are you currently working?

At what?
Salary?
Do you like it?
Do you do well at it?
What sorts of things give you trouble?
What sorts of things are easy for you?
How do you get along with the people at work?
Are any of them friends?
How do you get along with your boss or supervisor?
Are you doing the same thing that you did when we last talked?
When did the change happen?
What specially occurred?
How do you spend your leisure time?

School

Are you currently in school?
What grade are you in?
What are you majoring in?
Do you like school?
What sorts of things are easy for you?
What sorts of things give you trouble?
How do you get along with the people at school?
Are any of them friends?
How do you get along with your teachers?
What extracurricular activities do you do?
When will you finish school?
What will you do afterwards?
What would happen if you were to quit?
Do you know anyone who has quit?
What's happened to him or her?

Friends

How are you spending time with friends these days?
What activities do you engage in?
Are you still seeing the same people?
Are you seeing any new people?
When did this happen?
Are there any people you've stopped seeing?
When did this happen?
Have there been any changes in how you're spending time with people?
Please explain.

Has one friend or another become a best friend; or the other way around, has one best friend fallen from favor?
  Who? When?
Are you seeing one group of people or different groups?
  Do they know each other or do you keep them separate?
Are you seeing some friends or groups of friends more than you used to? Some friends or group of friends less than you used to?
  When did this happen?
If you're seeing different groups of friends, do you do the same things with them or do you have different activities for each group?
  What are the differences?
Does your drug use vary from group to group or is it consistent no matter where you are?
  Is this true for your friends also?
Did you meet your current friends mostly through work? Hanging around? School? Grew up with them? Other? Please explain.
Is there one place where you're inclined to hang out?
How long have you known your different friends?
Please describe your friends: age, sex, race, background, religion.
Are you spending more or less time alone these days than you used to?
Are you currently using more or fewer drugs than your friends?
Do some of your friends use more drugs than others?
  What are the differences?
  Have you some friends who use no drugs at all?
Have some of your friends stopped using drugs?
  When?
In what ways, if any, have your friends' drug-use patterns changed?
Have you ever run a group or felt that one revolved around you?
Are some of your friends either dead set against or really crazy for drugs?
What do your parents/spouse think about your friends?
  Have your parents/spouse changed their attitudes about your friends? When?

Boyfriend/Girlfriend, Husband/Wife

Do you currently have a boyfriend/girlfriend, husband/wife?
  How long have you been with him/her?
How many serious relationships have you had in the past?
  How long did they last? (and/or)
  Are you more inclined to have a variety of quick relationships?
Are you seeing the same person as when we last spoke?
If he or she is different from the previous person, or if you didn't have one last time, how did you meet?
  How's the relationship going?

How long have you been seeing each other?
Do you and your mate have a sexual relationship?
    Is it satisfactory, or are there a lot of problems?
Do you and/or your mate use drugs when you have sex?
    Most of the time?
    Sometimes?
    Never?
Compared to your friends of the same sex, did you have sexual relations with a mate relatively early? The same time as everyone else?
Later than everyone else?
Have you ever had homosexual relations?
    As a regular pattern?
    To the exclusion of or in addition to heterosexual relations?

General

In general, how have things been going for you?
What concerns or problems have come up during the last six months?
What things have gone well?
Have you tried any new activities or interests lately? For example, music, meditation.
    When?
Have you joined any groups, clubs, or organizations?
    When?
    What other ones do you belong to?
    Are you active?
Have you acquired any new possessions of note?
    Stereo? Car? House?
    Have you got rid of any?
    When?
How's your health these days? Physical? Emotional?
    If any major changes, when did they occur?
Have you done any traveling recently?
Are there any things you're particularly looking forward to doing?
    When?
Have you had any trouble with the law, school, or work?
    What was the nature of the difficulty? What happened?
    When did it happen?
Have you talked to a physician or counselor about your drug use since we last spoke?
    When did this happen?

Drugs

What drugs have you used in the last six months and with what frequency?

Alcohol?
Tobacco?
Marihuana?
Amphetamines? Cocaine?
Barbiturates, tranquilizers, Quaaludes?
Opiates, heroin, Dilaudid, etc.?
Are you using larger or smaller amounts of these drugs or using at a higher
or lower frequency than when we last talked?
Are you using with the same people, new people, no people?
    If any change from last time, please explain and indicate when the
       change occurred?
What drugs are your friends using that are new for them or that have come
back into use?
    For example, alcohol.
    When did this change occur?
Are your friends using any drugs that you're not using?
    Is this a change or has it always been that way?
    If a change, when did it happen?
Are your friends using more or less frequently than they used to?
    On different occasions or just anytime?
How does your use of drugs with your girlfriend/boyfriend, husband/wife
compare with your use with your friends?
    Greater than? Less than? Same as?
Has anybody who didn't know about your use before found out recently
that you use drugs? For example, your parents.
    When?
Is knowledge of your drug use a carefully guarded secret or do most people
you're in contact with know about it?
Is your use currently consistent or does it occur in fits and starts?
    Have you had any recent periods of heavy use? Light use? Absti-
       nence? Any periods of use that has been out of control?
    When did these changes occur?
    If you returned to using a drug, please explain why.
Do you find that you usually have one drug as a mainstay or do you switch
around?
Have you tried any new drugs since we last talked?
    Which one(s)?
    When?
    How often? What pattern of use did you establish?
Do you enjoy drug use more when you're alone or when you're with
others?
Do you usually plan when you'll use a drug or is it more by chance?
Are there some times during the day, week, month, or season when you're

more inclined to use one drug than another? For example, psychedelics
in good weather or the spring? Heroin on the weekend?
Marihuana before dinner? Daytime versus nighttime?
Which of the drugs that you either have used in the past or currently use do
you prefer?
    Why?
Do you mix drugs or do you prefer to keep them separate?
Have you in the past six months overdosed or had an adverse drug
reaction?
Do you have any rules about using drugs?
    Are there any things you check on before you use a drug?
Are there any activities that your use of drugs make more difficult or
impossible? Easier?
What activities do you particularly enjoy when you're high?
Are you likely to use drugs only in a particular place or will any place do?
Are there any activities, drug-related or not, that your friends enjoy that
you do not enjoy?
    For example, breaking and entering?
If you were to tell a new drug user three important things about using,
what would they be?
    Where did you get this information?
Do you have any rules about when or where to use, or do you pretty much
use when you feel like it?
Have you turned anybody on for the first time recently?
    When?
    How did it go?
Have you dealt drugs recently?
    When?
    Which ones?
    How often?
    To make money or to cover costs?
Where have you got your most reliable information about drugs?
    Least reliable?
Do you feel closer to the drug freak world or to the straight nondrug world?
What do you think about the laws relating to drugs?
    Have your opinions of them changed in the last six months?
    If so, when and how?
As you look back on your drug use, have there been changes in your
pattern of consumption?
    When?
    What has caused the change?
        A geographic move? Change in friends? Went to or left work or
            school? Broke up with or met a girlfriend/boyfriend, hus-
            band/wife? Change in health? Change in interests?

Do you plan to keep on using drugs?
How do you feel about your current pattern of use?
    Too much? Not enough?
    Why?

APPENDIX C

A Survey of Previous Research

For some drugs the practice of distinguishing among various using patterns is well established. Social drinking has been distinguished from alcoholism, for example, even if somewhat imprecisely. But for marihuana, psychedelics, and opiates, the importance of making such distinctions has only recently been recognized. A literature search using the computerized MEDLINE File (which catalogues articles from more than 1,000 journals) revealed only one study specifically concerned with occasional illicit drug use between January 1969 and November 1972. Until recently, research studies have tended to reflect in three related ways the reigning cultural belief that all illicit drug use is abusive.

First, many if not most investigators have not differentiated between moderate and excessive use. Margaret Heller, in her 1972 review of thirty-five studies of opiate use that had been published since 1954, concluded that their "most serious" flaw was that they "lumped together all drug users without considering the extent of their use."

Second, what few attempts were made to define the variety of drug-using styles only resulted in a proliferation of vague and confusing terms. This was most evident in regard to moderate patterns of use—ranging all the way from near-abstinence to near-compulsion—but it was also apparent in descriptions of extreme use (usually heroin addiction), which had been studied more carefully and intensively. The most inclusive terms, like "illicit drug use" and "nonmedical drug use," were too generic to have much descriptive value. More specific terms—such as "chipper," "experimenter," or "head"; "occasional," "habitual," "chronic," "heavy," "ritual," "recreational," "addicted," "committed," "casual," or "regular user"; "drug-dependent person"; and "abuser"—were employed to indicate the intensity and frequency of use or to describe some characteristic of the user. These terms, however, were applied so casually and inconsistently that, as the National Commission on

Marihuana and Drug Abuse reported (1973), "It is often difficult to ascertain who is being described, what kind of behavior is being evaluated . . . or what actual or potential risks of such behavior are likely." Isidore Chein et al. (1964) found that even the apparently precise term "heroin addict" was used in so many different ways that it was "meaningless to identify an individual as an 'addict.'" Bruce D. Johnson (1977) appropriately described "addict" as an "accordion word which expands or contracts to please the audience being played to" and which was sometimes defined "so broadly as to include anyone who was ever a daily heroin user."

Third, the few investigators who acknowledged the existence of moderate or noncompulsive using styles concentrated on marihuana and neglected the psychedelics and opiates, apparently because of the prevasive popular belief that the drug variable—that is, the chemistry of each drug—was the main determinant of the outcome of use. For example, sociologist Erich Goode (1969) defined the occasional marihuana smoker as "someone comparable to the social drinker, to whom marihuana is a pleasant but largely dispensable and not particularly important aspect of life," and he suspected that such benign using patterns predominated among marihuana users. Further, Herbert Blumer et al. (1967) noted the possibility of continued noncompulsive use of marihuana but believed that heroin could not be used on an occasional basis because it developed greater dependency. This failure to discern and describe moderate patterns of psychedelic or opiate use might be understandable if the ratio of moderate to compulsive users of these two types of drugs had been found to be low relative to the ratio for marihuana use. But satisfactory data were not yet available on those ratios; in fact, surveys of illicit drug use in the general population were not made until relatively recently. According to the National Commission on Marihuana and Drug Abuse (1973), no such studies were undertaken prior to 1965, and even though several were available by the mid-1970s, many of these had major shortcomings. "Most were studies of young populations . . . concerned with marihuana at the expense of both other illicit drugs and alcohol . . . . Simple measures of 'ever used' and 'present use' were obtained and finer distinctions were seldom made."

This failure of research studies to differentiate between moderate and excessive drug use, to develop a precise and accurate terminology, and to describe the moderate use of psychedelics and opiates was strikingly evident in 1972, when my DAC study was launched. Because that study and its successor (sponsored by NIDA), and therefore this book, place the main emphasis on the use of opiates, the following review of the research literature published between 1957 and 1981 focuses on studies of opiate use. It shows that although a growing number of investigators are now seriously considering the differences among various patterns of use, there is still a relative lack of information about nonaddictive use. Hundreds of studies deal with some aspect of addiction, but fewer than a dozen give substantial consideration to occasional use. In addition, a large number of the articles describing these studies deal solely with the "captive" or medical population of treatment centers while only a few are concerned with the nonmedical populations of users "at large."

Factors Inhibiting the Study of Occasional Opiate Use

There are at least four reasons why nonaddictive and nontreatment opiate use have not been adequately studied.

The first is related to the persistence of cultural beliefs that heroin is an inherently "bad" drug. Joseph R. Gusfield (1975) has noted that because researchers are not immune to the cultural atmosphere in which they work, the prevailing attitudes toward heroin use may have made it difficult for them to appreciate that much of the conventional wisdom contained in the literature was inaccurate. The tendency to regard any kind of heroin user as a "junkie" made it difficult for investigators to delineate groups that did not fit that cultural stereotype or to recognize how valuable the study of such groups could be.

A second, and probably more important, reason is that noncompulsive and therefore nontreatment users are very difficult to locate and study (Geber 1969; Catton & Shain 1976; Rittenhouse 1977). Opiate use is still so rare that the identification of users of any kind in the general population is a very expensive task. It is generally agreed that fewer than 1% of Americans are nonmedical opiate users: hence 10,000 persons would have to be interviewed to generate a representative sample of only 100 users, and only some of those would use the drug on an occasional basis. It is true, of course, that data on opiate users can be gathered efficiently from treatment, law-enforcement, correctional, and other captive populations. But such sources provide a highly selective sample of users who "have encountered significant personal, medical, social, or legal problems in conjunction with their drug use, and thus often represent the most pathological end of the using spectrum" (Greene, Nightingale & DuPont 1975).

Third, questions of ethical responsibility have probably impeded the study of nonaddictive use. Some researchers, aware of the popular belief that any use of heroin results in depravity and enslavement and that this belief undoubtedly serves to discourage heroin use, may have been reluctant to undertake the study of occasional use lest they undermine that attitude. Furthermore, some investigators may have feared that if they reported the existence of occasional users they might be accused of endorsing experimentation with opiates (Zinberg 1981). These ethical concerns have, of course, troubled me as well.

Fourth, the widespread confusion of terms relating to the level and quality of opiate use has been a substantial obstacle to research (Lasagna 1965; Smart 1974; Robins 1977; Apsler 1978). This confusion has not only complicated the comparison and interpretation of findings from different studies but has prompted at least one investigator to ask: "Is the occasional user of 'dangerous' or narcotic drugs an addict? Is the habitual user of heroin which is so 'cut' as to be incapable of creating serious tolerance or physical dependence 'addicted'? Is a person who has been off drugs for years and then takes one shot of heroin 'in relapse'?" (Lasagna 1965).

In the literature the terms "occasional use" and "chipping" are most often used to indicate a nonaddictive pattern of opiate use, but they do not necessarily connote moderate use. Rather, they tend to indicate less than daily use and the absence of physical dependence. Further, they do not necessarily imply anything about the consistency of use over time or about the frequency or quality of the concurrent use of other drugs.

The Emergence of Research Interest in Occasional Opiate Use

Alfred Lindesmith (1947), a pioneer in the study of heroin, was one of the first twentieth-century researchers to refer to nonaddictive use. He defined the "pleasure user" or "joy popper" as follows: "A 'joy popper' is simply an individual who uses the drug intermittently and *who has never been 'hooked'*" (original emphasis). Having only a few examples of joy poppers and no long-term data about them, Lindesmith speculated that most such users eventually became addicted. He did, however, emphasize the uniqueness of this group: "As long as they indulge in sufficient moderation to avoid severe withdrawal symptoms, they are sharply distinguished from those who have been 'hooked' and they do not regard themselves as addicts."

Jordan M. Scher (1961, 1966), through his work at the Cook County (Illinois) Narcotics Court and Jail, came in contact with "addicts" who had confined their use to weekends or parties. Although he felt that this pattern often progressed to more frequent use, he observed several cases "in which relatively gainful and steady employment has been maintained for two or three years while the user *was on what might be called a regulated or controlled habit*" (original emphasis).

Isidore Chein et al. (1964) stated that they had been able to establish the existence of "long continued nonaddictive users" of heroin, but not in sufficient numbers to permit a study of the type they wished to undertake.

When Harold Alksne, L. Lieberman and L. Brill discussed a model of the life cycle of addiction in 1967, they indicated that some drug-takers seemed able to "control their use" and to continue in occasional or limited use for "an indefinite period of time." The authors noted that "no research reports are available for this kind of use," and they felt it likely that these "experimental" users would either become more involved with opiates or stop using altogether. At the same time, however, they expressed the need for future research to document their theory.

Unlike many of the earlier investigators of occasional use, Erich Goode (1972) felt that "the occasional (weekend) heroin user is probably a good deal more common than most of us realize." He did not differ from most other investigators, however, in his view that the majority of occasional heroin users eventually become addicted. He based this opinion on the lack of cultural norms (which I call sanctions and rituals) to limit heroin use, the rapidity with which a user could become physiologically addicted, and the tendency of new users to discount the risk of becoming addicted. In elaborating the last point he referred to Alan G. Sutter (1969), who had argued that the "magical belief" that one could "chippy around" and still control heroin use was a self-deception that contributed to the development of addiction. "If a person knows from experience that he has always been able *to control his drug use* and still 'take care of business,' he will be convinced of his strong 'will power' and will believe that only 'weak-minded people get hooked.' This belief lays the groundwork for addiction" (original emphasis).

In view of these repeated declarations that in a majority of cases occasional use quickly leads to addiction, it is not surprising that the first study to focus specifically on occasional opiate use did not appear till 1973, when Douglas H. Powell published data on twelve occasional users who had responded to his newspaper advertisements. He concluded that these subjects had never become addicted even though they had all been using heroin for at least three consecutive years. Some of them, however, appear to have followed patterns of opiate use that, according to the standards of my project, could hardly be defined as "well controlled": one, for example, had used heroin for "six weeks straight" within the previous six months. Nor did Powell clearly describe the use of other intoxicants by the group. Nevertheless, his work established the existence of patterns of opiate use that differed significantly from the classic model of intensive and destructive heroin consumption. His investigation, which legitimized further studies (including my own) that were aimed at describing these alternative patterns, touched off increased research interest in occasional opiate use.

Occasional Opiate Users in Treatment Centers

The fact that occasional users turn up and are identified in treatment populations has raised concern about the propriety of giving treatment to such users. Guidelines suggested by the American Medical Association (1972), which state that the "mere" use of an opiate, "even if periodic or intermittent . . . cannot be equated with drug dependency," recommend that a specific medical diagnosis be made in each case. W. H. Dobbs (1971) warned that some people applying for methadone maintenance ought to be rejected because they were only occasional users. Paul H. Blachly (1973) demonstrated that Naloxone, an opiate antagonist, could be used, unlike urinalysis, to distinguish a person who was physically dependent from an occasional user, and he suggested that Naloxone should be administered for this purpose to those who applied for methadone maintenance. At one methadone clinic, he found that one-third of the applicants, who had no prior documentation of withdrawal in an institution, "showed no evidence of physical dependence"; and he concluded that there was "a significant hazard" that the treatment would addict these occasional users to methadone.

When Charles P. O'Brien (1976) administered Naloxone to applicants for methadone maintenance, he found that 55% gave positive responses for opiate dependence, 18% were weakly positive, and 15% were negative. The remaining 12% were not given Naloxone because they were "found not to be using heroin daily." Frederick B. Glaser (1978) suggested that only those who gave positive responses (55%) in O'Brien's study were definitely addicted and argued that the remaining 45% should have been regarded as addicted.

William L. Minkowski, R. C. Weiss and G. A. Heidbreder (1972) found more occasional heroin users than daily users in a random sample of clients at a Los Angeles Health Department youth clinic. Replies to 300 questionnaires and interviews with 100 subjects indicated that 12% had used it once a month or less, 1.1% had used it two to four times a month, and 1.2% every weekend or more; only 1.7% had used daily.

John Newmeyer (1974) of the Haight-Ashbury Free Medical Clinic also reported that individuals who could be "characterized as 'persons who sample heroin without becoming addicted'" self-refer for drug-related treatment.

In a study of 2,750 subjects aged eighteen or under who had received treatment in a drug program, Yoav Santo, E. C. Farley and A. S. Freedman (1980) reported that whereas 6.7% had "ever" used heroin within the three-month period prior to admission, only 4.3% repeated "weekly or more frequent use for at least four weeks" during the same period. Use of other opiates followed a similar pattern.

Occasional users may suffer from the dangers to health that are usually associated with heroin addiction. Edward Kersh (1974) found that 70% of the patients treated for narcotic overdoses in a particular New York hospital emergency room were occasional users. R. W. Light and T. R. Dunham (1974) commented on vertebral osteomyelitis due to septic intravenous administration of heroin in two individuals who had not used heroin for at least eight weeks preceding the onset of symptoms and who were "definitely not addicts." Roger Lewis, S. Gorbach and P. Altner (1972) reported on five occasional users they had encountered in one year who had spinal chondroosteomyelitis. These patients had all used heroin intravenously within the week prior to their hospital admission, but they were not addicted.

Marco Systems, Inc. conducted a study (1975) of admissions to New York City treatment programs in 1971 and found that approximately one-third of the sample had been categorized as less than daily users for the two months preceding treatment.

S. B. Sells (1977) has studied national data based on 27,460 drug admissions to a variety of treatment programs between 1 June 1969 and 31 March 1974. During this more than four-year period, from 8% to 12% of the patient population reported that they had been less than daily opiate users during the two months preceding treatment.

These studies raise the question, "Why do occasional users enter treatment?" There are many possible answers, each of which may be valid in specific cases.

1. As some of these studies suggest (Lewis, Gorbach & Altner 1972; Kersh 1974; Light & Dunham 1974; Macro Systems 1975), occasional users who are suffering from health problems associated with their drug use may self-refer for treatment. However moderate the use, the impurities in street heroin and the injection of opiates pose a serious risk of infection. In addition there is a risk of overdose when drugs of uncertain potency are used.

2. Although many studies report "nonaddicted" and "less than daily" users among their subjects, it does not necessarily follow that such use is nonabusive. Use in amounts and frequencies below those required for addiction may still interfere with work, marriage, and general functioning and thus may require treatment.

3. Occasional users may apply for treatment to help with personal problems that do not necessarily result from their use of drugs. For example, of the 2,750 adolescents who had been in one drug treatment program, almost half stated that they had applied for admission only to get help for personal problems (Santo, Farley & Friedman 1980).

4. At least some users report for treatment who believe they are addicted but in fact are not. O'Brien (1976) found that such users "became insulted if they were told they were not really dependent on drugs." These users may subscribe to the cultural mythology that even infrequent use of heroin will result in addiction. Alternatively, as articles by Frederick B. Glaser (1974) and by B. J. Primm and P. E. Bath (1973) suggest, some applicants who have used heroin frequently have not become physically dependent because of the low potency of the street drug.

5. For some occasional users (probably a small percentage), participation in treatment may provide the entree to a deviant drug-using subculture. Association with addicts in treatment offers the occasional user a new means of obtaining illicit drugs; in addition, a sense of belonging and the status associated with membership in a deviant group may be considered important rewards (Gay, Senay & Newmeyer 1974). A relevant case is reported in Zinberg and Lewis (1964): A twenty-four-year-old man who had been hospitalized for hepatitis and who claimed to be an addict finally confessed to a house officer that he had taken heroin only twice, but he cautioned the physician "not to tell his wife

because he pretended to her and to their 'cool' friends that he was 'hooked.'"

6. Many occasional users are coerced into treatment. Not infrequently, lawyers and "sympathetic" probation officers propose that the user enroll in a treatment program prior to criminal prosecution as a means of getting a lighter sentence. Dan Waldorf (1973) believed that as much as 27% of his treatment sample had not been addicted prior to treatment because "most of the sample had been committed to treatment under New York State civil commitment laws (89%), and actual physical addiction is not a necessary condition for treatment."

7. Finally, admission of nonaddicts may be encouraged by treatment-program recruiters. Treatment programs have an obvious interest in maintaining high enrollments because levels of funding are usually linked to the size of their patient population.

Treatment Data as a Measure of Occasional Use

If it could be assumed that all heroin users eventually seek treatment, data like those just considered would obviously be representative of the entire population of users and so would provide workable estimates of the number of occasional users. But in fact there is considerable evidence that many users apply for treatment.

A survey of heroin users in Wyoming identified a significant number of addicts who were unknown to the police and to the drug treatment centers of the community health facilities (Bourne, Hunt & Vogt 1975; Hunt 1977). Stuart Nightingale (1977) has also reported that according to national estimates, there are more opiate users out of treatment than in treatment: at any particular time, while 170,000 persons are in treatment for opiate addiction and 100,000 addicts are in jail, "another 300,000 to 400,000 are not in treatment," and "the majority . . . have never been in treatment."

In a smaller area Carl D. Chambers and John A. Inciardi (1972) conducted a study of active heroin addicts in Bedford-Stuyvesant, Brooklyn (New York), who had not been in treatment or in jail for six months prior to the interview. Analysis of the demographic characteristics of the ninety-five respondents "revealed nothing which would suggest that they were significantly different from the universe of 'heroin street addicts' in New York City." Seventy percent of them were males, and of these, 40% were black, 32% white, and 22% Puerto Rican. Their ages ranged from seventeen to forty-six (median age, twenty-four). All were reported to be addicted; they had used a median of four "bags" a day for periods from at least nine months to as long as twenty-three years. Yet almost half of the sample had never been treated for drug use.

In an epidemiological Chicago street study, Patrick H. Hughes et al. (1971) found that addicts occupying dealership roles were especially difficult to "involve in treatment and if involved, were unlikely to remain over time." By contrast, addicts who retained jobs were likely to participate and remain in treatment, usually for at least six months. A third category, "hustling addicts," fell between these two groups in terms of the likelihood of entering and remaining in treatment.

Andrew T. Weil (1972) discussed "stable addicts" he had encountered in San Francisco who were "hidden" from the attention of the social authorities. He described them as suburban working-class whites who were steadily employed and who purchased drugs with money they had earned. Their life-style was quite different from that of the stereotypic heroin addict. Some injected heroin once a day, others did it both morning and evening, and most "kept up these patterns for years."

It appears also that underrepresentation of the using population in treatment samples applies to both younger and older addicts. James V. DeLong (1972) has noted that the current approaches to treatment fail to attract a large number of the younger addicts. The reason for this, he says, is that most young addicts either are not "sufficiently disenchanted with either the life-style or the effect of heroin" to apply for treatment or "are as yet unconvinced that they are truly hooked." Similar conclusions have been drawn with respect to older users. Charles Winick (1974) reports that a "substantial proportion" of the 1,300 Metropolitan New York heroin users who came to the attention of correctional or treatment authorities "gave every indication of indefinitely continuing drug use." Earlier, W. C. Capel et al. (1972) had interviewed thirty-eight opiate users in New Orleans between the ages of forty-five and seventy-five, many of whom "have not stopped using opiates, but whose life-style has exhibited a protective adaptation that diverts attention from their illicit activity." Fewer than half (47%) of these older subjects used daily; the remainder reported various weekly patterns of use. Many had eluded arrest for years (some had never been arrested), and none were currently in treatment. Again, the authors concluded that neither methadone maintenance nor drug-free treatment groups appeared "to be attractive to men of this age group."

These studies support the commonsense view that treatment populations, which include fewer occasional users than addicts, underrepresent the at-large, active drug population. Although several reasons were given in the last section to explain why occasional users *might* come to treatment, it can be deduced from the data presented here that the proportion of occasional users who actually do enter treatment is much smaller than the proportion of heavy users (addicts) who enter treatment. To counteract this underrepresentation of occasional users in the treatment data, it is necessary to turn to another type of source material—data drawn from nontreatment (noninstitutionalized) samples.

Occasional Noninstitutionalized Users

Much of the data from studies of noninstitutionalized opiate users show that the proportion of occasional users in the community at large is greater than that in treatment populations. With one exception, these studies also reveal a higher proportion of occasional users than of addicts among users who are not in treatment. The study that constitutes the exception is one of the earliest surveys of drug use in a normal population, a sample of young Negro males in St. Louis. In that study, published in 1967, Lee N. Robins and G. E. Murphy found that of the 13% who had tried heroin, 10% had become addicted. In fact, no one who had used the drug more than six times had avoided addiction. Thus the St. Louis study indicated that nonaddictive use among blacks was infrequent between the 1930s and the 1950s. But since then the same investigator (Robins) found nonaddictive use to be far more commonplace (Robins 1979), and several other studies and surveys of noninstitutionalized users have supported this view.

In 1971 and 1972 Albert Levengood, P. Lowinger and K. Schooff (1973) interviewed sixty single, white male heroin users, aged fifteen to twenty-four, living in a Detroit suburb. Of these, twenty-two (37%) used "regularly or on a daily basis"; twenty-four (40%) used occasionally, with the quantity and frequency of use varying widely; and fourteen (23%) were considered "former users," having taken heroin within the previous year but not during the month preceding interview. The group of "former users" included some subjects who were recent daily users, but no one in that group had received any type of treatment. Levengood, Lowinger and Schooff mentioned that many occasional users had maintained "the same frequency and dosage" for at least one year, but they emphasized that all patterns of use were subject to change.

David S. Nurco et al. (1975) conducted a study of 267 noninstitutionalized males who had been known to the Baltimore police department as narcotic addicts. Eighty-six percent of the sample acknowledged at least one period of addiction. Data on frequency of use indicated that for any one of several time periods, subjects who had used less than daily within the previous month had always outnumbered daily users, constituting at least 56% of all users.

David B. Graeven and Andrew Jones (1977) examined adolescent heroin use in a suburban San Francisco high school between 1966 and 1974. Of the 294 heroin users identified during the study, the proportion not addicted ("experimenters") was almost equal to the proportion who had become addicted: 49% versus 51%. During the period of the study 38% of the experimenters had used heroin only once or twice, 33% had used it 3 to 33 times, 19% 31 to 100 times, and the remaining 10% more than 100 times. In the final year of the study, however, most of the original experimenters (60%) reported no use, 33% were using less than twice a month, and only 7% were using once or twice a week. The addict group had also significantly reduced its heroin use by the end of the study period: 20% reported no use, "8 percent reported modal use of one or two times per month, 16 percent had had modal use of one or two times per week, and 47 percent modal use of three or more times per week."

Perhaps the most prominent research dealing with occasional use is the series of studies of Vietnam veterans by Lee N. Robins (Robins 1973, 1974; Robins, Davis & Goodwin 1974; Robins, Helzer & Davis 1975; Robins et al. 1979). She interviewed 900 enlisted men twelve to eighteen months before their return from Vietnam in 1971 and then reinterviewed 617 (more than two-thirds) of the same men in 1974. In 1974 she also collected data on a comparable population of 284 nonveterans who were matched to the veterans in age, eligibility for service, education, and place of residence as of the verterans' dates of induction. Robins found that of all the men who had been addicted to opiates while in Vietnam, only 12% had relapsed into addiction within three years after leaving Vietnam. Still more relevant and surprising is her finding that although half of the veterans who had been addicted in Vietnam had used heroin since their return home, only 12% of them had become readdicted. "Even when heroin was used frequently, that is, more than once a week for a considerable period of time, only half of those who used it frequently became readdicted" (Robins et al. 1979). Data obtained from the matched sample of nonveterans led Robins to conclude also that the low level of addiction observed for veterans after leaving the battle area was consistent with the patterns of use prevailing in the larger U.S. population.

In a survey of noninstitutionalized users of illicit drugs in Ohio (Abt Associates, Inc. 1975), 1.4% of the respondents admitted that they had used heroin, a percentage much higher than any previous estimate. Of these, 8.7% used "several times per week or more," 18.7% "a few times per month," 17.4% "a few times per year," and 65.2% "less frequently."

In a national representative sample of twenty- to thirty-year-olds drawn in 1974 (N = 2,510), John A. O'Donnell et al. (1976) found that only 6% had "ever used" heroin (of these most had used on only a few occasions, that is, less than 10 times) and 76% had used less than 99 times (light use). The use of other opiates also tended to be occasional. Although only 31% of the sample had "ever used" opiates, 11% were using them "in a manner not far removed from legitimate medical use." The investigators found that only 20% of the sample used opiates "in a way that could reasonably be seen as abuse" and that only 8% exceeded the level of "experimental" use. Among all nonmedical opiate users, 61% were classified as having been experimenters (fewer than 10 occasions of use), 29% as light users (10 to 99 occasions), and only 10% as heavy users (100 or more occasions).

Annual survey data drawn from large samples of high-school seniors— more than 15,000 students in the classes of 1975 through 1979—also suggest that occasional opiate use predominated over heavy use throughout the entire five-year period (Johnston, Bachman & O'Malley 1982). For example, in 1979 0.5% of seniors used heroin in a thirty-day period, but the percentage who used daily was less than 0.1. Data on the number of using occasions, whether for the previous thirty days, twelve months, or a lifetime, also indicated that occasional use was more common than intensive use. For example, lifetime data for seniors in 1975, 1976, and 1977 show that approximately 1.6% of the sample had used opiates on from 1 to 19 occasions compared with 0.2% (at the most) who had used on more than 19 occasions.

In 1971 and 1972 two national drug surveys were completed by the Response Analysis Corporation for the National Commission on Marihuana and Drug Abuse. Since 1974, similar surveys have been made jointly by the Response Analysis Corporation and the Social Research Group at George Washington University, under the sponsorship of the National Institute on Drug Abuse (NIDA) (Cisin, Miller & Harrell 1979; Fishburne, Abelson & Cisin 1980; Miller & Associates 1983). All these surveys have also yielded data showing that occasional opiate use is more common than heavy use. The pre-1974 surveys, for instance, indicated that among students who had used opiates, most had used less than once a week (75% of high school users and 98% of college users) (National Commission on Marihuana and Drug Abuse 1973). According to a 1979 study of young adults aged eighteen to twenty-five, unselected for drug use, 2.5% reported on interview that they had used heroin less than 11 times, compared with 1.3% who had used 11 or more times (Fishburne, Abelson & Cisin 1980).

In 1975 survey data gathered on a regional basis from 1,426 youths living in Detroit, Baltimore, Cincinnati, and Providence also indicated that occasional use was relatively common (Watkins & McCoy 1980). This sample was divided into two groups for the purpose of analyzing ethnic differences in drug use: 31% of the subjects had been born in Appalachia or had "a relative no further back than a grandparent who had lived in rural Appalachia"; the other 69% were designated "non-Appalachian." Of the 17.1% of Appalachian youths who had used heroin and other opiates in the two months before being interviewed, almost 50% had used only once a week. Of the 8% in the non-Appalachian group who were current opiate users, an even larger proportion (59%) used only once a week.

In contrast to the one early survey that found a high rate of addiction among young Negroes in St. Louis (Robins & Murphy 1967), all the later data on the general (noninstitutionalized) population suggest that at any one time those who use opiates occasionally may constitute 40% or more of the total opiate-using population. One estimate based on recapture techniques goes far beyond that figure, claiming that nonaddicts outnumber addicts by as much as ten to one (Hunt & Chambers 1976; Hunt 1977, 1982). Even on the basis of combined data for populations in treatment and out of treatment, it is reasonable to conclude that the number of nonaddicted opiate users both in and out of institutions is roughly equal to or greater than the number of addicts. Although not all researchers would agree with this view, many of those who would not agree would admit that occasional use is not so rare as they once supposed. For example, in reviewing papers dealing with the epidemiology of heroin and other narcotics, Jane D. Rittenhouse (1977) has stated that "increasing evidence has shown that self-reported mild use without social and health problems is not uncommon." Similarly, Bruce D. Johnson (1977) concluded that the typical addict "is involved in relatively brief addiction episodes . . . interspersed with voluntary abstinence, irregular consumption, institutionalization, or admission to treatment."

Unresolved Questions about Occasional Use

Although in the past decade a great mass of data has been gathered about occasional opiate users, critical questions about *use* versus *abuse* among such users remain unanswered.

First, virtually nothing is known about the way in which occasional opiate consumption is patterned over time. Prior to 1970 most surveys did not go "beyond the simple fact of use to obtain data pertaining to patterns of use" (Rittenhouse 1977). In more recent work, data on the frequency of use are often reported in the form of the number of occasions of use within the previous month, year, or lifetime of the user but without indicating how such occasions are distributed. For example, an occasional user classified as having used fewer than ninety-nine times in one year may, hypothetically, have used three times daily for about one month, or he may have used once every three or four days throughout the year. Although these two hypothetical examples indicate two very different patterns of opiate use or levels of control, such differences are not revealed by the data.

Second, little is known about how stable the various patterns of occasional use are. There is some evidence (Powell 1973) that users may continue their nonaddictive use for years, but data are not yet available as to the proportions of occasional users who maintain this style for various periods of time. If occasional use is not a stable pattern—that is, if the majority of such users either quickly give up opiate use or eventually become addicted—it would seem that the apparent pattern of occasional use has little significance for policy formulation.

Third, none of the studies just reviewed consider a subject's level of *non*opiate drug use to be relevant to his or her classification as an occasional opiate user. Until recently the existence of occasional opiate users who might also be alcoholics or barbiturate addicts could hardly have been seen as having relevance for policy regarding opiate use.

Fourth, most of the available data do not clearly relate frequency of use to quality of use. (Robins's work is a notable exception.) Although it is tempting to assume that less frequent use is less abusive, this is not always the case. Except at the extremes (use once a year versus multiple daily use), frequency is not a reliable predictor of drug-related difficulties (Zinberg, Harding & Apsler 1978). Problem drinking, for example, occurs across a broad range of frequencies of use (Smart 1974; Pattison 1979). And as Jerome H. Jaffe has pointed out (1975), although the risk of adverse effects tends to increase with the level of drug involvement, there are important exceptions to this rule, such as the increased risk of overdose or of psychological discomfort among neophyte users. Because researchers have not consistently studied opiate-related problems in conjunction with the quality of opiate use (Smart 1974), no light has been shed on the numbers and characteristics of opiate users as opposed to the numbers and characteristics of opiate abusers.

Fifth, little is known about the demographic characteristics, social background, personality structure, and other pertinent factors that tend to be associated with different patterns of opiate use.

Glossary

Boosting:	The street term for shoplifting.
Booting:	The practice of pulling the plunger in and out during the intravenous injection of a drug—usually a narcotic—so that the user sees the blood go back and forth in the syringe.
Button:	A term applied to that part of the peyote cactus which is ingested as a psychedelic. Sometimes other psychedelics are referred to as buttons but not often.
Buzz:	One way of describing "feeling high," e.g., "having a buzz on."
Chipping:	The use of narcotics on an occasional basis in order to avoid addiction. A "chipper" uses narcotics in this fashion.
Cook:	The process of dissolving a powdered drug, usually a narcotic, in a few drops of water so that the drug can be injected conveniently.
Cop, copping:	A description of the process of obtaining an illicit drug. The term was originally used exclusively for narcotics but now is used generally for any illicit substance.
Dabbler:	A term generally used on the street to describe someone who has experimented with narcotics but whose occasional use is not consistent.
Dealer:	A person who sells illicit drugs.
Drop:	To use a drug, usually a psychedelic, e.g., "dropping acid."
Dropper:	A term that describes that part of the equipment ("the

	works") that holds the substance to be injected through a needle. Often an eyedropper is used, hence the term.
Getting off:	A phrase that describes the feeling of "getting high" on an intoxicant, e.g., "Oh, it took a long time, but I just got off."
Head:	The street term for someone who uses marihuana; sometimes applied to regular users of other illicit drugs.
High, getting high:	Originally the general description of the state of intoxication caused by the use of illicit drugs, but today it is commonly used to describe the changed state of consciousness, or euphoria, caused by any intoxicant use and sometimes by any effort to alter consciousness states.
Joint:	The street term for a marihuana cigarette.
Jones:	The street term for the awareness that one has a physiological addiction.
Junk:	The street term for narcotics, usually heroin.
Munchies:	The feeling of enhanced appetite that frequently follows the use of marihuana.
Nod off, go on the nod:	Drifting off into a stuporous state following the use of a narcotic.
Roach:	The very end of a marihuana cigarette after it has been smoked.
Rush:	The sudden, sharp shift in consciousness and body sensations that results from injecting, or less frequently after inhalation of a drug.
Score, scoring:	(See Cop, copping.)
Skin-popping:	The practice of injecting a drug, particularly heroin, just under the skin, i.e., subcutaneously, rather than into a muscle or vein.
Snort:	To inhale a drug through the nostrils, usually in powdered form, but occasionally as a liquid.
Sopers:	The street term for methaqualone (Quaaludes), a sedative-hypnotic, sometimes preferred by many users over barbiturates or benzodiazepines.
Spike:	The street term for the needle used to inject narcotics or other intoxicants.
Tab:	The usual term for a measured dose of the psychedelic LSD but also used now for other psychedelics.

Tie, tie off: The use of a belt, necktie, rope, etc., as a tourniquet to make the veins more prominent for injecting the needle.

Toke: The street term for inhaling marihuana from a joint (marihuana cigarette) or pipe.

Trip, tripping: The term for being high on a psychedelic drug.

Works: The equipment used for injecting drugs. This includes a hypodermic syringe and needle, or something similar such as a sharpened eyedropper; a small, metal container, known as a cooker, in which to dissolve and heat the drug; and some substance such as cotton to strain the drug. Sometimes considered part of the "works" are a thin wire used to clean out the hypodermic needle and a belt or rope, etc., known as a "tie."

Bibliography

ABT ASSOCIATES, INC. (1975), *Drug Use in the State of Ohio: A Study Based upon the Ohio Drug Survey*. Dr. Robert Jarrett, Principal Investigator. Cambridge, Mass.: Abt Associates, Inc.

ALCOHOLICS ANONYMOUS (1954), *Is A. A. for You?* New York: Alcoholics Anonymous Publishing, Inc.

ALKSNE, H., LIEBERMAN, L. & BRILL, L. (1967), A conceptual model of the life cycle of addiction. *Int. J. Addictions*, 2:221–240.

AMERICAN MEDICAL ASSOCIATION COMMITTEE ON ALCOHOLISM AND ADDICTION AND COUNCIL ON MENTAL HEALTH (1966), Dependence on amphetamines and other stimulant drugs. *JAMA*, 197:193–197.

AMERICAN MEDICAL ASSOCIATION COUNCIL ON MENTAL HEALTH AND COMMITTEE ON ALCOHOLISM AND DRUG DEPENDENCE (1972), Oral methadone maintenance techniques in the management of morphine-type dependence. *JAMA*, 219:1618–1619.

AMERICAN PHARMACEUTICAL ASSOCIATION (1967), *Handbook on Non-Prescription Drugs*. Washington, D.C.: American Pharmaceutical Association, 5th ed.

AMSEL, S., MANDELL, L., MATHIAS, L., MASON, C. & HOCHERMAN, I. (1976), Reliability and validity of self-reported illegal activities and drug use collected from narcotic addicts. *Int. J. Addictions*, 11:325–36.

An Evaluation of the Decriminalization of Marihuana in Maine (1978). Augusta, Maine: Office of Alcoholism and Drug Abuse Prevention.

APSLER, R. (1978), Untangling the conceptual jungle of "drug abuse." *Contemp. Drug Prob.*, 7:55–80.

BALL, J. C. (1967), The reliability and validity of interview data obtained from 59 narcotic drug addicts. *Amer. J. Sociol.*, 72:650–654.

BARR, H. L., LANGS, R. J., HOLT, R. R., GOLDBERGER, L. & KLEIN, G. S. (1972), *LSD: Personality and Experience*. New York: Wiley Interscience.

BAZELON, D. L. (1979), Risk and regulation. *Science*, 205:277–280.

BECKER, H. S. (1953), Becoming a marihuana user. *Amer. J. Sociol.*, 59:235–243.

—— (1963), *Outsiders: Studies in the Sociology of Deviance.* Glencoe, Ill.: Free Press of Glencoe.

—— (1967), History, culture and subjective experience: an exploration of the social bases of drug-induced experiences. *J. Health and Social Behavior*, 8:162–176.

BENVENUTO, J. A. & BOURNE, P. G. (1975), The federal polydrug abuse project. *J. Psychedelic Drugs*, 7:115–120.

BEXTON, W. H., HERON, W. & SCOTT, T. H. (1954), Effects of decreased variation in the sensory environment. *Canad. J. Psychol.* 8:70–76.

BIBRING, E. (1954), *Lectures on Psychoanalytic Ego Psychology.* Boston University, Graduate School of Psychology.

BIEBERMAN, L. (1967), *Session Games People Play.* Cambridge, Mass.: Psychedelic Information Center.

BLACHLY, P. H. (1973), Naloxone for diagnosis in methadone programs. *JAMA*, 224:334–335.

BLALOCK, H. M. (1979), *Social Statistics.* New York: McGraw-Hill, 2d ed. rev., pp. 160–161.

BLUMER, H., SUTTER, A. G., AHMED, S. & SMITH, R. (1967), Becoming hard-core narcotic addicts. In *The World of Youthful Drug Use.* Berkeley: University of California, School of Criminology, pp. 73–75.

BONITO, A. F., NURCO, D. N. & SHAFFER, J. W. (1976), The verticality of addicts' self-reports in social research. *Int. J. Addictions*, 11:719–724.

BORIS, H. N., ZINBERG, N. E. & BORIS, M. (1978), Social education for adolescents. *Psychiatric Opin.*, 15:32–37.

BOURNE, P. G., HUNT, L. G. & VOGT, J. (1975), *A Study of Heroin Use in the State of Wyoming.* Report for the Department of Health and Social Services, State of Wyoming. Washington, D.C.: Foundation for International Resources.

BRECHER, E. M. & THE EDITORS OF CONSUMER REPORTS (1972), *Licit and Illicit Drugs.* Boston: Little, Brown.

BRO, P. & SCHOU, J. (1975), Cannabis poisoning with analytical verification. *New Engl. J. Med.* 293:1049–1050.

BUNCE, R. (1982), Social and political sources of drug effects: the case of bad trips on psychedelics. In *Control over Intoxicant Use: Pharmacological, Psychological, and Social Considerations*, ed. N. E. Zinberg & W. M. Harding. New York: Human Sciences Press, pp. 105–125.

Cabinet Committee on Drug Abuse Prevention, Treatment, and Rehabilitation (1977), *Recommendations for Future Federal Activities in Drug Abuse Prevention.* Report of the Committee on Prevention. U.S. Department of Health, Education, and Welfare. Washington, D.C.: U.S. Government Printing Office.

CAPEL, W. C., GOLDSMITH, B., WADDELL, K. J. & STEWART, G. T. (1972), The aging narcotic addict: an increasing problem for the next decades. *J. Gerontol.* 27:102–106.

CATTON, K. & SHAIN, M. (1976), Heroin users in the community: a review of the drug use and life styles of addicts and users not in treatment. *Addictive Dis.*, 2:421–440.

CHAFETZ, M. E. & DEMONE, H. W., JR. (1962), *Alcoholism and Society.* New York: Oxford Univ. Press.

CHAMBERS, C. D. & INCIARDI, J. A. (1972), An empirical assessment of the availability of illicit methadone. In *Proceedings of the Fourth National Conference on Methadone Maintenance.* San Francisco, 8–10 January, pp. 149–151.

CHAMBERS, C. D. & TAYLOR, W. J. R. (1973), The incidence and patterns of drug abuse during maintenance therapy. In *Methadone: Experience and Issues,* ed. C. D. Chambers & L. Brill. New York: Behavioral Publications.

CHEIN, I., GERARD, D. L., LEE, R. S. & ROSENFELD, E. (1964), *The Road to H.* New York: Basic Books.

CHRISTIE, N. & BRAUN, K. (1969), Alcohol problems: the conceptual framework. In *Proceedings of the 29th International Congress on Alcohol and Alcoholism,* vol. 2. Highland Park, N.J.: Hillhouse.

CISIN, I., MILLER, J. & HARRELL, A. (1979), *Highlights from the National Survey on Drug Abuse: 1977.* DHEW Publication No. (ADM)79–620. Washington, D.C.: U.S. Government Printing Office.

CLAUSEN, J. A. (1968), Drug addiction: social aspects. In *International Encyclopedia of the Social Sciences,* vol. 4, ed. D. L. Sills. New York: Macmillan, pp. 298–304.

COHEN, S. (1968), The cyclic psychedelics. *Amer. J. Psychiat.*, 125:394–395.

COHEN, M. M., KIRSCHHORN, K. & FROSCH, W. A. (1967), In vivo and in vitro chromosomal damage induced by LSD–25. *New Engl. J. Med.*, 277:1043–1049.

COHEN, M. M., MARINELLO, M. & BACH, N. (1967), Chromosomal damage in human leukocytes induced by lysergic acid diethylamide. *Science,* 155: 1417–1419.

DELONG, J. V. (1972), Treatment and rehabilitation. In *Dealing with Drug Abuse: A Report to the Ford Foundation.* New York: Praeger Publications, pp. 173–254.

——— (1974), Introduction. In *"High" States: A Beginning Study,* N. E. Zinberg. Drug Abuse Council Publication #SS–3. Washington, D.C.: The Drug Abuse Council, Inc.

DE RIOS, M. D. & SMITH, D. W. (1976), Using or abusing? An anthropological approach to the study of psychoactive drugs. *J. Psychedelic Drugs,* 8:263–266.

DOBBS, W. H. (1971), Methadone treatment of heroin addicts. *JAMA,* 218: 1536–1541.

DOLE, V. P. & JOSEPH H. (1977), Methadone maintenance: outcome after termination. *N. Y. State J. Med.* 77:1409–1412.

DOLE, V. P. & NYSWANDER, M. E. (1965), A medical treatment for diacetylmorphine (heroin) addiction. *JAMA*, 193:646–648.

—— (1966), Rehabilitation of heroin addicts after blockade with methadone. *N. Y. State J. Med.*, 66:2011–2017.

—— (1967), Heroin addiction—a metabolic disease. *Arch. Int. Med.*, 120:19–24.

DOLE, V. P., NYSWANDER, M. E. & WARNER, A. (1968), Successful treatment of 750 criminal addicts. *JAMA*, 206:2708–2711.

Drug Abuse Films (1973). Washington, D.C.: National Coordinating Council on Drug Education.

DUPONT, R. L. (1983), Letter to the Editor. *New York Times*, 15 January.

EDDY, N. B., HALBACH, H., ISBELL, H. & SEEVERS, M. H. (1965), Drug dependence: its significance and characteristics. *Bull. World Health Org.*, 23:721–722.

EDWARDS, G. F. (1974), Drugs, drug dependence, and the concept of plasticity. *Q. J. Studies on Alcohol*, 35:176–195.

ERIKSON, K. T. (1964), Notes on the sociology of deviance. In *The Other Side: Perspectives in Deviance*, ed. H. S. Becker. Glencoe, Ill.: Free Press of Glencoe.

—— (1966), *The Wayward Puritan*. New York: Wiley.

Federal Strategy for Drug Abuse and Drug Traffic Prevention (1977). Report for the President by the Strategy Council on Drug Abuse. Washington, D.C.: U.S. Government Printing Office.

FISHBURNE, P. M., ABELSON, H. I. & CISIN, I. (1980), *National Survey on Drug Abuse: Main Findings, 1979*. DHEW Publication No. (ADM)80–976. Washington, D.C.: U.S. Government Printing Office.

FOOD AND DRUG ADMINISTRATION (1977), Safety and effectiveness of over-the-counter drugs: the FDA's OTC drug review. *Pediatrics*, 59:309–311.

FORT, J. (1969), *The Pleasure Seekers: The Drug Crisis, Youth and Society*. New York: Bobbs-Merrill.

FREEDMAN, D. X. (1970), Drugs and culture. *Triangle*, 10:109–112.

GAY, G. R., SENAY, E. & NEWMEYER, J. A. (1974), The pseudo junkie: evolution of the heroin life style in the non-addicted individual. *Anesth. Analg.*, 53:241–247.

GEBER, B. A. (1969), Non-dependent drug use: some psychological aspects. In *Scientific Basis of Drug Dependence*, ed. H. Steinberg. London: J. & A. Churchill, pp. 375–393.

GILL, M. M. & KLEIN, G. S. (1964), The structuring of drive and reality: Rapaport's contributions to psycho-analysis and psychology. *Int. J. Psycho-Anal.*, 45:483–498.

GLASER, F. B. (1974), Psychologic vs. pharmacologic heroin dependence. *New Engl. J. Med.*, 290:231.

_____ (1978), Personal communication. 9 January.

GLASSCOTE, R. M., SUSSEX, J. N., JAFFE, J. H., BALL, J. & BRILL, L. (1972), *The Treatment of Drug Abuse: Programs, Problems, Prospects.* Washington, D.C.: Joint Information Service of the American Psychiatric Association and the National Association for Mental Health.

GOODE, E. (1969), Multiple drug use among marihuana smokers. *Social Problems,* 17:48–64.

_____ (1972), *Drugs in American Society.* New York: Knopf.

_____ (1973), *The Drug Phenomenon: Social Aspects of Drug Taking.* New York: Bobbs-Merrill.

GOODMAN, L. S. & GILMAN, A. (1975), *The Pharmacologic Basis of Therapeutics,* New York: Macmillan, 5th ed.

GOTTLIEB, D. (1970), Alienation and rebellion among the disadvantaged. In *Drug Dependence: A Guide for Physicians.* Chicago: AMA.

GRAEVEN, D. B. & JONES, A. (1977), *Addicts and Experimenters: Dynamics of Involvement in an Adolescent Heroin Epidemic.* Paper presented at National Drug Abuse Conference, San Francisco.

GREENE, M., NIGHTINGALE, S. & DuPONT, R. L. (1975), Evolving patterns of drug abuse. *Ann. Int. Med.,* 83:402–411.

GRINSPOON, L. (1971), *Marihuana Reconsidered.* Cambridge, Mass.: Harvard Univ. Press.

_____ (1974), Personal communication, 20 March.

GRINSPOON, L. & BAKALAR, J. (1979), *Psychedelic Drugs Reconsidered.* New York: Basic Books.

GUSFIELD, J. R. (1972), *Symbolic Crusade: Status Politics and the American Temperance Movement.* Chicago: Univ. Illinois Press.

_____ (1975), The (f)utility of knowledge: the relation of social science to public policy toward drugs. *Ann. Amer. Acad. Polit. Soc. Sci.,* 417:1–15.

HARDING, W. M. & ZINBERG, N. E. (1977), The effectiveness of the subculture in developing rituals and social sanctions for controlled use. In *Drugs, Rituals and Altered States of Consciousness,* ed. B. M. du Toit. Rotterdam: Balkema, pp. 111–133.

HARDY, T. (1895), *Jude the Obscure.* New York: Norton, 1978.

HARTMANN, H. (1939), *Ego Psychology and the Problem of Adaptation,* tr. D. Rapaport. New York: Int. Univ. Press, 1958.

HELLER, M. (1972), *The Sources of Drug Abuse.* Addiction Services Agency Report. New York: Addiction Services Agency.

HELLMAN, A. D. (1975), *Laws Against Marihuana: The Price we Pay.* Chicago: Univ. Chicago Press.

HELMER, J. (1975), *Drugs and Minority Oppression.* New York: Seabury Press.

HEPLER, R. S. & FRANK, I. R. (1971), Marihuana smoking and intraocular pressure. *JAMA,* 217:1392.

HERMAN, C. P. & KOZLOWSKI, L. T. (1982), Indulgence, excess, and restraint: perspectives on consummatory behavior in everyday life. In *Control over Intoxicant Use: Pharmacological, Psychological, and Social Considerations*, ed. N. E. Zinberg & W. M. Harding. New York: Human Sciences Press, pp. 77–88.

HERON, W., BEXTON, W. H. & HEBB, D. O. (1953), Cognitive effects of a decreased variation in the sensory environment. *Amer. Psycholog.*, 8:366–372.

HERON, W., DOONE, B. K. & SCOTT, T. H. (1956), Visual disturbances after prolonged perceptual isolation. *Canad. J. Psychol.*, 10:13–18.

HERSHEY, N. & MILLER, R. D. (1976), *Human Experimentation and the Law.* Germantown, Md.: Aspen Systems Corporation.

HUGHES, P. H., CRAWFORD, G. A., BARKER, N. W., SCHUMANN, S. & JAFFE, J. H. (1971), The social structure of a heroin copping community. *Amer. J. Psychiat.*, 128:551–558.

HUNT, L. G. (1977), Prevalence of active heroin use in the United States. In *The Epidemiology of Heroin and Other Narcotics*, ed. J. D. Rittenhouse. NIDA Research Monograph No. 16. DHEW Publication No. 78–559. Washington, D.C.: U.S. Government Printing Office.

⸺ (1982), Growth of substance use and misuse: some speculations and data. In *Control over Intoxicant Use: Pharmacological, Psychological, and Social Considerations*, ed. N. E. Zinberg & W. M. Harding. New York: Human Sciences Press, pp. 149–157.

HUNT, L. G. & CHAMBERS, C. D. (1976), *The Heroin Epidemics: A Study of Heroin Use in the United States, 1965–1975.* Holliswood, New York: Spectrum.

HUXLEY, A. (1954), *The Doors of Perception.* New York: Harper & Row.

Impact Study of S. B. 95 (1976). Sacramento: California Health and Welfare Agency, Office of Narcotics and Drug Abuse.

INGELFINGER, F. J. (1977), The handbook on non-prescription drugs. *New Engl. J. Med.*, 297:48–49.

JACOBSON, R. C. & ZINBERG, N. E. (1975), *The Social Basis of Drug Abuse Prevention.* Drug Abuse Council Publication No. SS–5. Washington, D.C.: The Drug Abuse Council, Inc.

JAFFE, J. H. (1975), Drug addiction and drug abuse. In *The Pharmacological Basis of Therapeutics*, ed. L. S. Goodman & A. Gilman. New York: Macmillan, 5th ed., pp. 284–324.

JOHNSON, B. D. (1977), *Once an Addict, Seldom an Addict.* Paper presented at the National Drug Abuse Conference, San Francisco.

JOHNSON, B. D. & GOLDSTEIN, P. J. (1979), *What is an Addict? Empirical Patterns and Concepts of Addiction.* Paper presented to the Drinking and Drugs Section of the Society for the Study of Social Problems. Boston, Mass., 26 August.

JOHNSTON, L. D., BACHMAN, J. G. & O'MALLEY, P. M. (1980), *Drug Use among American High School Students, 1975–1977.* Rockville, Md.: National Institute on Drug Abuse.

———— (1982), *Student Drug Use in America, 1975–1981.* DHHS Publication No. (ADM)82–1221. Rockville, Md.: National Institute on Drug Abuse.

JOSEPHSON, E. (1974), Trends in adolescent marihuana use. In *Drug Use: Epidemiological and Sociological Approaches,* ed. E. Josephson & E. E. Carroll. New York: Wiley, pp. 177–205.

KAFKA, J. S. (1964), Technical applications of a concept of multiple reality. *Int. J. Psycho-Anal.,* 45:575–578.

KAFKA, J. S. & GAARDER, K. R. (1964), Some effects of the therapist's LSD experience in his therapeutic work. *Amer. J. Psychother.,* 18:236–243.

KAPLAN, E. H. & WIEDER, H. (1974), *Drugs Don't Take People, People Take Drugs.* Secaucus, N.J.: Lyle Stuart.

KAPLAN, J. (1983), *The Hardest Drug: Heroin and Drug Policy.* Chicago: Univ. Chicago Press.

KENISTON, K. (1969), Heads and seekers: drugs on campus, countercultures, and American society. *Amer. Scholar,* 38:97–112.

KERSH, E. (1974), Narcotic overdosage. *Hosp. Med.,* 10:3.

KHANTZIAN, E. J. (1975), Self-selection and progression in drug dependence. *Amer. J. Psychother.,* 36:19–22.

———— (1978), Drug-alcohol problems in women: a clinical perspective. *Psychiatric Opin.,* 15:18–20.

KHANTZIAN, E. J., MACK, J. E. & SCHATZBERG, A. F. (1974), Heroin use as an attempt to cope: clinical observations. *Amer. J. Psychiat.,* 131:160–164.

KNIGHT, R. P. (1937), Psychodynamics of chronic alcoholics. *J. Nerv. Ment. Dis.,* 9:538–548.

KRYSTAL, H. & RASKIN, H. A. (1970), *Drug Dependence: Aspects of Ego Functions.* Detroit: Wayne State Univ. Press.

LASAGNA, L. (1965), Addicting drugs and medical practice: toward the elaboration of realistic goals and the eradication of myths, mirages, and half-truths. In *Narcotics,* ed. D. M. Wilner & G. G. Kassebaum. New York: McGraw-Hill, pp. 53–66.

LASCH, C. (1979), *Culture of Narcissism.* New York: Norton.

LEAVITT, F. (1974), *Drugs and Behavior.* Philadelphia: W. B. Saunders.

LETTIERI, D. J., SAYERS, M. & PEARSON, H. W., eds. (1980), *Theories on Drug Abuse: Selected Contemporary Perspectives.* NIDA Research Monograph 30. DHHS Publication No. (ADM)80–967. Washington, D.C.: U.S. Government Printing Office.

LEVENGOOD, A., LOWINGER, P. & SCHOOFF, K. (1973), Heroin addiction in the suburbs—an epidemiologic study. *Amer. J. Pub. Health,* 63:209–213.

LEWIS, D. C. & ZINBERG, N. E. (1964), Narcotic usage: II. A historical perspective on a difficult medical problem. *New Engl. J. Med.,* 270:1045–1050.

LEWIS, R., GORBACH, S. & ALTNER, P. (1972), Spinal pseudomonas chon-droosteomyelitis in heroin users. *New Engl. J. Med.*, 286:1303.

LIGHT, R. W. & DUNHAM, T. R. (1974), Vertebral osteomyelitis due to pseudomonas in the occasional heroin user. *JAMA*, 228:1272.

LILLY, J. C. (1956), Mental effects of reduction of ordinary levels of visual stimuli on intact healthy persons. *Psychiatr. Res. Rep.*, 5:1–9.

LINDESMITH, A. R. (1947), *Opiate Addiction.* Evanston, Ill.: Principia Press.

――― (1965), *The Addict and the Law.* Bloomington: Indiana Univ. Press.

LIPINSKI, E. (1972), Motivation in drug misuse: some comments on agent, environment, host. *JAMA*, 219:171–175.

LOLLI, G. (1970), The cocktail hour: physiological, psychological, and social aspects. In *Alcohol and Civilization*, ed. S. P. Lucia. New York: McGraw-Hill.

LOLLI, G., SERRIANNI, E., GOLDER, G. & LUZATTO-FEGIZ, P. (1958), *Alcohol in Italian Culture.* Glencoe, Ill.: Free Press.

MACRO SYSTEMS, INC. (1975), *Three-Year Followup Study of Clients Enrolled in Treatment Programs in New York City.* Rockville, Md.: National Institute on Drug Abuse.

MADDUX, J. F. & DESMOND, D. P. (1975), Reliability and validity of information from chronic heroin users. *JAMA*, 228:1272.

MADDUX, J. F., WILLIAMS, J. E. & LEHMAN, P. E. (1969), Results of a pre-release program for narcotic addicts. *Int. J. Addictions*, 4:203.

Maine: A Time/Cost Analysis of the Decriminalization of Marihuana in Maine (1979). Augusta, Maine: Office of Alcoholism and Drug Abuse Prevention.

MALOFF, D., BECKER, H. S., FONAROFF, A. & RODIN, J. (1982), Informal social controls and their influence on substance use. In *Control over Intoxicant Use: Pharmacological, Psychological, and Social Considerations*, ed. N. E. Zinberg & W. M. Harding. New York: Human Sciences Press, pp. 53–76.

MANN, P. (1978), *The Washington Post.* 23 July.

MARCOVITZ, E. (1969), On the nature of addiction to cigarettes. *J. Amer. Psychoanal. Assn.*, 17:1094–1096.

MARCUSE, H. (1955), *Eros and Civilization.* New York: Vintage Books.

Marihuana Survey—State of Oregon (1977). Washington, D.C.: The Drug Abuse Council, Inc., 28 January.

Marijuana and Health (1982). Report of a Study by a Committee of the Institute of Medicine, Division of Health Sciences Policy. Washington, D.C.: National Academy Press.

MCAULIFFE, W. E. & GORDON, R. A. (1975), A test of Lindesmith's theory of addiction: the frequency of euphoria among long-term addicts. *Amer. J. Sociol.*, 79:795–840.

MCGLOTHLIN, W. H. (1974), The epidemiology of hallucinogenic drug use. In *Drug Use: Epidemiological and Sociological Approaches*, ed. E. Josephson & E. E. Carroll. New York: Wiley, pp. 279–301.

McGLOTHLIN, W. H. & ARNOLD, D. O. (1971), LSD revisited—a ten-year followup of medical LSD use. *Arch. Gen. Psychiat.*, 24:35–49.

MEAD, G. H. (1934), *Mind, Self and Society.* Chicago: Univ. Chicago Press.

MILLER, J. D. & ASSOCIATES (1983), *National Survey on Drug Abuse, Main Findings, 1982.* Washington, D.C.: U.S. Government Printing Office.

MINKOWSKI, W. L., WEISS, R. C. & HEIDBREDER, G. A. (1972), A view of the drug problem: a rational approach to youthful drug use and abuse. *Clin. Pediatr.*, 11:376–381.

MOGAR, R. E. & SAVAGE, C. (1954), Personality change associated with psychedelic (LSD) therapy: a preliminary report. *Psychother.: Theory, Res. Pract.*, 1:154–162.

MOORE, M. H. (1982), Limiting supplies of drugs to illicit markets. In *Control over Intoxicant Use: Pharmacological, Psychological, and Social Considerations,* ed. N. E. Zinberg & W. M. Harding. New York: Human Sciences Press, pp. 183–200.

MUSTO, D. F. (1973), *The American Disease: Origins of Narcotic Controls.* New Haven: Yale Univ. Press.

NAHAS, G. G. (1976), *Keep off the Grass.* New York: Reader's Digest Press.

National Commission on Marihuana and Drug Abuse (1972), *Marihuana. A Signal of Misunderstanding.* Washington, D.C.: U.S. Government Printing Office.

―――― (1973), *Drug Use in America: Problem in Perspective.* Washington, D.C.: U.S. Government Printing Office.

National Council on Alcoholism (1975), *13 Steps to Alcoholism: Which Steps Are You on?* New York: National Council on Alcoholism.

National Institute on Drug Abuse (1977), *Marihuana and Health.* Sixth Annual Report to the Congress from the Secretary of Health, Education, and Welfare. DHEW Publication No. (ADM)77–443. Washington, D.C.: U.S. Government Printing Office.

―――― (1980), *Marihuana and Health.* Eighth Annual Report to the Congress from the Secretary of Health, Education, and Welfare. DHEW Publication No. (ADM)80–945. Washington, D.C.: U.S. Government Printing Office.

NEWMAN, R. G., CATES, M., TYTUN, A. et al. (1976), Reliability of self-reported age of first drug use: analysis of New York City narcotics register data. *Int. J. Addictions,* 11:611–618.

NEWMEYER, J. (1974), Five years after: drug use and exposure to heroin among the Haight Ashbury Free Medical Clinic clientele. *J. Psychedelic Drugs,* 6:61–65.

NEWMEYER, J. & JOHNSON, G. (1982), Drug emergencies in crowds: an analysis of "rock medicine," 1973–1979. In *Control over Intoxicant Use: Pharmacological, Psychological, and Social Considerations,* ed. N. E. Zinberg & W. M. Harding. New York: Human Sciences Press, pp. 127–137.

New York Times (1974), Interview with G. G. Nahas. 4 February.

―――― (1974), Interview with R. C. Kolodny. 9 April.

NIGHTINGALE, S. (1977), Treatment for drug abusers in the United States. *Addictive Dis.*, 3:11–20.

NURCO, D. N., BONITO, A. J., LERNER, M. & BALTER, M. D. (1975), Studying addicts over time: methodology and preliminary findings. *Amer. J. Drug Alcohol Abuse*, 2:183–196.

O'BRIEN, C. P. (1976), Experimental analysis of conditioning factors in human narcotic addiction. *Pharmacol. Rev.*, 27:533–543.

O'DONNELL, J. A., VOSS, H. L., CLAYTON, R. R., SLATIN, G. T. & ROOM, R. G. W. (1976), *Young Men and Drugs—A Nationwide Survey*. NIDA Research Monograph No. 5. Rockville, Md.: National Institute on Drug Abuse.

O'NEILL, E. (1956), *Long Day's Journey into Night*. New Haven: Yale Univ. Press.

ORWELL, G. (1949), *1984*. New York: Harcourt Press.

PARRY, H. J., BALTER, M. D. & CISIN, I. H. (1970), Primary levels of underreporting psychotropic drug use. *Publ. Opinion Q.*, 34 (Winter).

PATTISON, E. M. (1979), The selection of treatment modalities for the alcoholic patient. In *The Diagnosis and Treatment of Alcoholism*, ed. J. H. Mendelson & N. K. Mello. New York: McGraw-Hill, pp. 126–227.

PEELE, S. (1975), *Love and Addiction*. New York: Signet.

PEKANNEN, J. & FALCO, M. (1975), Sweet and sour. *Atlantic*, 236:50–53.

PERT, C. B., PASTERNAK, G. & SNYDER, S. H. (1973), Opiate agonists and antagonists discriminated by receptor binding in brain. *Science*, 182:1359–1361.

POWELL, D. H. (1973), A pilot study of occasional heroin users. *Arch. Gen. Psychiat.*, 32:955–961.

PRIMM, B. J. & BATH, P. E. (1973), Pseudoheroinism. *Int. J. Addictions*, 8:231–242.

RADO, S. (1958), Narcotic bondage. In *Problems of Addiction and Habituation*, ed. H. Hock & J. Zubin. New York: Grune & Stratton.

RAPAPORT, D. (1958), Theory of ego autonomy: a generalization. *Bull. Menninger Clinic*, 22:13–35.

———— (1959), A historical survey of psychoanalytic ego psychology. In *Identity and the Life Cycle* [Psychological Issues, Monograph 1], E. H. Erikson. New York: Int. Univ. Press, pp. 5–17.

———— (1960), On the psychoanalytic theory of motivation. In *Nebraska Symposium on Motivation*, ed. M. R. Jones. Lincoln, Neb.: Univ. Nebraska Press, pp. 173–247.

Report of the Liaison Task Panel on Psychoactive Drug Use/Misuse (1978). In *Vol. IV, Appendix: Task Panel Reports Submitted to the President's Commission on Mental Health*. Washington, D.C.: U.S. Government Printing Office, pp. 2103–2140.

RITTENHOUSE, J. D., ed. (1977), *The Epidemiology of Heroin and other*

Narcotics. NIDA Research Monograph No. 16. DHEW Publication No. (ADM)78–559. Rockville, Md.: National Institute on Drug Abuse.

ROBBINS, E. S., FROSCH, W. A. & STERN, M. (1967), Further observations on untoward reactions to LDS. *Amer. J. Psychiat.*, 124:393–395.

ROBINS, L. N. (1973), *A Followup of Vietnam Drug Users.* Special Action Office Monograph, Series A, No. 1. Washington, D.C.: U.S. Government Printing Office.

———— (1974), *The Vietnam Drug User Returns.* Special Action Office Monograph, Series A, No. 2. Washington, D.C.: U.S. Government Printing Office.

———— (1977), Brief terms of reference. In *The Epidemiology of Heroin and Other Narcotics*, ed. J. D. Rittenhouse. NIDA Research Monograph No. 16. DHEW Publication No. (ADM)78–559. Rockville, Md.: National Institute on Drug Abuse.

———— (1979), Addict careers. In *Handbook on Drug Abuse*, ed. R. L. DuPont, A. Goldstein & J. O'Donnell. Washington, D.C.: U.S. Government Printing Office, pp. 325–336.

———— (1980), Proposal to National Council, National Institute on Drug Abuse.

ROBINS, L. N., DAVIS, D. H. & GOODWIN, D. W. (1974), Drug use in U.S. Army enlisted men in Vietnam: a follow-up on their return home. *Amer. J. Epidemiology*, 99:235–249.

ROBINS, L. N., HELZER, J. E. & DAVIS, D. H. (1975), Narcotic use in southeast Asia and afterward. *Arch. Gen. Psychiat.*, 32:955–961.

ROBINS, L. N., HELZER, J. E., HESSELBROCK, M. & WISH, E. (1979), Vietnam veterans three years after Vietnam. In *Yearbook of Substance Abuse*, ed. L. Brill & C. Winick. New York: Human Sciences Press.

ROBINS, L. N. & MURPHY, G. E. (1967), Drug use in a normal population of young Negro men. *Amer. J. Publ. Health*, 570:1580–1596.

ROSENFELD, H. A. (1960), On drug addiction. In *Psychotic States*, ed. H. A. Rosenfeld. New York: Int. Univ. Press, 1965, pp. 128–143.

SALLAN, S. E., ZINBERG, N. E. & FREI, E. III (1975), Antiemetic effects of delta-9-tetrahydrocannabinol in patients receiving cancer chemotherapy. *New Engl. J. Med.*, 293:795–797.

SANTO, Y., FARLEY, E. C. & FREEDMAN, A. S. (1980). Highlights from the national youth polydrug study. In *Drug Abuse Patterns among Young Polydrug Users and Urban Appalachian Youths.* National Institute on Drug Abuse, Services Research Report. DHHS Publication No. (ADM)80–1002. Washington, D.C.: U.S. Government Printing Office.

SAVAGE, C. (1952), Lysergic acid diethylamide (LSD): a clinical and psychological study. *Amer. J. Psychiat.*, 108:896–900.

SCHER, J. (1961), Group structure and narcotics addiction: notes for a natural history. *Int. J. Group Psychother.*, 2:221–240.

——— (1966), Patterns and profiles of addiction and drug abuse. *Arch. Gen. Psychiat.*, 15:539–551.

SCHULTES, R. E. (1972), The utilization of hallucinogens in primitive societies—use, misuse, or abuse? In *Drug Abuse: Current Concepts and Research*, ed. H. Keup. Springfield, Ill.: C. C. Thomas.

SELLS, S. B. (1977), Reflections on the epidemiology of heroin and narcotic addiction from the perspective of treatment data. In *The Epidemiology of Heroin and Other Narcotics*, ed. J. D. Rittenhouse. NIDA Research Monograph No. 16. DHEW Publication No. (ADM)78–559. Rockville, Md.: National Institute on Drug Abuse.

SINGLE, E., KANDEL, D. & JOHNSON, B. D. (1975), The reliability and validity of drug use responses in a large-scale longitudinal survey. *J. Drug Issues*, 5:426–443.

SMART, R. G. (1974), Addiction, dependency, abuse, or use: which are we studying with epidemiology? In *Drug Use: Epidemiological and Sociological Approaches*, ed. E. Josephson & E. E. Carroll. New York: Wiley.

SMITH, D. E. (1975a), Personal Communication, 17 June.

SMITH, D. E. (1975b), North American Congress on Alcohol and Drug Problems—A Report to the American Psychiatric Association.

SOBELL, L. C. & SOBELL, M. B. (1975), Outpatient alcoholics give valid self-reports. *J. Nerv. Ment. Dis.*, 161:32–42.

SOBELL, M. B., SOBELL, L. C. & SAMUELS, F. (1974), Validity of self-reports on alcohol-related arrests by alcoholics. *Q. J. Studies on Alcohol*, 35:276–281.

STEPHENS, R. (1972), The truthfulness of addict respondents in research projects. *Int. J. Addictions*, 1:549.

SUTTER, A. G. (1969), Worlds of drug use on the street scene. In *Delinquency, Crime, and Social Process*, ed. D. Creasey & D. A. Ward. New York: Harper & Row, pp. 802–829.

SZASZ, T. (1975), *Ceremonial Chemistry: The Ritual Persecution of Drugs, Addicts and Pushers*. Garden City, N.Y.: Anchor Press/Doubleday.

TINKLENBERG, J. R. (1975), *Marihuana and Health Hazards*. New York: Academic Press.

TREBACH, A. A. (1982), *The Heroin Solution*. New Haven: Yale Univ. Press.

U.S. Bureau of the Census (1980a). 1980 Census of Population, Supplementary Reports. Persons of Spanish Origin by State. PC80–S1–3. Washington, D.C.: U.S. Government Printing Office.

——— (1980b). 1980 Census of Population, Supplementary Reports. Race of Population by States. PC80–S1–7. Washington, D.C.: U.S. Government Printing Office.

VAILLANT, G. E. (1978), Alcoholism and polydrug dependence. In *Harvard Guide to Modern Psychiatry*, ed. A. M. Nicholi. Cambridge, Mass.: Harvard Univ. Press.

———— (1983), *The Natural History of Alcoholism*. Cambridge, Mass.: Harvard Univ. Press.

WALDORF, D. (1973), *Careers in Dope*. Englewood Cliffs, N.J.: Prentice Hall.

WALDORF, D. & BIERNACKI, P. (1982), Natural recovery from heroin addiction: a review of the incidence literature. In *Control over Intoxicant Use: Pharmacological, Psychological, and Social Considerations*, ed. N. E. Zinberg & W. M. Harding. New York: Human Sciences Press, pp. 173–182.

WALDORF, D., ORLICK, J. & REINARMAN, C. (1974), *Morphine Maintenance: The Shreveport Clinic, 1919–1923*. Drug Abuse Council Publication No. SS–1. Washington, D.C.: The Drug Abuse Council, Inc.

WATKINS, V. M. & McCOY, C. B. (1980), Drug use among urban Appalachian youths. In *Drug Abuse Patterns among Young Polydrug Users and Urban Appalachian Youths*. DHHS Publication No. (ADM)80–1002. Rockville, Md.: National Institute on Drug Abuse.

WEIL, A. T. (1972), *The Natural Mind*. Boston: Houghton Mifflin.

WEIL, A. & ROSEN, W. (1983), *Chocolate to Morphine: Understanding Mind-Active Drugs*. Boston: Houghton Mifflin.

WEIL, A. T., ZINBERG, N. E. & NELSEN, J. (1968), Clinical and psychological effects of marihuana in man. *Science*, 162:1234–1242.

White Paper on Drug Abuse (1975), Report to the President from the Domestic Council Drug Abuse Task Force. Department of Health, Education, and Welfare. Washington, D.C.: U.S. Government Printing Office.

WHITEHEAD, P. C. & SMART, R. G. (1972), Validity and reliability of self-reported drug use. *Canad. J. Criminol. Correct.*, 14:83–87.

WILKINSON, R. (1970), *The Prevention of Drinking Problems*. New York: Oxford Univ. Press.

WINICK, C. (1974), Some aspects of careers of chronic heroin users. In *Drug Use: Epidemiological and Sociological Approaches*, ed. E. Josephson & E. E. Carroll. New York: Wiley, pp. 105–128.

WISHNIE, H. (1971), Opioid addiction: a masked depression. In *Masked Depression*, ed. S. Lesse. New York: Jason Aronson, 1974.

World Health Organization, Expert Committee on Mental Health (1957). *Addiction Producing Drugs*. 7th Report of the WHO Expert Committee. WHO Technical Report Series No. 116. Geneva, Switzerland: World Health Organization, pp. 17–25.

YOUNG, J. (1971), *The Drugtakers: The Social Meaning of Drug Use*. London: MacGibbon & Kee.

ZALEZNIK, A. & SCHWABER, E. (1976), Discussion of ORNSTEIN, P. H. & ORNSTEIN, A., On the continuing evolution of psychoanalytic psychotherapy: reflections and predictions. *Annual of Psychoanalysis*, 5:329–370.

ZETZEL, E. R. (1949), Anxiety and the capacity to bear it. *Int. J. Psycho-Anal.*, 30:1–12.

ZINBERG, N. E. (1972), Heroin use in Vietnam and the United States. *Arch. Gen. Psychiat.*, 26:486–488.

———— (1974), *"High" States: A Beginning Study.* Drug Abuse Council Publication No. SS–3. Washington, D.C.: The Drug Abuse Council, Inc.

———— (1975), Addiction and ego function. *Psychoanal. Study Child*, 30:567–578.

———— (1976), The war over marijuana. *Psychology Today.* April. pp. 10, 14, 52, 102–106.

———— (1981), Social interactions, drug use, and drug research. In *Substance Abuse: Clinical Problems and Perspectives*, ed. J. H. Lowinson & P. Ruiz. Baltimore: Williams and Wilkins, pp. 91–108.

ZINBERG, N. E. & DeLONG, J. V. (1974), Research and the drug issue. *Contemp. Drug Prob.*, 3:71–100.

ZINBERG, N. E. & FRASER, K. M. (1979), The role of the social setting in the prevention and treatment of alcoholism. In *The Diagnosis and Treatment of Alcoholism*, ed. J. H. Mendelson & N. K. Mello. New York: McGraw-Hill, pp. 359–385.

ZINBERG, N. E. & HARDING, W. M. (1982), Introduction—control and intoxicant use: a theoretical and practical overview. In *Control over Intoxicant Use: Pharmacological, Psychological, and Social Considerations*, ed. N. E. Zinberg & W. M. Harding. New York: Human Sciences Press, pp. 13–35.

ZINBERG, N. E., HARDING, W. M. & APSLER, R. (1978), What is drug abuse? *J. Drug Issues*, 8:9–35.

ZINBERG, N. E., HARDING, W. M., STELMACK, S. M. & MARBLESTONE, R. A. (1978), Patterns of heroin use. *Ann. N.Y. Acad. Sci.*, 311:10–24.

ZINBERG, N. E., HARDING, W. M. & WINKELLER, M. (1981), A study of social regulatory mechanisms in controlled illicit drug users. In *Classic Contributions to the Addictions*, ed. H. Shaffer & M. E. Burglass. New York: Brunner/Mazel, pp. 277–300.

ZINBERG, N. E. & JACOBSON, R. C. (1975), The social basis of drug abuse prevention. In *Developments in the Field of Drug Abuse.* Proceedings of the National Drug Abuse Conference, 1974. Cambridge, Mass.: Schenkman, pp. 3–13.

———— (1976), The natural history of chipping. *Amer. J. Psychiat.*, 133:37–40.

ZINBERG, N. E., JACOBSON, R. C. & HARDING, W. M. (1975), Social situations and rituals as a basis of drug abuse prevention. *Amer. J. Drug Alcohol Abuse*, 2:165–182.

ZINBERG, N. E. & LEWIS, D. C. (1964), Narcotic usage: I. A spectrum of a difficult medical problem. *New Engl. J. Med.*, 270:989–993.

ZINBERG, N. E. & ROBERTSON, J. A. (1972), *Drugs and the Public.* New York: Simon & Schuster.

ZINBERG, N. E. & WEIL, A. T. (1970), A comparison of marijuana users and non-users. *Nature*, 226:119–123.

Index